RADICAL SPACE

RADICAL SPACE

BUILDING THE HOUSE OF THE PEOPLE

Margaret Kohn

CORNELL UNIVERSITY PRESS

ITHACA AND LONDON

First published 2003 by Cornell University Press
First printing, Cornell Paperbacks, 2003

Printed in the United States of America

Library of Congress Cataloging-in-Publication Data

Kohn, Margaret, 1970–
  Radical space : building the house of the people / Margaret Kohn.
    p. cm.
Includes bibliographical references and index.
  ISBN 0-8014-3992-2 (cloth : alk. paper) — ISBN 0-8014-8860-5 (pbk. : alk. paper)
    1. Cooperation—Italy—History. 2. Cooperative
societies—Italy—History. 3. Friendly societies—Italy—History. 4.
Municipal government—Italy—History. 5. Local
government—Italy—History. 6. Socialism—Italy—History. I. Title.
  HD3343 .K64 2003
  306.3'44'0945—dc21

                                                          2002154275

Cornell University Press strives to use environmentally responsible suppliers and materials to the fullest extent possible in the publishing of its books. Such materials include vegetable-based, low-VOC inks and acid-free papers that are recycled, totally chlorine-free, or partly composed of nonwood fibers. For further information, visit our website at www.cornellpress.cornell.edu.

Cloth printing   10 9 8 7 6 5 4 3 2 1
Paperback printing   10 9 8 7 6 5 4 3 2 1

CONTENTS

ILLUSTRATIONS

ACKNOWLEDGMENTS

I have always dreaded the responsibility of properly acknowledging the people who have most contributed to this project because I fear that I will inevitably leave out many whose influence and support, while indirect, was nevertheless crucial. These include members of the political theory/philosophy faculty at Williams College, my colleagues at the University of Florida, my family, and the Italian friends who first brought me to the *casa del popolo* (house of the people). With that caveat, I particularly thank the following individuals who had the most profound influence on every stage of the research and writing process: Susan Buck-Morss, Sidney Tarrow, Anna Marie Smith, and Jonas Pontusson. Isaac Kramnick, Keally McBride, and Ryan Hurl also read the entire manuscript. Along with the three anonymous readers at Cornell University Press, and my editor Catherine Rice, they deserve much credit for the transformation that this project has undergone since its birth many years ago. William Cortlett, Leslie Paul Thiele, and Francesco Ramella also offered useful feedback on individual chapters. More generally, the Critical Theory Working Group at the European University Institute (EUI) provided the intellectual context and inspiration that made this research possible.

I owe a special debt of thanks to the following institutions that provided funding and institutional support for this research: the Fondazione Luigi Einaudi, the Fulbright Foundation, the EUI, and the Center for European Studies at Cornell University. Most of chapter 6 and a short section of chapter 8 were previously published. I thank the journals *Polity* and *Political Power and Social Theory* for allowing me to draw on this material for chapters 6 and 8, respectively.

RADICAL SPACE

1

INTRODUCTION

It is a question of giving history a counter-memory.

—Foucault

One evening in July of 1997 I found myself eating in a Communist pizzeria. Some Italian friends had suggested this spot—San Martino alla Palma—because of its stunning view of Florence and absence of foreign tourists. Almost a decade after the fall of the Berlin Wall and five years after the dissolution of the Italian Communist Party, I was somewhat surprised to see a large picture of Antonio Gramsci in the entrance. We were eating at the Circolo ARCI—the local headquarters of the Italian Communist Recreational Association, still the largest social center in the village. Although hardly a hotbed of ideological ferment, this *casa del popolo* (house of the people) continued to sponsor political lectures and outings while providing space to a variety of organizations.

I had come to Italy to study the political economy of the cooperative movement, hoping that it could shed light on the feasibility of market socialism. What I had found in the archives, however, puzzled me. Although the economic advantages of cooperative membership were fairly well documented, they did not seem central to the self-understanding of the cooperative movement. Unlike traditional firms, the early cooperatives were primarily concerned with commercial viability in so far as it served to sustain the broader social and political functions. My interest in the cooperatives as economic institutions was overshadowed by a growing fascination with the politics that emerged out of this distinctive social space.

The two questions that guide this book emerged out of reflection on the theoretical significance of these houses of the people. The first question is simply whether place matters for politics. The linguistic turn in contemporary political theory—both in its Habermasian and Foucaultian variants—has generated a rich theoretical literature that analyzes discourse. But is there something about shared physical presence that intensifies or transforms political experience? The second question follows the first: could particular spaces serve a transformative political project as well as a disciplinary regime? These questions engage some of the core concerns of political theory, yet to answer them I had to look for new (or overlooked) concepts and sources.

The significance of the house of the people was an enigma to decipher. In some ways the *casa del popolo* with its restaurant and courtyard, meeting rooms and terrace, seemed like the product of utopian socialists' fantasies, a small-scale version of Fourier's phalanstery. But certain details undermined this interpretation. The vernacular style, with its characteristic stone walls, ochre painting, green shutters, fluorescent lights, and eclectic, old-fashioned furniture hardly suggested careful social engineering. On the contrary, the building seemed to blend into the town and did not obviously symbolize an alternate social order. Nonetheless, its very existence was disconcerting; it complicated the tourists' map of Florence on which the church, the state, and the bourgeoisie had left the only traces of power. It served as a reminder that under adverse conditions, the subaltern classes created political spaces that served as nodal points of public life.

In Italy the houses of the people captured something distinctive about the political transformation that took place at the turn of the century. They were one piece of a collective history, a kind of fossil that remained incarnate even after the spirit that animated it—the people, their clubs, and their speeches—had disappeared or changed. The houses of the people made visible to me a set of social and political tactics that transformed power relations between the rich and the poor in Italy in the period between national unification and fascism. This book analyzes the topography of that political transformation.

The motivation for this study is the hope that a careful analysis of the sites of resistance that flourished in turn-of-the-century Italy might strengthen a conception of democracy that is useful today. (The reasons for focusing on Italy are outlined in appendix 1.) Looking at the practices of mutual aid societies, cooperatives, *case del popolo*, and municipalities could reinforce the normative core of democratic theory by recovering the political logic of a particular moment of the process of democratization. This does not mean, however, that the strategies appropriate to the past can be applied directly today. The past does not provide formulas for the future, but it can supply reference points for the present. Theory is the mechanism through which sediments of past struggles over power and interpretation can transcend their immediate context to illuminate new conjunctures.

Space

From the polis to the public sphere, political theorists have shared the intuition that space is crucial to democracy.[1] Whether the goal is to create a unified demos or to empower the disenfranchised, shared places help forge communities by enabling and constraining the way in which people come together. Particular places orchestrate social behavior by providing scripts for encounters and assembly. The built environment shapes individuals' actions and identities by reinforcing relatively stable cues about correct behavior. Space also functions symbolically, as "a repository of historical meanings that reproduce social relations" and as a "mnemonic device for recovering memories."[2] In his seminal work *The Collective Memory*, Maurice Halbwachs explained that the only way to recapture the past is by understanding how it is preserved in our physical surroundings.[3] Buildings, architectural plans, sacred space, boundaries, public/private domains, and ruins can be read as texts that communicate important elements of culture and patterns of power.[4] They are also ways of enacting and thereby reproducing power relations.[5]

The textual dimension, however, does not exhaust the meaning of space.[6] Conveying a message is only one of several functions of space. A building also serves pragmatic needs; for example, it may provide shelter or serve as a visual barrier preventing outsiders from looking in. Because space has been most thoroughly theorized in the discipline of architecture, there is a tendency to think of it primarily in terms of blueprints, designs, and physical properties, but space is also lived and experienced. It has a corporeal as well as a symbolic or cognitive dimension.

Space affects how individuals and groups perceive their place in the order of things. Spatial configurations naturalize social relations by transforming contingent forms into a permanent landscape that appears as immutable rather than open to contestation.[7] By providing a shared background, spatial forms serve the function of integrating individuals into a shared conception of reality. Architecture produces bodily practices in a way that is not always visible or legible "for it reproduces itself within those who *use* the space in question, within their lived experience."[8] The body can serve as a very powerful mnemonic device because the embodied principles are beyond the grasp of consciousness and therefore cannot be voluntarily transformed. Thus, constructed social spaces and their corresponding bodily practices (modes of living in them) appear naturalized. By fixing patterns of domestic life and work, space enacts crucial social distinctions such as the boundary between kin and outsider, production and reproduction, individuality and collectivity. The home and the factory are the material form of institutions such as family and work. We often experience these constructions with an implicit sense of inevitability. A spatial heuristic can illuminate domains of political experience that have hitherto remained obscured in a culture that emphasizes visual and linguistic knowledges.

The social and symbolic properties of space can also be important resources for transformative political projects. Political spaces facilitate change by creating a distinctive place to develop new identities and practices. The political power of place comes from its ability to link the social, symbolic, and experiential dimensions of space. Transformative politics comes from separating, juxtaposing, and recombining these dimensions.

The social dimension of space reflects the way in which places encourage or inhibit contact between people. Linguists have identified the "phatic aspect of speech," terms like "hello," "how are you?" which initiate, maintain, or interrupt contact.[9] Particular spaces serve a similar function. They aggregate or exclude, and they determine the form and scope of the interactions. These effects may be achieved through physical properties such as the accessibility of a courtyard, the arrangement of chairs, or the presence of a pulpit. New urbanist planners such as Andres Duany feature front porches in their designs in order to build community by facilitating informal, unplanned contact between neighbors.[10]

The significance of a place may be a product of the traditions and rituals it invokes as much as it is a product of the physical layout. Even if residents of expensive new urbanist communities do not have the time to linger on porches or prefer the air-conditioned interior, they still may appreciate the front porch because it evokes an idealized image of small-town life. It can function as the backdrop for a fantasy, a kind of dream image, rather than as a functional architectural feature. The meaning of a space is largely determined by its symbolic valence. A particular place is a way to locate stories, memories, and dreams. It connects the past with the present and projects it into the future. A place can capture symbolic significance in different ways: by incorporating architectural allusions in the design, by serving as a backdrop for crucial events, or by positioning itself in opposition to other symbols. Its power is a symptom of the human propensity to think synecdochically; the chamber of labor, like the red flag, comes to stand for socialism or justice. It is a cathexis for transformative desire.

In addition to the social and symbolic aspects of space, there is an intuitive, experiential dimension that is particularly difficult to put into words because it involves perception rather than cognition. Phenomenologist Alfred Schutz designates it "kinesthetic experience."[11] William Connolly uses the term "visceral register" to distinguish the characteristics of physical co-presence.[12] It is made up of the gestural, symbolic, and affective planes. The visceral register encompasses the precognitive impact of things such as greeting, focus, tone, posture, and inflection. Space is one of the key ways in which the body perceives power relations. The physical environment is political mythology realized, embodied, materialized. It inculcates a set of enduring dispositions that incline agents to act and react in regular ways even in the absence of any explicit rules or constraints.[13]

One initial objection to this approach is that spatial analysis is superfluous because it is a subset of the highly theorized category of discourse analysis. According to this position, Foucault included spaces such as the clinic and the prison under the rubric of discourse. In fact, Foucault was careful to distinguish between discourse (informal rules for the production of specialized knowledge) and other elements of disciplinary power such as sites and institutions.[14] He concluded that discursive formations link together the diverse field of power relations.[15] While studying the spaces of resistance of early-twentieth-century Italy, I found space to form connections. There was a great deal of heterogeneity in leftist discourse during the transitionary period before World War I. Scientific socialism coexisted uneasily with peasant millenarianism and petit-bourgeois radicalism. Social spaces rather than shared languages linked coalitions together.

Another objection is that cooperatives, houses of the people, and chambers of labor are actually associations, not spaces. Although there is some overlap between the two categories, associations and spaces are not synonymous. There are associations that have no spaces, for example, groups such as the American Association of Retired People (AARP) or the American Automobile Association (AAA), which provide services for a fee but do not facilitate the co-presence of their members. There are also spaces that are not created by associations: places such as airports, bars, and theaters, where people come together without having formal ties, sustained contact, or shared purposes. The political spaces studied in this book tend to fall into the overlapping category; they are spaces that are formed by associations. Although it is sometimes necessary to use associational membership as a proxy for "spaces of resistance" because the latter is extremely hard to measure, it is important not to loose sight of the difference between the two concepts. The people who attended literacy courses or played cards at houses of the people did not necessarily belong to any group. These spaces provided informal opportunities to encounter new ideas, recognize commonalities, debate tactics, and maybe then engage in political activity. They were the lifeworld out of which more formalized associations emerged. Associations that are not "spatial," in other words, that do not facilitate co-presence, are seldom constitutive of identity. They do not build dense, overlapping social bonds. The connections they forge, if any, are organized around narrowly conceived interests. Although they contribute to democratic processes such as interest representation, they seldom create forums for political debate or contexts for action.[16]

Radical Democracy

State powers have long known how to manipulate space for political purposes. Governments erect monuments and palaces to encourage emotional identification with the state. They also plan and restructure roads, neighborhoods, and fortifications in order to channel, control, or prevent potentially disruptive crowds. Many influential studies—from Michel Foucault's *Discipline and Punish* to Mike Davis's *City of Quartz*—have focused on the use of space to expand normalization and control. This attentiveness to space has deepened our understanding of the circulation of power. Foucault showed that Bentham's Panopticon was not only a metaphor for the disciplinary nature of modern power but also a spatial practice, an architectural *technē* designed to reinforce a new experience of the self, to create docile bodies, and to interpolate an introspective soul. The Panopticon was a symbol of a new society and a tool for building it. To understand the circulation of modern power, it is illuminating to look at disciplinary spaces. But space is not just a tool of social control. This book shows how spatial practices can contribute to transformative politics. All political groups—government and opposition, right and left, fascist and democratic—use space, just as they all employ language, symbols, ideas, and incentives. Studying how they transform and appropriate space is one way of understanding the character of these movements.

The sites of sovereign power are easy to recognize: the White House, the Winter Palace, Wall Street. Their monumental forms dominate the skyline. The street-level perspective, however, allows us to see the rhizomatic structures that are equally important. The power they exert is not sovereign power but rather the capillary action of diverse and multiple forces that combine and intersect to produce systematic effects. These micropowers are easily overlooked, yet they are crucial for understanding politics. To discern them we must look at the diverse places where politics takes place: festivals, town squares, chambers of labor, mutual aid societies, union halls, night schools, cooperatives, houses of the people. I call these radical democratic spaces because they are political sites outside of the state where the disenfranchised generated power.

Radical democracy was not a prominent political category in Europe at the turn of the century. It is a designation that I employ retrospectively to group together a variety of movements that shared the common goal of engaging in politics at the level of everyday life and transforming the social and economic bases of political power.[17] The word *radical* comes from the Latin *radicalis*, meaning root. Radical democracy is the attempt to return to the original meaning of the term, which referred to the power of the common people.[18] Another sense of the term is "far reaching," understood here as the attempt to reach beyond currently accepted limitations placed on democracy. The radicalization of democracy can occur in several different ways: by linking diverse democratic struggles,[19] creating new sites for more effective political participation,[20] extending collective control into previously excluded domains such as the workplace,[21] and expanding the understanding of citizenship to accomplish meaningful inclusion of previously marginalized groups.[22]

The resurgence of interest in radical democracy is indebted to Ernesto Laclau and Chantal Mouffe's use of the concept in *Hegemony and Socialist Strategy*. There they trace the concept of radicalism from the early 1800s, when it served as the discursive framework for working-class politics, through the writings of renegade socialists such as Bernstein, Luxemburg, Sorel, and especially Gramsci.[23] Radical democracy was the product of a period in which the people rather than the proletariat were imagined to be the agent of social and political transformation. This heritage, however, is an asset rather than a liability.[24] Like Laclau and Mouffe, I reject the assumption that an evolutionary process transformed primitive populist struggles into the disciplined tactics of a unified industrial working class. Radical democracy means political struggle with neither a privileged agent of emancipation nor a group necessarily excluded from participation.[25] Democracy becomes a way of articulating the link that relates pluralistic modes of struggle to one another.[26] If democracy is to be substantive and not merely formal, it cannot be something that takes place exclusively on the terrain of the state, nor can it be reasonably isolated from economics, one of the most significant sources of power.

Radical democracy is Janus-faced; it looks both to the past and to the future. It transmits a vision of democracy that is distinct from both liberalism and Marxism. Radical democrats were the subaltern classes, that is, they included not only workers in industrial enterprises but all those who were excluded from citizenship and struggled for inclusion.[27] The term is also forward looking. The idea of radical democracy suggests an alternative to social democracy, which has come to connote statist strategies and technocratic management. In contrast, radical democracy evokes the self-organization of society and the transformative potential of social movements, without losing sight of the way in which existing concentrations of power, especially in the economic arena, are still a primary barrier to fundamental political change.

Democratic theorizing can be understood as a dialectical process whereby the normative core of the concept and its particular manifestations continually transform one another. What is the normative core of democracy? If there is one theme unifying the diverse threads of democratic theory it is the idea of rule by the people,[28] which must include widespread sharing in both the production and exercise of power. This general formulation, however, offers limited guidance for specifying which institutions are best suited to realize the ideal of self-government. The real meaning of radical democracy can only emerge by studying the process of democratization. Tracing that process involves discovering how the dominant interpretation of democracy and its specific institutional forms generate a tension that can only be reconciled through a reinterpretation of the concept's normative core. The unfolding of democracy is neither reductionist nor teleological. It does not follow a predetermined logic. The open-ended interaction between the normative principle and historical form leaves both transformed. The role of the democratic theorist is to uncover the submerged counterhistory of democratic practice that confounds or expands our existing definition of the term.

Critical Theory and History

Pre-fascist Italy may seem an unlikely place to look for a paradigm of radical democracy. Although it is true that Italy's democratic movements were destroyed by fascism, fascism targeted workers' spaces precisely because they posed a formidable alternative to existing powers.[29] These spaces reflected new ideas about the relationship between economics and politics and embodied these ideas in realities. The claim that radical-democratic movements failed is only partially true. Despite twenty years of repression under fascism, institutions such as cooperatives and *case del popolo* provided networks that were important in the resistance movement at the end of World War II. Furthermore, this red subculture experienced a strong resurgence during the postwar period and generated political effects (from successful urban planning to innovative social programs and regional industrial policy) that endure to this day.[30]

Even an unsuccessful movement may reveal democratic possibilities. Its disappointment does not necessarily invalidate the dream. For if we doubt that history has an underlying internal logic developing toward greater good and progress, then success or failure should not be the ultimate arbiter of normative validity. With this in mind, the role of the critical theorist is not to show that things had to be the way they are but rather to reveal that they could have been different. Denaturalizing dominant relations is the first step toward imagining the possibility of transformation. For Walter Benjamin, unlike Gramsci, mass adhesion to an ideology does not guarantee its rationality. Historical competition does not ensure that "arbitrary constructions" will be eliminated and emancipatory projects will triumph.[31] Sometimes it is the marginal or vanquished practices that contain traces of emancipatory praxis. In a vision of history without an evolutionary logic or telos, defeats as well as victories can provide the "retroactive force" that illuminates and guides future struggles. In the "Fourth Thesis on the Philosophy of History," Benjamin explains that "the class struggle, which is always present to a historian influenced by Marx, is a fight for the crude and material things without which no refined and spiritual things could exist. Nevertheless, it is not in the form of the spoils which fall to the victor that the latter make their presence felt in the class struggle. They manifest themselves in this struggle as courage, humor, cunning, and fortitude."[32]

This passage suggests the importance of the utopian-transformative dimension of immanent critique. Benjamin also expresses the idea that emancipatory ideals are embodied in material struggles, not merely the history of ideas. If our goal is a more nuanced theory of democracy, the most appropriate method of investigation involves studying actual struggles as well as philosophical discussions. Recovering a vanquished ideal may be important simply because it sustains a vision of an alternative. Normative principles such as democracy are dangerous; they may serve to mask forms of domination, contain dissent, or become empty rhetorical mantras of legitimation. But such ideals also animate struggles, help articulate alternatives, expose forms of domination, and make it possible to imagine a better future. In other words, they open the conceptual space for change, which is fundamental to politics. These only partially realized normative ideals, which by definition exceed the actuality of the practices that embody them, must be retained as a set of tools to be employed under more favorable historical circumstances. They are all we have to combat the quietism of accepting the merely existent.

The method of this study brings theoretical and empirical analyses into conversation with one another. Although this hybrid may be unfamiliar to some readers, it reflects the three dimensions of critical theory: it is inspired by the tradition of continental philosophy; it employs historical and empirical techniques to deepen our understanding of social reality; and it is motivated by normative concerns.[33] Although my goals are primarily theoretical, the mode of theorizing involves reading material culture and historical practices as well as written texts.

My approach is indebted to the critical theory tradition of immanent critique.[34] This historical-critical method is an alternative to the dominant methods in political theory, that is, the generation of normative theory through abstract reflection and deduction or the critical exegesis of canonical texts. Rather than positing an ideal alternative to existing political reality, I assume that a close reading of social and political practices provides the most compelling normative guidelines. My approach is also inspired by Foucault's genealogical method in that it aspires to tell a history of the present that recovers subaltern practices in order to break the "discursive lock" of the dominant paradigms in political theory.[35] This project is historical; it is based on faithful reconstruction of the way in which the subaltern classes constructed new political spaces and practices. It is also normative because it is an intervention that calls for revitalizing this democratic tradition that has been both marginalized as the result of repression and superseded by its own successes.

The task of immanent critique is not to juxtapose an ideal to existing reality. Instead, it reveals traces of an underlying emancipatory possibility, through a thorough interrogation of actual practices.[36] The traditional tactic of immanent critique as practiced by Marx was to contrast the normative self-understanding of bourgeois society with its own actual effects. He revealed how the legal freedom of exchange within the market place was based on sustained violent dispossession of labor power and served to reproduce relations of structural dependence. Similarly, Foucault showed how the humanistic impulses of prison reformers could serve to expand disciplinary forms of social control. Although scholars such as Foucault and Adorno tried to denaturalize the existing forms of domination, they were not equally successful at establishing the basis for the "utopian-transformative dimension" of critical theory, that is, identifying the forces and practices capable of resistance. Whereas critical theory usually reveals how democracy masks actual domination, I show how an overemphasis on domination can mask emancipatory moments.[37] I demonstrate that this historical-archeological approach can be used for discovering practices of resistance as well as those of domination.

This research is inspired by the passage in "Thesis on the Philosophy of History" in which Benjamin calls for a project of theory capable of appropriating submerged resources from the past and recasting them as tools in contemporary struggles. This does not imply that there is a guiding rationality contained in past practices that needs only to be excavated and polished up so that its universal validity can shine through. It aspires to acquire knowledge of past struggles in order to see how they suggest submerged possibilities for thought and praxis.[38]

Spatial analysis is not an alternative to social and political theory but an overlooked dimension of it. By paying more attention to the role of place in politics, I hope to better understand the character of working-class social movements. Specifically, the task of chapter 2 is to defend the proposition that space is not synonymous with stasis and therefore not antithetical to transformative politics. Chapters 3 and 4 evaluate two prominent theories linking particular spaces to politics: the public sphere (Habermas) and the factory (Gramsci and Marx). Chapters 5–7 each analyze a different site of resistance: the cooperative, the house of the people, and the chamber of labor. These historical investigations serve to elucidate the salience of encounter, proximity, concentration, simultaneity, and symbolism for political identity and participation. In chapter 8 I introduce the concept of municipalism, a theoretical elaboration based on the experience of radical democracy at the local level. Derived from *municipalis* meaning free city, the concept is a distinctly political approach to community. In the areas of Italy where municipalism flourished, clientelistic ties of dependence were permanently broken. Even though many sites of resistance were destroyed under fascism, they created geographies of popular power that endure in the present.

This book emphasizes the social and political dimensions of the built environment, its capacity to shape individuals' actions, identities, and interpretations. It looks at sites that provided an opportunity to encounter new people and ideas, to communicate controversial theories under conditions of relative security, and to experiment with new identities. These spaces linked pragmatic and symbolic functions. They served to locate stories, preserve memories, and embody utopian desires. During the day, workers were quite literally "objects," inputs in the production process with only instrumental value. At the cooperative or at the house of the people they became subjects, co-creators of an alternate world.

2

SPACE AND POLITICS

To construct the city topographically . . . from out of its arcades
and its gateways, its cemeteries and bordellos, its railroad
stations . . . , just as formerly it was defined by its churches and its
markets. And the more secret, more deeply embedded figures of
the city: murders and rebellions, the bloody knots in the network
of streets, lairs of love, and conflagrations.

Walter Benjamin, *The Arcades Project*

Contemporary Western nomenclature for politics has two roots: *polis*,
the term designating the spatial location of the city-state, and *politeia*.
This later term, although usually translated as "constitution," also connotes the multiple institutions, practices, habits, and laws that characterize social life.[1] The relationship between these two aspects has been
one of the central dilemmas in political theory. Political life, with its
concomitant dissentions and solidarities, arises from the necessity of living together in a particular location. But this premise does not determine the boundaries that define exclusion or inclusion, let alone the
rules and habits that regulate collective life.

In Ancient Greek thought, the relationship between the citizen and
the polity was mediated by specific sites—the city walls, market place,
gymnasium, forum, the temple—and the types of subjectivity and solidarity these sites engendered. Following the ancient Greeks, Rousseau
reflected on the relationship between spatial design, community, and
democracy. According to Rousseau, simple proximity did not guarantee
community. In *Letter to D'Alembert*, Rousseau argued that the theater
creates the illusion of community and communication because it concentrates people in one place.[2] But, in fact, it fosters isolation. The space is
structured to encourage each individual to focus attention on the stage

instead of engaging with his fellow citizens. It breeds an attitude of passivity and reinforces hierarchy. The theater is the opposite of the agora, an open forum that fosters participation, communication, and solidarity. For Rousseau, certain spatial configurations could strengthen radical democratic politics, whereas others reinforced social hierarchies.

The importance of a spatial dimension to politics is prominent in some strains of communitarian thought, where community is conceived as constitutive of both subjectivity and citizenship.[3] Although community is not necessarily limited to people who share a given locality, the concept usually evokes the texture of small-town life: dense social ties that emerge organically out of physical proximity. According to its critics, the communitarian ideal connotes a more conservative position, that is, a greater readiness to defer to tradition and a nostalgic desire for stable foundations. Some critics argue that this approach to collective life involves a rejection of politics (understood as an arena of contention, pluralism, and dissent) and the substitution of a prepolitical consensus rooted in the supposedly natural solidarities of family and homeland.[4] Through a logic of equivalence, space has become associated with this "apolitical" strand of communitarianism.

Yet such a simple equation is problematic. The spatial dimension of politics is no more intrinsically static than history, language, law, discourse, or any other dimension. Teleological approaches to history are more fixed than space, at least if space is theorized as a surface inscribed with tensions and contradictions. Similarly, language may serve as the basis for limiting disruptive and polarizing claims. Some deliberative democrats envision political consensus as the product of discursive practices governed by necessary, universal presuppositions. This reflects a desire for rootedness that is not present in the idea of political space, understood as an open arena of contestation. This "agonistic" conception of political space is explicit in the work of Hannah Arendt, who argued that the polis made pluralism, distinction, and action possible. She insisted that "before men begin to act, a definite space had to be secured and structure built where all subsequent actions could take place."[5] Political space is a place where people speak and act together rather than a static physical location.

Neither the general term *space* nor more specific concepts such as *locality, place,* or *site* should be assumed to connote tradition, closure, and stasis. The terms *place* and *site* designate bounded, marked spaces, contexts for proximity and encounter between people; a locality is the nexus of several broader structures and practices. These definitions are similar to those used by Sheldon Wolin in his approach to political space, which he called "the locus wherein the tensional forces of society are related, as in a courtroom, legislature, an administrative hearing, or the convention of a political party."[6] According to this definition, political space can facilitate either domination or resistance.

This chapter argues that space is an element of politics that can contribute to social change as well as social control. Before looking at the political effects of specific spatial formations, it is necessary to consider the political salience of space as a category of analysis. This is crucial because the vocabulary of spatiality has recently gained currency but is seldom employed in a rigorous manner. Whereas geographers had traditionally used the term to denote a purely physical location, contemporary theorists have taken the opposite extreme and evacuated any sense of rootedness, sometimes using the word "space" as a synonym for discourse. Instead, we need a mediating position that acknowledges that space is a product of social practices but one that has particular properties precisely because of its embodiment in specific types of places. Such a mediating position neither reduces space to a purely physical category nor evacuates its material dimension. This project shows the distinctive results of taking space as more than just a metaphor.

Space and Social Movements

Spatial designations are common in everyday language. There are terms such as *place, location, nodal point, milieu, position, structure*, and *locality* that indicate abstract spatial concepts by suggesting a general sense of their boundedness. Then there are other words such as *neighborhood, road, town, village, workplace*, or *state* that designate specific, potentially identifiable locations. Finally there are additional terms such as *turf, home, cyberspace, nation*, and *global market* that refer to places strongly marked by their association with specific social formations.[7] These terms remind us that subjectivity itself is, in part, a product of spatial practices. For example, an individual defines herself by saying: "I am American" or "I am Florentine" or "I'm from the West Side." It is taken for granted that localities and territories are deeply implicated in the meaning of citizenship and, more generally, the process of self-definition.

Epoch-making events are often remembered by spatial markers: the fall of the Berlin Wall, Tiananmen Square, the taking of the Bastille. Perhaps this is because humans have a tendency to think in images, and memory is most effectively triggered by material traces rather than abstract notions. But this also reflects a strategy employed by groups struggling for social change, which attempt to reappropriate the spaces that most embody power. The spatialization of resistance is an enduring motif in collective action, which may take several forms. There is the use of public places, usually historical or monumental sites, to frame or dramatize a particular issue. Because monuments are themselves concentrations of symbolic power, they are particularly open to symbolic appropriation or challenge. By far the best-known "spatial repertoires" (sit-ins, demonstrations in the piazza, marches on the capital, pilgrimages to monuments) fall into this category because their goal is to communicate a message to the public or to the powerful.[8] But another spatial category is equally important. These semipublic spaces allow for people to come together in places that are insulated from surveillance and control. Charles Tilly argues that safe spaces of one kind or another are a sine qua non of social movements. Oppositional movements need to control spaces in order to organize their activities without being subject to repression.[9] Similarly, James Scott emphasizes the importance of "off-stage social spaces." He argues that no effective resistance is possible without some form of communication and coordination among the members of a subordinate group. This in turn requires social spaces that offer some protection from persecution and repression.[10]

Space is implicated in processes of creation, reappropriation, and change; therefore it cannot be a static realm that is antithetical to politics. According to Hannah Arendt, building political spaces reflects the desire to create something enduring, but what is erected as a result of the desire is a context for future contestation. The marketplace, town square, school, forum, community center, and the city itself are not necessarily places of closure but can be nexuses that open up the possibility of interaction between diverse groups.[11] At this point it would be premature to argue that space in general has any particular political effects. Instead, my claim is purely formal. Just as history is intuitively understood as the record of change over time, so must we begin to think of architecture, geography, and urbanism as traces of spatial transformations.

The Political Salience of Spaces of Resistance

Particular places or sites are the concrete modalities through which individuals experience power. Anthropologists have long emphasized that the internal structure of domestic space (the home) and its relationship to other places (the village) communicate important information about culture and power. Only recently, however, have scholars begun to apply this insight to the relationship between the individual, the home, and the social institution of the family in modern Western societies. The home is one of the places in which the individual experiences the hierarchies, rules, and conventions of family life. It distinguishes "familiarity from strangeness, security from insecurity, certainty from doubt, order from chaos, comfort from adventure, settlement from wandering, here from away."[12] But the home does not only mark the distinction between inside and outside. It also materializes power relations within the family. For example, the home regulates the dispersion of people into particular rooms. There are places that are forbidden, and accessibility is contingent upon status differences.[13] Also, certain spaces are designated as the legitimate place for particular activities.[14] Consider how the father's study or workshop typically exudes its aura of power and privilege. Moreover, particular spaces constrain the range of acceptable behaviors. The formal parlor of the bourgeois home is a place where one must tread carefully not only because of the valuable furnishings but also because it is a stage for performing the formal behaviors required when entertaining guests. Gestures, practices, and social roles become embodied as they are performed in particular places. Before or beyond cognition, they exert a particularly enduring influence on social relations.

In his analysis of the home in *The Poetics of Space*, Bachelard argues that "imagination augments the values of reality."[15] But the reverse is also true. Reality also augments imagination. How we imagine ourselves and our relationship to others, our capacities and limitations, and the legitimate principles that govern our living together are profoundly shaped by concrete spaces. The church dominates the town square, and the sanctuary achieves a distinctive arrangement of symbols, sanctity, and bodies. These spatializations affect the relationship between ecclesiastical authority and parishioners. Piety emerges from church going, and nationalism is a product of the barracks and the village school.

Although domestic space plays a powerful role in embodying and reproducing certain social roles, certain subjectivities if you will, it cannot be understood in isolation from broader structures. This is the error of a naïve phenomenological approach that analyzes the experience of consciousness without considering the underlying structures that give rise to modes of experience.[16] The principles and practices that govern domestic space are clearly connected to broader structural dynamics: the nuclear family, the real estate market, suburbanization, the rhetorical power of family values, zoning laws, mortgage deductions, property devaluation.[17] The particular form of the single-family home and its prominent position as the dominant feature of the American landscape are products of both intended and unintended factors, including technological development (automobiles, roads), political choices (federal subsidization of highway building), low population density, and the postwar policy of inclusion (a stakeholder society or co-optation, depending on your point of view).[18] Once established, this spatial formation serves to reinforce the ideology of privatization and a certain image of family life that exerted wide-reaching influence beyond the confines of suburbia.[19]

Like the home, the school, the prison, and the factory are sites where individuals come into contact with and experience power relations. Social or political structures are reproduced through bodily practices. By bodily practices I mean the often pre-reflective ways in which the body experiences the space around it. In *Discipline and Punish*, Foucault turns to an analysis of spatial formations to account for "a transformation of the way in which the body itself is invested by power."[20] His analysis of Bentham's Panopticon reveals how the disciplinary prison captures the process through which modern society politically invests the body. The power of spatial formations such as that of the prison or school arises from the fact that even before the development of particular notions of subjectivity, the body is inserted into a particular place. The way in which place frames images, controls sensations, and mandates characteristic gestures is crucial to the formation of individuals. Under industrialization, the control of the most minute gestures became profitable; simultaneously, prisons, factories, and schools proliferated. Although institutions such as the prison often escaped or subverted policy makers' original intentions, they were available to intensify other forms of social control by creating docile workers, manageable pathologies, and regular habits. According to Foucault, these factories, schools, and hospitals were realities that determined how people imagined themselves and others.

The power of place comes from the fact that social relations are directly experienced as inevitable and immutable, an extension of the world we inhabit. A common error reflected in both theory and "naïve" experience is to mistake the apparent stability of the natural and built environments for immutability. Although language, morality, art, discourse, and literature also generate fields of power relations, there is something particularly powerful about space precisely because of its irreducible physical component. Orientation in a landscape is the way in which the body experiences the world around it, thereby coming to know itself as an individual. Its power arises from the fact that space is lived and not merely perceived in a cognitive manner. It provides a place and a backdrop for a set of habits through which individuals recognize themselves in their social roles, as doctors, professors, workers, or women. Such sites also create order in a complex society; they are literally where people come to know their place. If space were conceived abstractly, it would be possible to change one's mind, but given that space is *lived* it becomes necessary to change reality.

Space as Displacement of Politics

Why has modern political theory, until quite recently, overlooked the power of place? There are several possibilities: the mind-body dualism that dismissed space as part of the material world; the Cartesian, scientific attitude with its aspirations to universality and abstraction at the expense of locality; the Derridean critique of "pure presence"; the current obsession with globalization.[21] Michel Foucault suggested two reasons for the long-standing dismissal of space in political theory: "Space used to be either dismissed as belonging to 'nature'—that is, the given, the basic conditions, 'physical geography,' in other words a sort of 'prehistoric stratum'; or else it was conceived as the residential site or field of expansion of peoples, of a culture, a language or a State."[22] In other words, space is conceived of either as nature or community. This means that space is either incidental or antithetical to the qualities of change, disruption, and innovation that are critical for political transformation. If, as Marx (following Shakespeare) put it, "all that is solid melts into air," then specific places, sites, and nodal points are at best incidental to the study of the structures that are genuinely constitutive of society.[23]

Both liberalism and Marxism have associated progress with rationalization and universalization, which undermine the relevance of situated knowledges and local practices. The tendency to conflate the masculine qualities of progress, universality, politics, and history together and set them in opposition to the feminine domain of tradition, stasis, and locality is one of the reasons why space often connotes conservatism. In Marxist theory, the dialectic is historical and thus temporal. Progress and emancipation are posited in the future. For Marxist-influenced thinkers such as Ernesto Laclau, space is static, conservative, and opposed to change.[24] Laclau explicitly argues that "politics and space are antinomic terms. . . . Politics only exists insofar as the spatial eludes us."[25] Such a position is consistent with Feuerbach's claim that "time is the privileged category of the dialectician, because it excludes and subordinates where space tolerates and coordinates."[26]

Contemporary theory has also tended to privilege time and language over space.[27] Coming from very different philosophical traditions, Habermas's work on the ideal speech situation, the Derridean critique of "pure presence," and Foucault's exploration of discursivity have fostered an interest in language and writing at the expense of space and material culture.

Michel de Certeau's *The Practice of Everyday Life* illustrates the critical orientation toward space that is widespread in much of poststructuralist and Marxist thought. His text provides an ideal focus for analysis because it reflects a set of assumptions that are widespread but implicit in other works. The core of his approach is to assimilate space to fixity, stasis, and control, a set of properties with negative connotations. According to Certeau, place implies "flattening out" difference, containing flux, and limiting change. It is associated with statistics, graphs, modern science, control, and military strategy.[28] Certeau believes place can "serve as the base from which relations with an exteriority composed of targets or threats can be managed."[29] In other words, place is a locus of control; its expression is the Panopticon.

Although Certeau does not make a sustained argument to justify this approach to space, he draws on widely shared intuitions, starting with the binary opposition between space and time. The logic goes like this: if space is the opposite of time, then it must be opposed to change. Certeau writes that a spatial sequence of points "is thus a mark in place of acts, a relic in place of performances." Whereas temporality is associated with freedom, the endless possibility of progress, or at least transformation, spatiality is linked to control and closure. Space is conflated with domination and homogeneity and juxtaposed with the transformative, plural qualities of temporality. Certeau fails to recognize the subversive and disruptive sides of space, concluding that the "'proper' (e.g. the domain of calculation and control) is a victory of space over time."[30]

Given this theoretical position, it is puzzling that Certeau devotes several chapters to spatial practices such as "walking in the city" and "spatial stories." By looking at the city, he discovers a complex interrelationship between place, memory, narrative, and meaning. While castigating *space* as a synonym for *closure*, he celebrates particular places such as the city as sites of transformation and irreducible plurality. He recognizes the way that the city opens up a kinesthetic world of experience to the modern-day *flaneur*. To reconcile the apparent contradiction between these two positions, he suggests that these spatial practices "refer to another spatiality (an anthropological, poetic or mythic experience of space)."[31] Later in the essay he reverses himself, insisting that "to walk is to lack a place. . . . The moving about that the city multiplies and concentrates makes the city itself an immense social experience of lacking a place—an experience that is, to be sure, broken up into countless tiny deportations, and compensated for by the relationships and intersections of these exoduses that intertwine and create an urban fabric."[32] His argument follows a flawed deductive logic. The premise is that space and place are static. Because the city is an opportunity for experience, diversion, disruption, self-presentation, and self-discovery, it cannot be "a place." But why not reverse the equation and start with the more plausible premise that the city is a place (a specific space) and conclude that space cannot be conflated with stasis and fixity?

My objection is that equating space with domination, stasis, and control is arbitrary, and in fact illogical, given that the city, the one place that Certeau discusses, exhibits none of those qualities. One possible solution to this paradox is that the terms *space* and *place* are meant metaphorically not literally. They are just poorly chosen metaphors for a politics of domination or nostalgia.

Although Certeau does not address this possibility, Ernesto Laclau, in his defense of a similar position, denies that the term *space* is meant metaphorically. He explains that "when we refer to space, we do not do so in a metaphorical sense, out of analogy with physical space. There is no metaphor here. . . . If physical space is also space, it is because it participates in this general form of spatiality."[33] For Laclau, the general form of spatiality is fixity. To understand this claim, we must consider why he concludes that space and politics are antinomic. For Laclau, politics becomes possible at a moment of dislocation, when an external element disrupts the ability of the dominant structure to contain and subsume all alternatives. Previously fixed elements are freed from the existing ordering principle; contestation and struggle ensue as rival possibilities compete to reestablish a new order. Dislocation is definitive of politics because different elements are no longer fixed in their predetermined place and must be reordered, rearranged into a new logic. According to Laclau, temporality is a constitutive aspect of dislocation because temporality suggests the possibility of something that exceeds the present. It is a way of expressing contingency or disruption. Disruption is that which comes from outside, the unknowable, the future, and therefore the temporal.[34]

There is nothing illogical about thinking of space rather than time as the site of dislocation, rupture, contradiction, and contingency. Trotsky's theory of combined and uneven development emphasized that the contradictions of capitalism do not necessarily come in temporal succession but can instead manifest themselves in the relationship between different geographical locations. The link between temporality and dislocation is also inconsistent with many philosophical treatments of time. History is often theorized as the way of overcoming existing contradictions. Both Nietzsche's eternal return and Hegel's end of history are different manifestations of this idea of time as a principle of fixity. Some versions of the dialectic imagine the future as a time when present contradictions will be reconciled. Space does not facilitate these illusions.[35]

Urban space is often characterized by contrasts and contradictions that exist side by side: rich and poor; production, consumption, and reproduction; decay, renewal, and reappropriation. Their juxtaposition in space is a glaringly visible reminder of the impossibility of achieving complete control, order, and homogeneity. It is this quality that makes urban space at once so threatening, fascinating, and haunting.[36] The Situationists coined the term *derive* (literally, "drifting") to describe "a technique of transient passage through varied ambiances."[37] Their goal was simply to become cognizant of the terrain of the city, letting go of habitual forms of blindness, thereby acquiring insight into its tensions, possibilities, and meanings.

Geography is the record of different levels of development at a given moment in time; it contains the sediments of alternate ways of building, elements of diverse modes of production, and evidence of the appropriation or destruction of nature. In any urban landscape there are the traces of historical struggles, that is, monuments, including both consciously erected memorials and stubbornly lingering scars. Nor are such layers of meanings restricted to urban landscapes; small villages and towns also reflect the tensions between different axes of power and resistance. The church, dissenters, commercial elite, local and central government, police, bandits, and foreign conquerors all build their monuments—the cathedral, barracks, fortress, central market, men's club—places that concentrate, mark, symbolize, and reproduce their powers. In fact, space provides a stage, juxtaposing these contradictions. It is a surface upon which one can map dislocations.[38]

Attempts to engage in critical theorizing often emphasize a spatial dimension. Foucault turns to "local knowledges" as a way of undermining authority and establishing the contingency of dominant theories.[39] Feminist and postcolonial theorists suggest that writings from the margins or transgressing borders may offer some leverage for undermining the universal practices that have served to reinforce domination. These are attempts to appropriate or subvert traditions that used spatial location as a way to authorize privilege: the center versus the periphery, the public versus the private sphere, the first versus the third world.[40] Space is not inherently liberatory. It is an element of both order and chaos. My suggestion is not that we reverse the dichotomy and privilege space as the ultimate embodiment of dislocation. Both time and space contain elements of fixity and flux. Rather than reestablishing a hierarchy between the two terms, it would be more fruitful to analyze how these two dimensions converge, contradict one another, and thereby reconstitute new political possibilities.

The House of the People

Stone and mortar are particularly potent symbols. Monumental buildings such as churches or palaces can convince both allies and enemies of a group's strength and power. But it would be a mistake to conclude that these buildings simply reflect existing power relations. They can also serve as a tool or even an inspiration for action and change. Political spaces can function as focal points for organizing otherwise dispersed energies. Although the power of place is often taken for granted, the connection between space and subjectivity can also be a tool for change. The socialist newspaper *La Giustizia* (1906) suggested that the workers' cooperative polished its members like the Po River polished stones. According to the piece, the refined atmosphere of the cooperative embodied the capacities of the most advanced workers and then inspired others to live up to this standard. The article particularly emphasized that the building—its cleanliness and décor—functioned as an element of social change.[41]

The buildings of the cooperatives and chambers of labor also reflected the aspirations of their members and their desire to make something collectively that they could not achieve individually. They materialized the workers' dreams, thereby sustaining those dreams. Writing in 1899, Jacques Greux described the experience of first entering Victor Horta's Maison du Peuple in Brussels:

> It is an impression of surprise and marvel that invades everyone who enters, passing by the great monumental door, that supports its roof at a great height, you penetrate in the construction where one accesses it by eight doors and there the vast proportions reveal themselves immediately. There are corridors that open up everywhere, stairways that wind, passages that intercross and recede, then halls, stores, large meeting rooms, offices, . . . what more can I say? And all these places that at first glance seem confused in an inextricable labyrinth are so logically, so appropriately combined that all it takes is to stop and think for a bit to immediately comprehend the practicality and ingenuity of the combinations. It is really imposing and one feels small, really small and almost crushed in front of the impressive majesty of the monument. It is rightly this, the "house" grand and powerful, that the people deserved, that [shows that] this people are themselves totally powerful and grand. . . . And everywhere, right down to the smallest corner, the clarity of day penetrates, emerges, and diffuses through the large windows and openings and brings to it its joy and its life, turning the new house of the people a veritable palace of light.[42]

Although it is tempting to dismiss this accolade as socialist propaganda, such a reaction would overlook the way the passage captures the experience of a monumental space. Anyone who has entered a cathedral, or palace, or magnificent municipal building can probably recognize the sensation that Greux tries to evoke. He describes the way that proportions, light, and organization of space converge to create an awe-inspiring, transformative effect. Although this experience was by no means unique to a house of the people, it was exceptional for workers to feel ownership over such a space. It inspired a sense of entitlement that is a precondition to rule. Because workers were positioned in the roles of petitioners at government offices or servants in grand palaces, monumentality usually functioned to make them aware of their powerlessness. The houses of the people had the opposite effect. Often compared with churches, they were organized for earthly rather than heavenly salvation.

The architectural significance and monumentality of Victor Horta's famous Maison du Peuple, of course, was not typical. Only one other workers' space—Konstantin Melnikov's constructivist Workers' Club, built in Moscow in the 1920s— would attain similar renown. Most of the cooperatives, chambers of labor, and houses of the people were modest constructions, built in vernacular styles by carpenters rather than architects. Nevertheless, the same principle was at stake; the builders believed that a microcosm of their ideal would help materialize their vision on a broader scale. They believed in the transformative effects of space, insisting,

> Our *case di tutti* [houses of everyone] must be beautiful, not for monumental vanity, not so that it will be the only thing seen from far away, while it overshadows the houses of our members. . . . That is a vain and ambitious civilization made for others. We should want to make our cooperative beautiful, for the same reasons that we want to improve our house. It must be the place where we learn to become more demanding, that is to say, more civilized.[43]

According to *La Giustizia*, the atmosphere of the cooperative elevates and influences the conduct of the members by inciting their desire for a better life. This desire starts out as an inchoate longing, inspired by the monumental beauty of the Maison du Peuple in Brussels, or pride in the local cooperative, and is channeled into the political activities those places provide.

Certain places are highly implicated in the process of forming identity and establishing solidarity. Furthermore, particular kinds of space, their taken-for-granted exclusions and inclusions, are important for politics. Subsequent chapters look at particular places—the factory, the cooperative, the chamber of labor—to analyze the forces they brought together. This chapter has challenged the assumption that spatiality implies stasis and therefore has an essentially conservative dimension. This assumption takes two forms. The more sweeping claim is that space is antithetical to politics. The more moderate version reflects a suspicion that locality and situatedness usually reflect an ultimately exclusionary longing for home. This chapter has demonstrated that space is no more intrinsically static than any other category such as time or language, thereby laying the groundwork for the much more difficult task of investigating how particular spaces enable or constrain popular participation in politics.

3

THE BOURGEOIS PUBLIC SPHERE

We live in a world in which the best becomes the worst, where
nothing is more dangerous than heroes and great men; where
everything, including freedom and revolt, changes into its own
opposite.

Henri Lefebvre, *Critique of Everyday Life*

Carlo Goldoni's comedy *The Coffee-House* (1755) depicts the romantic
intrigues and social hierarchies of a group of people who assemble daily
at Ridolfo's café. The characters include obsequious shopkeepers and
their servants, dissolute noblemen, pretentious bourgeoisie, and ladies
of ambiguous virtue. Members of different classes meet at the café; they
read the newspapers, gossip, and even discuss politics.[1] The bourgeois
public sphere that Goldoni parodies, however, is different from the one
of our theories and imagination.

The plot of the play, although extremely complicated, is fairly conventional. An unfaithful husband has deserted his wife, assumed the
false identity of Count Leandro, and flourished in Venice as a professional gambler. Don Mazio, the archetypical gossip, troublemaker, and
regular café patron complicates the situation by falsely accusing both
Count Leandro's wife and his new mistress of infidelity. Following a
convention typical of farce, the protagonists' identities are confused, in
part because it is Carnival, and the deserted wife wears a mask in the
hope of catching her straying husband.

In *The Coffee-House*, Goldoni parodies the secrecy, hypocrisy, and pre-
tense characteristic of the new bourgeois mode of sociability. The interdependence of secrecy and openness, publicity and privacy is the main

theme of the play. This is apparent in the stage design, which ingeniously juxtaposes the public and private, inside and outside, while emphasizing the permeability between them. The action of the play takes place on a small public square in Venice. There are three shops on the little piazza: a barber, a coffee shop, and a gambling house. Above the shops are a series of private rooms whose windows open out onto the street. Throughout the play, different characters draw attention to the way the private rooms both determine and contradict the public facade. Pandolfo, the owner of the gambling shop, challenges the supposedly greater respectability of the café, insisting, "You [Ridolfo, the proprietor of the café] have private rooms, like the others."[2] Another recurrent motif is Don Mazio's suggestion that the count's mistress has a back door to her apartment. Even though the count is the only visitor who has entered publicly, everyone believes the rumor than there must be a second, hidden entrance. The play provides a counterpoint to Habermas's more idealized vision of café life in *The Structural Transformation of the Public Sphere*. This chapter highlights the secrecy and exclusion that undermine the politics of the public sphere.

The Bourgeois Public Sphere

The café of late-eighteenth-century Europe was the paradigmatic site of the bourgeois public sphere. The café was a political space, a particular place with its own characteristic rules, informal practices, and scripted behaviors. It brought together certain people, divided others, and did so in regularized ways. The café was also political in so far as it was the social milieu of the new liberal politics.

According to Jürgen Habermas, the public sphere of the late eighteenth century was made up of places such as London's thousands of cafés, where artisans and intellectuals could meet, and the Parisian salons, which brought the nobility together with artists, intellectuals, and literati.[3] Habermas's analysis of the bourgeois public sphere is a model of critical social theory because of its attentiveness to the locations out of which a new mode of power arose. The bourgeois public sphere, which found its fullest realization in eighteenth- and nineteenth-century England, was an arena of rational-critical discussion about the common good. Habermas defined the public sphere as "a realm of our social life in which something approaching public opinion can be formed."[4] After analyzing the coffeehouses, salons, clubs, and journals,

Habermas concluded that the public sphere existed wherever private individuals engaged in critical debate that exerted a certain influence over government. It provided a link between the established channels of political authority and purely private economic and domestic interests.

The concept of the bourgeois public sphere theorized the political significance of civil society in a new way. The approach located liberal politics in a particular social milieu rather than simply an intellectual field or historical period. It linked two different dimensions of politics that have traditionally been investigated in isolation: ideas and institutions. For Habermas, the public sphere was not a physical place. It was an analytic construct that could not be reduced to a particular location such as the café or club. Like a Weberian ideal type, it abstracted from empirical regularities in order to highlight their salient features.

Social milieu is one component of this idealized model, arguably the most innovative one. Yet Habermas did not explicitly theorize the characteristics of social milieu. He analyzed "social structures of the public sphere," which he later called institutions, grouping the café, salon, club, family, and world of letters together as examples of institutions. The concept of the public sphere elides the distinction between very different kinds of spaces. The café, a widely accessible public accommodation, was a very different kind of space than the private gentleman's club, the more exclusive alternative that quickly replaced it. John Timbs describes how the two thousand coffeehouses found in London in 1715 were replaced by clubs, primarily because the cross-class nature of the coffeehouse was uncongenial to many patrons: "Our clubs are thoroughly characteristic of us. We are a proud people . . . and have a horror of indiscriminate association, hence the exclusiveness of our clubs."[5] Whereas the café opens onto the street, the club constructs barriers to entrance. Although both may create an opportunity for conversation, they constitute their respective publics in very different ways. The types of spaces that make up the public sphere reveal much about a society. As one English commentator wrote in 1899, "in an age of utilitarianism and the search for the comfortable like ours there is more to be learned [by looking at the club] than in the ruins of the Coliseum."[6]

Whereas the concept of the bourgeois public sphere links the theoretical elaboration of liberalism (through readings of Kant, Mill, and Tocqueville) and its social spaces, I propose to disaggregate the two components. Bracketing liberalism's idealized self-understanding and looking inside the closed doors of its salons, clubs, and cafés, we might discover a new understanding of the politics of the bourgeois public sphere. This chapter studies the bourgeois public sphere in order to understand its limitations. In the first section, to rethink the *publicness* of the public sphere, I analyze the role of secret societies in promulgating the Enlightenment. In subsequent sections I focus on its *bourgeois* character in order to uncover the relationship among class interests, universal principles, and the standard of rationality. In the final section I outline the distinctive characteristics of the popular public sphere.

Secrecy and the Public Sphere

Habermas recognized the irony that the public sphere existed "largely behind closed doors."[7] He concluded, however, that the "secret promulgation of enlightenment typical of lodges . . . had a dialectical character."[8] Initially, reason needed to be protected from publicity "because it was a threat to existing relations of domination." When repression subsided, the importance of secret societies diminished. According to Habermas, the capacity for reason was nurtured in secret before ultimately emerging in the light of public and vanquishing the forces of censorship and persecution. The need for "demonstrative fraternization ceremonies" disappeared, and a more rational, accessible, and enlightened form of sociability triumphed.

If there were an evolutionary dynamic as Habermas suggests, then secret societies would present no fundamental problem for his concept of the public sphere. If, however, the mystical, ritualistic, hierarchical, and hidden dimensions of societies such as the Masons remained a crucial element of bourgeois sociability well into the nineteenth century, then we have reason to question the publicness, the universality, and the rationality of the public sphere.

The historical record of secret societies in eighteenth- and nineteenth-century Europe raises doubts about Habermas's narrative of evolution from secrecy to publicity.[9] Speculative Masonry arose in England in the late seventeenth century as a form of sociability that brought together men from different social classes and religious creeds.[10] The Masonic lodge was the prototypical site of the bourgeois public sphere, a place where members of different social classes, committed to education, science, reason, commerce, friendship, religious toleration, social equality, and public service could forge a new, more enlightened politics. European Masonry, however, was an extremely complex phenomenon. Associated with both Newtonian physics and alchemy, Masonry pared reason and science with mysticism and hermetics. It created a context for egalitarian encounters only to reassert hierarchy through its constantly expanding number of grades and titles. It emphasized the values of universalism and inclusivity while tenaciously guarding its privileges and secrecy. So perhaps Lessing was correct in calling Freemasonry the inner truth of bourgeois society. The post-structuralist truism that the character of the enlightenment is determined by its constitutive outside, its secretive, hierarchical, and exclusionary dark side, is transparent in the phenomenon of Masonry.

The paradox underlying European secret societies was that the ideal of universalism was realized through an adaptation of the model of the guild, a typically feudal structure. Speculative Masonry was the progeny of operative Masonic lodges, artisanal guilds where practicing stonemasons socialized, provided mutual aid, protected their interests, and sacralized the secrets of their craft. Masonry reflected the corporate logic,[11] which was dominant in early modern Europe. Its purpose was to form a unified collectivity in which distinct parts would work together for the same goal. The metaphor of the body also emphasized "the indissolubility of human ties." According to the corporatist vision, collectivities rather than individuals were the basic components of society.[12] Guilds, like the operative Masons, were formed to defend particular interests, most notably to limit access to a segment of the labor market; they were one component of the hierarchically ordered society of feudalism. Yet the network of Lodges of Speculative Freemasonry provided the social context for the diffusion of Enlightenment principles.

Another similar question at the heart of Masonry is why the movement strove to realize principles of equality through a hierarchical system of grades, titles, and levels. The distinctions between Apprentice, Master, Warden, Fellow, Grand-Master, and Grand-Warden seemed more appropriate to a conservative aristocratic society than to a liberal and reformist movement. The fundamental differentiation between Apprentice and Master was a remnant of the traditional nomenclature used in artisanal trades. But rather than minimizing this distinction over the course of time, the Masons multiplied the levels and titles to create a highly stratified society, with many lodges and sects having as many as seven or eight different grades. These symbolic distinctions often reproduced existing social hierarchies and regulated access to the order's ritual knowledge.

The paradoxical nature of Masonry is also manifest in its symbolic and ritual systems. In the ritual in which an Apprentice was promoted to

Master, the Brothers all wore aprons, ceremonial garb evocative of the "craftsman as hero" ideal. As Masonry evolved, however, many orders replaced the artisanal symbols such as the apron, ax, and workbench with aristocratic images of knighthood such as swords and armor. Others adopted names that proclaimed them to be the Knights of ——. The so-called Scottish Masons were particularly known for embracing mysticism and hermetics. "Scottish" Masonry was committed to avenging of the assassins of Hiram, architect to King Solomon, and traced its lineage through the medieval Templars and the Crusaders. Their rituals involved drawn swords, skeletons, horrific oaths, and symbolic acts of vengeance. Orders of the Grades of Vengeance such as the Chevalier Kadosh became extremely popular in France in the prerevolutionary period.[13] Although the Grades of Vengeance might have been an extreme tendency, all Masonic orders elaborately ritualized and mystified even their worship of nature and reason.

One possible explanation for these tensions is that Masonry grafted two disparate elements: Enlightenment ideals and "archaic" forms of social organization. But this seems unlikely given the bourgeois roots of secret societies. Although it is true that Masonry emerged out of the guild structure, it fundamentally transformed the structure and function as well as the social and economic bases of the original lodges. Despite its claims to antiquity, which are endlessly repeated in Masonic lore and mythology, Masonry was a modern phenomenon that originated in the early eighteenth century. It flourished under the new economic and social circumstances of mercantile England and benefited from the gradual abolition of restrictions on secular sociability. Although maintaining symbolic links to traditional identities and associations, Masonry was distinctly a product of the growth of urbanism, leisure, and cosmopolitanism.[14] The world of secret societies provides glimpses of the future more than it reveals traces of a feudal past. The Masons' characteristic hierarchy, secrecy, exclusiveness, power politics, and irrationality were at the heart of the newly emergent public sphere.

The contradictions and tensions that are so apparent in the phenomenon of secret societies were also true of other sites that made up the public sphere. The ideal of universalism was celebrated in exclusive clubs and salons that transgressed the boundary between noble and bourgeois only to reassert new, more refined divisions. Reason, objectivity, and science were worshipped not just as modes of enlightenment but also as privileges and instruments of power.

The paradoxical nature of the politics of the public sphere is particularly apparent in the history of the Carbonari, a secret society that flourished in Italy at the beginning of the nineteenth century. Like other variants of Masonry, the Carbonari espoused both liberal, egalitarian principles and secret teachings that were only accessible to members initiated into the higher ranks.[15] Unlike earlier secret societies, however, the Carbonari developed a mass base rooted in its genuinely popular constituency. In Naples, the epicenter of the movement, there were 340 lodges, called *vendite*, meaning "shops." A conservative estimate places the total membership between 50,000 to 60,000 in 1816.[16] The Carbonari was also nationalist in character, reflecting its anti-Napoleonic origins.[17]

Although rumors connecting secret societies to political upheaval have been widespread since the French Revolution, only one case has convinced historians: the Carbonari provided the political leadership and the mass support for the Neapolitan revolution of 1820.[18] Throughout the preceding decade, the political program of the Carbonari called for the unity, liberty, and independence of the Italian people, with some members advocating constitutional monarchy as a way to further this agenda and others advocating a republican form of government. One document specifies that the goal was to "destroy tyrants and overthrow absolutist governments"; another clarified that the organization's aim was to "restore to the citizen that liberty and those rights which Nature bestowed on us."[19] Unlike previous secret societies, the Carbonari recruited heavily among the lower classes, including domestic servants, soldiers, and fishermen. Rituals included the provision that the initiate could make the sign of the cross if he could not sign his name. On the eve of the 1820 revolution, estimates of membership ran from 300,000 to 642,000 members.[20]

It would seem as the if the hut (*baracca*) and shop (*vendita*) of the Carbonari were among the first sites of radical democratic practice in Italy. Overtly political and socially embedded, these places facilitated the formation of a cross-class alliance. Yet the terms of such an alliance were never openly negotiated. The secrecy protecting the oaths and principles of the higher grades institutionalized and intensified existing inequalities in the distribution of knowledge. The Carbonari created a widely shared myth of fraternalism and equality that masked the actual dispersion of power. An 1821 account of the Carbonari suggested that "the main object [of different levels] was to secure a number of satellites, ready to obey invisible superiors and directions which they cannot understand."[21] Although such an assessment initially sounds paranoid, it helps explain the puzzling reality of a "secret" society with half a million members. This number only makes sense if the important secrets were accessible to only a small percentage of the mass membership.

If the characteristics of secrecy, hierarchy, and mysticism were unique to secret societies, then they would only be historical curiosities. But what if the practices of secret societies revealed some general truths about the bourgeois public sphere? Groups like the Masons and the Carbonari emphasized a theoretical commitment to equality while relying on elaborate forms of hierarchy. Their unity was forged through mythic rendering of particular (usually class-specific) interests as sacred, universal, transcendent truths. Finally, their lodges facilitated genuinely cross-class coalitions, but such coalitions were structured to reinforce the hegemony of the elite rather than to create a popular forum. There is no doubt that these sites of resistance to the old regime were fundamental in diffusing liberal ideas, establishing new alliances, and reinforcing new identities. These political effects were usually not so much the product of conspiracy as they were the indirect result of new forms of sociability. Analyzing the bourgeois public sphere from the standpoint of the secret societies yields the conclusion that such a public sphere could not realize its own aspirations to rationality, inclusiveness, and universality.

Bourgeois and Citizen

Although the "publicness" of the bourgeois public sphere is debatable, its class character is uncontestable. In fact, it is the sociological sophistication and nuance of the model that makes Habermas's analysis exemplary. He uses the adjective *bourgeois* to emphasize that despite its universalistic pretensions, the public sphere was the product of specific historical experiences and corresponding class interests. He draws attention to the cultural and economic structures that were necessary preconditions of the public sphere. For example, the public sphere was premised on the idea that rational individuals could enter into a distinctive arena characterized by its publicness. This in turn presupposed a realm of interiority, subjectivity, and privacy in which the bourgeois man experienced himself as an individual and developed the convictions that he would bring into public debate. This capacity for judgment, while not the exclusive privilege of birth or lineage, was linked to the cultural, economic, and social structures of bourgeois life.

Habermas emphasizes the connection between economic position and citizenship. During the period when the public sphere flourished, property qualifications explicitly excluded the working classes from political participation. But such suffrage restrictions were manifestations of a more deeply rooted link between economic status and political participation. The problem was not only that workers were not allowed to vote but also that their interests were assumed to challenge both order and prosperity. In other words, the relationship between economic position and participation in the public sphere was not merely contingent. The bourgeois could conceive of his interests as universalizable because they were already reflected in the structure of the economic system. As long as the public good was defined as the aggregate national income and the bourgeoisie were those who owned and controlled this income, there was no reason to perceive private and public good as conflicting. Class interests could only be perceived as generalizable interests as long as conflicting visions were excluded. This means that the political inclusion of the working class could not leave the public sphere intact but would necessarily introduce an element of conflict; once fundamental economic interests were no longer shared, they could not be taken for granted as premises but had to be thematized as interests.

The ideal of universalizability is problematic when it is based on masking a series of prior (and often violent) exclusions. The public sphere was fragmented from the outset, and therefore power and conflict were never exogenous.[22] More strident critics of Habermas go a step farther, suggesting that the idealized image of the bourgeois public sphere served to reinforce the power differentials.[23] By aiding in the masquerade whereby private economic concerns were disguised as general interests, the public sphere served to strengthen particularistic interests of the elite. Returning to these themes in a 1989 essay, "Some Further Reflections on the Public Sphere," Habermas acknowledges this point. He recognizes that the issue of exclusion is fundamental when the excluded groups "play a constitutive role in the formation of a particular public sphere."[24] A constitutive (as opposed to merely incidental) exclusion puts into question whether the ideal of universalizability is really the appropriate standard for transformative political change, given that the interests of those excluded socially are almost never defined by existing structures as generalizable and hence relevant to the "universalist" project.[25]

Workers and the Public Sphere

The crucial question is whether democratizing the public sphere destroys it, whether a deliberative politics is necessarily elitist.[26] To answer this question it is necessary to turn to the debate surrounding the political inclusion of the working classes. This, in turn, involves evaluating the existence and distinctiveness of a popular public sphere. Was there an arena outside the state in which workers could formulate and articulate challenges to abuses of authority by dominant power? If so, how did it differ from the bourgeois public sphere? In *The Structural Transformation*, Habermas claims the plebian public sphere, which manifested itself in movements such as Chartism and anarchism, "remains oriented toward the intentions of the bourgeois public sphere."[27] Essentially, Habermas makes two arguments about the role played by the public sphere in the struggle for political inclusion of the working classes. First, he insists that popular democratic mobilization was not distinct from earlier bourgeois forms. Second, he claims that political participation on the part of workers effectively destroyed the public sphere. He states unequivocally, "In reality, however, the occupation of the political public sphere by the unpropertied masses led to an interlocking of state and society which removed from the public sphere its former basis without supplying a new one."[28] Paradoxically, Habermas asserts that popular participation involved both the extension and destruction of the public sphere as a distinctive sphere of rational-critical consensus. In both cases, the possibilities for democracy seem bleak. Either the inclusion of the majority leaves the real basis of power intact or it undermines the basis for a rational-critical debate all together.

Are these the only two choices? Must the popular public sphere be either derivative or destructive? Scholars such as Geoff Eley, Günther Lottes, Oskar Negt, and Alexander Kluge have challenged this characterization of the effects of popular participation. Like Habermas, these scholars use the ideal of a public sphere to criticize the impoverished nature of public life under late capitalism. Unlike Habermas, they argue that the nostalgia for a lost reign of rationality is counterproductive for social change. Not only have the structural changes, most notably the extension of mass consumerism, completely transformed the conditions of cultural production but the bourgeois public sphere was also a flawed model from the outset.

Social historians such as E. P. Thompson and Maurice Agulhon have made important albeit implicit contributions to this debate by documenting the links between the cultural aspects of workers' lives and forms of political mobilization.[29] They have discovered a distinctive, diverse, and vibrant working-class culture. Thompson in particular has identified the way in which collective political action both relied on and reconstituted preexisting English cultural traditions. Public theater, ritual shaming, and anonymous sabotage were characteristic of popular action before the industrial period and came to serve as protest strategies against the social dislocations of early capitalism.

At first it appears conceivable that these studies could be incorporated into Habermas's framework. The account would follow an evolutionary logic; during the nineteenth century, the lower classes learned increasingly sophisticated strategies, ultimately adopting the modern political forms of the bourgeoisie.[30] It is true that working-class politics originated in taverns, the functional equivalent of the bourgeois coffeehouses, eventually becoming formalized in associations, study groups, and corresponding societies. French historian Maurice Agulhon suggests that the history of workers' associations reflects a "dialectic between old-fashioned and modern" rather than an evolutionary logic. He argues that the "eruption of democratic ideas" among workers in Provence in the mid-nineteenth century had three roots: bourgeois associations such as the *cercle*, bourgeois culture (transmitted through the mediation of educated artisans), and autonomous mutual insurance companies.

Some forms of protest were embedded in a distinctively plebian culture. The bread riot and the demonstration, for example, emphasized the public display of force and resolve rather than the public exercise of reason. Alongside liberal discourse and parliamentary procedures, workers used songs and satire. Günter Lottes argues that what may initially appear like a pure assimilation of bourgeois practices was actually a reappropriation of the dominant norms that yielded distinctive political forms.[31] Furthermore, workers' use of apparently primitive tactics such as mob violence or anonymous vandalism was sometimes based on necessity rather than political immaturity. Often it was the only effective method of political action under the adverse conditions of government repression. E. P. Thompson emphasizes that the person who took part in a mob or acted under the cover of darkness did not open himself up for individual punishment.[32] Public criticism of the existing power structure is almost always a luxury. This luxury was seldom enjoyed by workers, who still relied on the bourgeoisie for employment and survival. Furthermore, without political rights, workers were especially vulnerable to state repression. This vulnerability constrained the repertoires of collective action.

These theoretical criticisms and historical investigations force us to reevaluate the public sphere as a normative category for political critique. Did the public sphere, with appropriate modifications and reforms, serve as the medium for the radicalization of democracy at the onset of the twentieth century? Can it today? Did the intellectual journals, clubs, and cafés continue to serve as a space for rational critical debate about the common good? Can the public sphere still serve as a nodal point for linking the power of citizens' rational, critical capacities to the service of universal ideals?

The Habermas of *The Structural Transformation of the Public Sphere* was pessimistic. The book could easily have been called the "degeneration" of the public sphere. Influenced by the Frankfurt school's criticisms of the culture industry and postwar social theory's attack on mass society, Habermas painted a bleak picture of civil society under late capitalism. He concluded that in the twentieth century, the boundary separating the private from the public had been effectively dissolved, leaving in its wake self-interested bargaining and technical administration, "without involving any rational-critical political debate on the part of private people."[33] This was in part the result of the commodification of culture, which turned critical citizens into passive consumers of entertainment, anaesthetized by increasingly alien spectacles.[34] No longer capable of either critical engagement or individuality, public life lost its distinctive quality, leaving only the anemic togetherness of mass consumption in the mall, movie theater, or soccer stadium.

Or at least that is the story Habermas tells at the conclusion of *The Structural Transformation of the Public Sphere*. His recent work, however, is more optimistic about the capacity of civil society to renew its vital function of mediating between the private individual and the state. This optimism reflects a new, quasi-transcendental foundation for the ideal of the public sphere: discourse ethics.[35] Although the details of the theory of discourse (or communicative) ethics have undergone various modifications, the essence of Habermas's position is that the premises of communication (things such as the truthfulness of the propositional content, the authenticity of the speaking subject, and so forth) contain the possibility of reaching consensus.[36] Consensus is possible because understanding is the telos inherent in human speech. The shift here is crucial: Habermas moves from a historically and spatially specific way of locating social integration to an abstract, universal basis. In his middle period, Habermas links the individual to the community by showing that normative validity is not the result of the individual's monological reason but the intersubjective process of dialogue. Although Habermas explicitly acknowledges that few cases of communication actually embody this ideal, he emphasizes that the "ideal speech situation" nevertheless serves as a compelling standard for criticizing distorted communication.

In more recent works, such as *Between Facts and Norms* and *The Inclusion of the Other*, Habermas has returned to the political implications of his work on language. He offers a deliberative model of politics in which deliberative forums could enhance political legitimacy by strengthening the procedural fairness and rational content of democracy.[37] The premise underlying deliberative democracy is that the rational consensus engendered through discussion should serve as the normative guide for democratic politics.[38] Although this shift from discourse ethics to deliberative democracy appears to be a return to the theme of the public sphere, methodologically it is still a departure from the earlier work. Whereas the original concept of the public sphere served to illuminate how specific social forces, institutions, and spaces contributed to the process of democratization, the more abstract idea of rational discourse obscures these political elements. *Structural Transformation* emphasized the specific economic and social preconditions that made a distinctive form of criticism and control possible. The ideal of discourse ethics, in contrast, relies on an abstract notion of consensus, thereby obscuring the way in which power structures limit the range of possible outcomes. The spatial nature of the metaphor of the public sphere lends itself to analysis of specific sites of public opinion formation as well as their relative accessibility or closure. Deliberative democracy's emphasis on the general structure of communication as the basis of democratic politics, however, hides the fact that even linguistic competence is hierarchically distributed and implicated in the reproduction of dominant exclusions.

The Enlightenment public sphere was progressive in a political context in which power was a prerogative of inherited status. Juridical equality was an immense improvement over a political system based on an elite monopoly of power and authority. In the nineteenth century, a universalistic concept of rationality furthered democracy because the primary forms of exclusion were justified through an explicit defense of hierarchy and privilege. The error comes in universalizing this particular moment and reifying it as the enduring legacy of democracy. Under current conditions, such an abstract notion of rationality may indeed be counterproductive. Formal equality masks the barriers to effective participation that continue to determine the outcomes of supposedly democratic processes. Appeals to generalizable interests are the sine qua non of discussion in the public sphere. But social and economic structures constrain what seems generalizable. The standard of universalizability overlooks the fact that the interests of the marginal and disempowered are precisely those that are not defined as generalizable under dominant definitions.

These criticisms by no means imply that the concept of the public sphere should be abandoned. The resurgence of interest in the public sphere, as well as the prominence of related concepts such as discursive democracy and civil society, indicates the need to theorize the relationship between informal mechanisms of public opinion formation, representation, and authorized decision making. Instead of abandoning this project, critical social theory would need to radicalize it. This involves recovering the original critical intent of the concept of the public sphere.

The Popular Public Sphere

In *The Public Sphere and Experience*, the German social critics Negt and Kluge make a strong argument in favor of the political salience of a proletarian public sphere, that is, a place where the subaltern classes can determine their own experience, thereby learning to formulate an autonomous political agenda. The problem with Negt and Kluge's use of the term is that it remains extremely abstract. The proletariat public sphere is easily romanticized because it is an ideal rather than a recognizable place. Furthermore, their terminology raises the issue of whether the public sphere is confined to the proletariat (industrial workers) or includes what Gramsci called the subaltern (or popular) classes.

Is there such a thing as a popular public sphere? The concept of the public sphere has at least two meanings. It is the sphere in which private people come together to engage in reasoned debate about the general rules governing social and political life.[39] The public sphere can also designate the place where the hegemony (or counterhegemony) of a social class is achieved by integrating elements of other classes and formulating a worldview capable of assimilating some of their values. According to both of these definitions, a popular public sphere flourished in pre-fascist Europe. Its constitutive social spaces were taverns, cooperatives, wine circles, and chambers of labor.

One difference between the bourgeois public sphere and its popular progeny was the relationship between the public and private dimensions. Although politics takes place in the public sphere, a crucial precondition of political participation is the sense of autonomy and subjectivity (collective or individual) cultivated in the private domain. The motivation, strength, and resolution to engage in protracted struggles with opposing forces in the public arena come from experiences that take place in the "back regions."[40] In these back regions, it is possible to fortify claims and concepts that are defined as irrational or illegitimate from the hegemonic perspective.

The popular "private sphere" differed from its "bourgeois" corollary (see table 1). According to Habermas, discussions in the public sphere reflected the capacity for individual judgment and subjectivity that was nurtured in the bourgeois home.[41] Only individuals with distinctive views and experiences could enter into rational critical debate. These individuals developed a capacity for autonomy and judgment in the private home, where, unlike at court, they were not bound by conventional ideas and behaviors.[42] In the twentieth century, the disappearance of a distinctive private realm caused the transformation of the public sphere. Mass-based, consumer culture insinuated itself into the home, breaking down the realm of "interiority" and undermining the public sphere. The mass media eviscerated the line between public and private, subordinating both to the homogeneous standards of consumer culture.

For workers, however, the private home was never the basis of interiority and critical consciousness. The crowded and poorly lit home was the site of production and reproduction, not leisure and reflection. The capacity for political judgment was nurtured instead in places such as union halls and cooperatives. In Habermas's model, only the individual who "attained clarity about itself" by "communicating with itself" could participate in the public sphere.[43] But this vision is excessively individualistic and still influenced by the Cartesian mythology of the autonomous intellect. In popular politics, the line between public and private is transgressed, but this is a sign of the popular public sphere's viability rather than its failing. By communicating with others, not in isolation, disenfranchised workers could attain clarity about their shared interests, including class interests. These encounters took place in "primary associations"—places such as the neighborhood *circolo* or mutual

Table 1. Differences between the Bourgeois and Popular Public Spheres

	Bourgeois Public Sphere	Popular Public Sphere
Constitutive private spaces	Home	*Circolo*, mutual aid society, trade union
Constitutive public spaces	Café, salon, club, Masonic lodge	Chamber of labor, house of the people
Economic theory	Individualistic, free-market	Cooperative
Political theory	Liberalism	Socialism, radical democracy
Political institution	Parliament	Municipalism, councils

aid society, where individuals of similar backgrounds formed relatively homogeneous groups. These "primary associations" helped sustain a diversity of viewpoints and ensured political socialization, thus playing a role analogous to that of the "private" home. The more public side of the equation took place in spaces such as the chamber of labor, where different social groups (industrial workers, artisans, laborers) and factions (minimalists, maximalists, syndicalists) fought for ideological and institutional leadership over the workers' movement.

The popular public sphere also had economic and political characteristics that differed from the bourgeois public sphere. Whereas the bourgeois public was based on the illusion that the roles of *bourgeois* and *citoyen* did not conflict, the popular public sphere emphasized the tension between them. In the cooperative movement, workers experimented with alternate economic structures that overcame the opposition. Whereas bourgeois subjectivity was guaranteed by private property, the subaltern classes' structural position foreclosed a political identity based on economic autonomy. The alternative to individual private property was "social wealth," an economic structure based on collective resources. Fourier's phalansteries, Owen's New Lanark, as well as the less grandiose and utopian but more prolific consumer cooperatives that spread across Europe were part of this social economy. Even though these economic alternatives never replaced or even seriously threatened capitalism, the desire for collective control over economic life was a widely shared aspiration that unified different class fragments, generated resources for oppositional projects, and provided a base for political struggle.

The popular public sphere also had a political dimension. Whereas liberalism was the political theory of the bourgeois public sphere, radical democracy and socialism were the political theories of the popular public sphere. The institutional manifestation of liberal democracy was

Parliament, a body explicitly committed to talk over action and deliberation about the common good instead of strategic struggles for power. In effect, it consolidated the power of the emerging national bourgeoisie. Municipalism was the institutional achievement of the popular public sphere. By creating new representative institutions such as the chamber of labor and integrating them into the system of local government, municipalism facilitated popular participation not only in voting but also in governing.

This book focuses on the spatial dimension of the popular public sphere rather than on its more familiar ideological side. It explores the way that social spaces create "solidarity that can be grasped with the senses."[44] Most people, especially poor people, have few individual resources, and therefore their power comes from numbers. Solidarity is their greatest strength, and atomization is their greatest weakness. Physical places that bring people together to experience, celebrate, and reinforce their unity are of utmost political importance.[45] According to Negt and Kluge, that is the significance of the barricade. The barricade is of more moral than military importance; it is a performance of solidarity, a material embodiment of cooperation and mutual protection. Physical proximity creates solidarity by facilitating the implicit processes whereby individuals share and constantly revise interpretations. The concentration of bodies is the only available tactic of resistance for those who do not (either literally or metaphorically) carry weapons. Public or quasi-public space is crucial because "massing together serves as a mutual confirmation of their own reality, for who else but the other workers can confirm that their struggle is not a mere illusion. . . . It is only in this reaffirmed reality that an atmosphere of collective revolt comes about, that the workers begin to talk, make suggestions, and become active."[46] Neither the private sphere of the workplace (symbolized by the factory) nor the atomized arena of mass communication can create the space for solidarity, critique, and experimentation characteristic of the popular public sphere.

The concept of the public sphere has been an important contribution to political and social theory. The strength and the weakness of Habermas's approach was his attempt to link together intellectual and social history. The Enlightenment ideal of the public sphere was eloquently articulated by Kant in his essay "What Is Enlightenment," but it was also lived by thousands of upwardly mobile artisans, intellectuals, shopkeepers, artists, and déclassé aristocrats, who gathered together in cities.

In thousands of cafés they established new modes of social interaction that were still improvised rather than scripted. They took these protean encounters and created formal and exclusive associations: Masonic lodges, salons, political clubs. Although the concept of "the public" has a long and complex history, Habermas contributed fresh sociological insight into the properties of "the public sphere." Not a physical space or a cultural code or an ideology, the idea of the public sphere was an attempt to link these elements.

Under an avowedly hierarchical and aristocratic political system, the bourgeois public sphere was a site of resistance to the existing monopoly on power. But after the consolidation of liberal-capitalist regimes, the ideal of "reasonable" public debate became a justification for excluding those issues that threatened the existing consensus and those individuals who challenged its premises. The idealized aspirations to rationality, publicity, and universality obscured the ambivalent elements of its legacy—the reconstituted hierarchies, myths, and exclusions of bourgeois sociability.

The public sphere links together political ideologies and practices, ideas and spaces. The danger is that when the two diverge, the ideological component tends to obscure the social realities. We associate the Enlightenment more with the theories of Kant than with the realities of the Masonic lodge. One reason is that the history of ideas is easier to study. Scholarly treatises are relatively coherent and explicit, and they are more accessible than the illusive records of popular political practices and their meanings. Spatial analysis provides an opportunity to recover the material basis of politics and a motivation to read different types of sources, including the tactical, engaged theorizing that challenges political philosophy's self-understanding.

4 / THE DISCIPLINARY FACTORY

Fritz Lang's *Metropolis* (1927) provides a vivid, expressionistic optics of the dark side of factory production. It captures a sinister world of powerful machines and desperate, downtrodden men simmering underneath a fantastic, futuristic city. The opening scenes juxtapose two opposed yet interlinked spaces: a Baroque pleasure garden for the rich and a dark, subterranean prison-cum-factory for the poor. The only force capable of bridging the barrier between the two worlds is the privileged but kindhearted Freder's love for Maria, the saint of the poor. The message of the film, however, is by no means the need for class struggle. In the logic of *Metropolis*, breaking machines is tantamount to self-destruction, and collective action easily degenerates into mass hysteria and irrational mob violence. The solution is found in Freder's benign intervention; his good heart unifies the workers ("hand") and the bourgeoisie ("brain").

Metropolis effectively illustrates the ambivalent status of the factory in the cultural production of the interwar period. The factory functioned as a symbol of oppression and social control. But the film also captures the fascination with the machine that was characteristic of the 1920s—a fascination that was shared by workers and the wealthy, as well as Russian revolutionaries, Italian fascists, and American industrialists. The treatment of the factory in political theory reflects this same ambivalence.

Adam Smith was one of the first theorists to recognize the paradoxical legacy of the division of labor, which could lead to fantastic increases in productivity while reducing the workers to idiocy.[1] Marx, Lenin, and Gramsci each struggled with the dual nature of the factory.[2] In different ways, each suggested that the factory, symbol of the ascendancy of industrialism, could also be the most important site of resistance to capitalism.

Was the factory an effective site of resistance? Socialist critics of the bourgeois public sphere embraced the factory as the most promising site of political mobilization. Some even suggested it was the nodal point of a new society. Unlike the world of the bourgeois public sphere, however, the factory was not imagined as an ideal realization of rationality and consensus. The factory was a site of domination, which played a fundamental role in motivating the struggle against capitalism. The dystopian properties of the factory made it a potential site of resistance to the capitalist system. Marx argued that the experience of the factory illuminates the actual conditions of work under capitalism, thereby augmenting class consciousness and facilitating class struggle. This chapter shows that the factory was also a particularly refined spatial system for isolating and controlling workers.

Socialist theorists have treated the factory as a metaphor for a moment in the logic of capitalism, a system of production that we sometimes call Fordism. This highly abstract and metaphoric approach makes it possible to see the factory alternately as the germ of a new producerist society (Lenin and the early Gramsci) or the site of the destruction of capitalism (Marx). From the perspective of the spatial heuristic, the contradictory and complex nature of the factory is more easily recognized.[3] This chapter shows that in the initial stages of industrialization, the factory was essentially a spatial arrangement created to increase surveillance and control over the labor process, which inhibited collective action on the part of workers. The factory as an experience, however, is not the same as the factory as a place enclosed by four walls. Although the factory did not prove to be the exclusive or even primary site of political mobilization, factory workers brought their experiences into the tavern, the *casa del popolo*, the club where they forged links, gained allies, and assimilated new ideas.

The Logic of the Factory

Although Marx never used the term *space of resistance*, it was implicit in his analysis of capitalism, class conflict, and revolution. As a prominent critic of utopian communes, he was acutely aware of the relationship between place and power.[4] Marx saw that a crucial step in motivating collective action was recognizing individual experiences of exploitation as manifestations of a broader structural dynamic. Concentration and dispersion of workers as well as the visibility or opacity of economic structures were of foremost importance for political transformation. Although Marx did not believe that a new arrangement of social space would change humanity, he did note that the spatial practices of capitalism could affect class consciousness. Marx's analysis of the dystopia of the factory is one of the most important theories linking microspaces to emancipation; however, the link between the factory and a transformative politics is paradoxical because it is premised on the intensification of exploitation.

There is a profound tension within the Marxist tradition about the role of the factory in the process of social transformation. While many early socialists and even communists were nostalgic for the creativity and autonomy of artisanal labor, subsequent thinkers embraced the modern, mechanized factory as the basis of a distinctive proletarian identity and power. This tension is apparent in the difference between the much-commented-on romanticism of the early Marx, who imagined that it would be possible to "hunt in the morning, fish in the afternoon, rear cattle in the evening, criticise after dinner,"[5] and the almost futurist tone of Gramsci's celebration of the factory as site of proletarian unity. Although these two positions may initially seem like opposite poles, I suggest that we read them as two particularly prominent manifestations of a conceptual dilemma. How can the factory, the site of disciplinary power and exploitation par excellence, serve as a nodal point in the struggle against workers' subordination?

Both Marx and Gramsci assumed that the factory produced not only capitalist commodities but also revolutionary subjects. For Marx, class consciousness arose in response to the alienation of the factory. For Gramsci, proletarian identity was more a direct extension of the factory's discipline and unity. Both positions present highly idealized and stylized visions of the factory. They posit the factory as the structural basis of the revolutionary subject, the proletariat, without investigating the factory as a place with its own material specificity. To unravel the difficulties implicit in the idea of the factory as a potential site of resistance, I consider Marx and Gramsci's theoretical analyses in light of the historical record of factory life in Italy at the turn of the century. This involves two steps: going *inside* the factory to uncover the types of political subjectivity that were produced there and stepping *outside* the factory to assess its relationship to other sites of political power.

Marx on the Factory

For Marx, the factory was both the site of exploitation as well as the basis of eventual emancipation. His criticism of the factory system drew on descriptions of inhuman conditions of labor exposed in pamphlets and newspapers. Early socialist critics focused attention on the oppressive conditions of modern factory labor: extremely long hours; repetitive, stressful work; appalling violations of the most minimal health and safety standards; and complete subordination to the unceasing rhythms of machines. Although Marx and Engels embraced the increase in productive forces engendered by capitalism, they did not romanticize factory life.

In *The Condition of the Working Class in England in 1844,* an exposé of conditions in British factories and slums, Engels called preindustrial life "idyllic."[6] Although they criticized other socialist thinkers for just this kind of nostalgia, Marx and Engels often reproduced it, especially in their early work. Although the *Communist Manifesto* highlights the achievements of capitalism, it has little positive to say about the factory system. Marx and Engels argue that "owing to the extensive use of machinery and to division of labour, the work of the proletarians has lost all individual character, and consequently, all charm for the workman. He becomes an appendage of the machine. . . . Masses of laborers, crowded into the factory, are organised like soldiers."[7] They compare the proletarian to the slave who is in bondage not to a single master but to the machine itself, the bourgeois class, and the bourgeois state. Marx and Engels recognize that the factory system is based on the science of exploitation; by increasing the control of management, facilitating the use of machinery, and thus deskilling labor, the bourgeoisie can appropriate the spiraling profits necessary to compete in the capitalist market.

The factory system, however, sows the seeds of its own destruction. Like the dynamics of exploitation and resistance that characterize the capitalist system in general, the factory produces its own gravediggers. The paradoxical benefit of the hyper-exploitation achieved in the totally controlled environment of the factory is that the real nature of capitalism, which is obscured in the marketplace, becomes easy to see. Marx and Engels suggest that "the more open this despotism proclaims gain to be its end and aim, the more petty, the more hateful and the more embittering it is."[8] The factory system increases exploitation, but it makes such exploitation more visible and transparent. Even though all previous forms of capitalist production also subordinated human labor to the instruments of labor, the factory system is unique because in the factory "this inversion for the first time acquires technical and palpable reality."[9] The factory worker knows that she is just another "input" in the production process and that she is even more expendable than the complex, expensive machinery. No longer blinded by relations of personal obligation and dependence, the proletariat can see the growing cleavage between the interests of management and labor. This knowledge is the crucial first step in developing class consciousness and eventually engaging in revolutionary action.

A second result of the factory is that it contributes to the increasing homogeneity of the working class. In the *Communist Manifesto*, Marx and Engels explain that modern machines undermine the importance of the skills and training that previously differentiated workers. Strength, precision, calculation, and creativity are all nullified by the single imperative of tending the machine. As control over the work process is wrested from the artisans and craftsmen, differentiation among workers declines. Under these conditions, workers no longer consider each other potential competitors but rather members of the same class, undergoing the same experience of exploitation. Precisely because the factory is a site that concentrates and accelerates the exploitation of labor, it is also the nodal point of resistance. The unceasing competition of capitalism with its concomitant commercial crises and cyclical recessions makes workers' lives ever more precarious, but the factory system also reveals that these experiences are shared by the proletariat as a class.

Writing in 1848, Marx and Engels were optimistic that the experience of the factory would give birth to oppositional trade unions and eventually national or international, class-based, and politically oriented organizations:

With its [the proletariat's] birth begins its struggle with the bourgeoisie. At first the contest is carried on by individual labourers, then by the workpeople of a factory, then by the operatives of one trade, in one locality, against the individual bourgeois who directly exploits them. . . . But with the development of industry the proletariat not only increases in number; it becomes concentrated in greater masses, its strength grows, and it feels that strength more. The various interests and conditions of life within the ranks of the proletariat are more and more equalised, in proportion as machinery obliterates all distinctions of labour, and nearly everywhere reduces wages to the same low level. . . . Thereupon the workers begin to form combinations (Trade Unions) against the bourgeoisie.[10]

The narrative of the *Communist Manifesto*, part history and part prognostication, culminates in class consciousness, workers' political parties, and class struggle. In retrospect, such a vision seems unduly mechanistic. Even if the technical exigencies of production did tend toward a homogeneous, hyper-exploited, and class-conscious proletariat, the vision underestimates the capacity of the bourgeoisie to respond to challenges through a strategy combining co-optation and coercion.[11] Marx defines the factory as "machinery organised into a system" but then overlooks the implications of this crucial insight.[12] The factory was a site of struggle for control of the production of commodities and of docile workers, a struggle in which managers had almost all of the advantages. Marx uses political language to draw a connection between the technical possibilities of the machine and the effect of increased, hierarchical control, claiming that "the central machine from which the motion comes [is] not only an automaton but an autocrat."[13] The factory was not simply the aggregation of new machines but also the refinement of a system of power.

Inside the Italian Factory

The factory was a highly adaptable form, varying in size, level of mechanization, complexity of division of labor, management structure, and type of production process. Under capitalism, however, these variations had one unifying purpose: the rationalization of production as a way to increase profitability. Numerous studies have shown that this goal was achieved by introducing machines and disciplining factory operatives to be wholly subordinate to the rhythms of those machines.[14] Although there is extensive documentation of the appalling factory conditions in Italy at the turn of the century, the details of factory life have been used to support very different conclusions.[15] Rural reactionaries stressed the promiscuity of the factory in an attempt to reassert the moral order of semifeudalism;[16] urban reformers recounted the details of squalor, disease, and danger in order to build consensus in favor of some form of benign government oversight. Working conditions also varied. The experience of highly skilled male metal workers in the expanding heavy industries was very different from the experience of women and children employed in vast numbers in labor-intensive trades such as tobacco processing, spinning, dying, straw weaving, food processing, and sewing. Nevertheless, the factory was the apogee of social control and exploitation for most workers in fin-de-siècle Italy. Rather than functioning as a site of resistance, the factory was the nodal point of a highly coercive system that served to produce docile bodies rather than militants.[17] The nearly despotic power of factory owners and management was a very effective break on the struggle for popular enfranchisement, at least until the authoritarian character of the factory was challenged by political forces that had organized outside its walls.

Initially, the despotic factory was protected by the convergence of liberalism and naked power distinctive of post-unification Italian politics. Liberal ideology defined conditions in the factory as private matters while power politics guaranteed the intervention of the state to break strikes and dissolve "subversive" workers' organizations. For example, in 1880 the municipal government of Biella, an industrialized area in northern Italy, described factory inspections as an "attack on the inviolability of the home."[18] In 1897 a newspaper representing the interests of the industrialists admitted frankly that "thanks to God and to our fathers we can say also in Italy, paraphrasing the famous phrase of Louis XIV ['l'état, c'est moi'], the state, it is us. Since the government which rules is a direct emanation of our will and our desires."[19]

Discipline in the factory was guaranteed by a complex set of often draconian rules, which were enforced by a system of fines and punishments for any violations. The rules encoded the workers' position at the bottom of a hierarchical system. For example, the regulations of the cement factory De Filippis in Bari specified that "superior to the workers are (a) the owners of the firm; (b) the manager and his agents; (c) the foreman, shift supervisor and his assistants; (d) the door-keeper in the execution of his duties [presumably recording workers' arrival and departure]."[20] Factory rules did not simply detail the correct procedure for performing an individual's tasks but represented an attempt to ensure a strict hierarchy and a docile workforce. According to one textile factory in Bergamo, "all workers must always be docile and subordinate to their superiors but without delay, hesitation, or comment and full of good faith they should carry out all of the tasks assigned to them." In addition, "they should keep themselves clean and behave correctly." The regulations also specified that workers must enter and leave the factory "without making noise."[21] In the tobacco industry, suspensions or fines were also levied for offenses such as the following: "eating fruit or other such things . . . during working hours," bringing "alcoholic beverages" to work, "smoking or chewing tobacco," "singing or making noise," "arbitrary changing in the use of machinery," and sitting down.[22] At Stigler in Milan the workers entered the factory at seven in the morning and left at eight in the evening, and during the entire time they were prohibited from speaking, singing, or "making noise." A foundry at Bologna simply forbade "discussing any topic on the premises of the foundry unrelated to the industry."[23] (See figs. 1 and 2.)

The most powerful means of enforcing these rules was the deposit system. Workers would leave part of their pay in deposit, and this would be forfeited if they violated regulations. They would also loose access to the social insurance funds that employers sometimes deducted from the workers' pay; this proved to be a particularly effective way to prevent strikes or work stoppages. According to one employer, "Abandoning work, even collectively, without at least eight days of warning will result in the loss of the deposit."[24] Other regulations were stricter, specifying that work stoppage for any reason would incur forfeiture of the deposit as well as immediate dismissal.[25] Even "showing solidarity with colleagues who were punished or fired" was itself an act subject to disciplinary response.[26]

Nor did the discipline and surveillance stop at the factory gates. "Unfaithfulness, insubordination, [and] lack of respect toward the bosses also outside the factory" were violations of the factory rules. Workers could be fired for "promoting or taking part in discussions or meetings that cause disruption or damage the interests of the firm or the reputations of the people trusted with its direction."[27] La Galileo, a factory in Florence, fired workers for "indecorous" or "dishonorable" acts, even those committed after working hours.[28] The real motivation for such rules, however, was less a traditional paternalistic-feudal sense of responsibility for the moral character of inferiors and more the desire to clamp down on subversive organizations such as political parties and leagues of resistance. The factory rules of a wool-spinning mill in Bellano, owned by Rossi di Schio, stated that "outside of the wool factory the workers must conduct themselves with morality and decorum." They could be fired for criminal acts against property or public disorder as well as "membership in societies or attendance at meetings in which people are present who sow the seeds of hate instead of charity, and, with the pretext of doing good, cause evil to the damage of workers or

Fig. 1. The spatial organization of factory work. *Source*: Aris Accornero, Uliano Luca, and Giulio Sapelli, eds., *Storia fotografica del lavoro in Italia, 1900–1980* (Bari: De Donato, 1981).

Fig. 2. The spatial organization of home work: a group of seamstresses (ca. 1900). *Source*: Accornero, Luca, and Sapelli, *Storia fotografica del lavoro in Italia*.

claim doctrines to this effect."[29] Not only were factory workers given no opportunity to discuss working conditions on the premises but they were forbidden from taking part in the most basic political activities outside work during their "free" time. In his analysis of the factory regulations, Stefano Merli concludes that this is why as late as 1901 the 10,000 to 12,000 workers at the Rossi mill had not yet formed a union. "The women did not even dare to cross the street to where the seat of the socialist circle (which had only 24 members) was located."[30]

These workers did not need Foucault to draw the links between discipline in the factory and the prison. Some examples of the coercion, discipline, and surveillance in the early factories were reported in a newspaper column titled "The Prisons of Industry." In 1887 the socialist newspaper *Fascio Operaio* documented a hat factory in Naples that locked the workers in the factory.[31] Others would not allow workers to leave the premises, even during the designated break time. This was a point of particular concern to women, who often had to return home to care for sick children or relatives. The workers who lived in dormitories provided by the factory were vulnerable to greater levels of control. Even after the working day, the management would regulate employees' movements to ensure that workers would not "steal" their own labor power from the company by expending it on leisure activities. In one silk factory, the workers were not allowed to go to bed as late as they wanted; to ensure that no one violated the rules, the management engaged a nighttime supervisor, who in turn employed the following strategy for rationalizing the intensity of social control. To hide her precise location from the workers, the nighttime supervisor generally "kept two or three lamps lit" and changed position every once in a while. Furthermore, "to make sure that the supervisor herself did not fall asleep," the management created a primitive punch-clock made up of "a special mechanism with a pendulum" that could make a verifiable imprint at given times throughout the night.[32]

In labor-intensive sectors such as textiles and food preparation (which employed the majority of Italian factory workers), the distinguishing character of the factory was not the level of technological modernization but rather new forms of social control and innovative ways of "rationalizing" labor. In Milan, the employers' association of confectioners instituted a centralized system for recording and tracking all employees across the industry. Each member agreed to keep records of the conduct and movements of employees.[33] Another mechanism for increasing control over labor was to take impoverished children and confine them in "trade schools," where they worked extremely long hours for little or no pay. The line between school, prison, and factory became obscured in these places, where, in the words of Alessandro Cabrini, a representative in the Chamber of Deputies, "impoverished girls are forced to work sometimes as much as eighteen or twenty hours per day without any pay or a few pennies of remuneration."[34]

Although the worst abuses were originally in the less mechanized industries such as spinning, weaving, sewing, and mining, factory discipline was increasing in the more "high-tech" sectors of heavy industry. In the metal-working industry, the production process was reorganized to undermine the control of autonomous work groups and master craftsmen. In his study of the new industrial factories outside of Milan, Donald Bell explains the changes in the following terms:

[Previously] in small plants master manufacturers directed teams of skilled puddlers and foundrymen—themselves controlling groups of assistants—in the complex process of producing high-quality metals. At every stage of manufacture, well-trained operatives would be engaged in the forging, casting, and rolling of molten metal by handwork methods requiring considerable physical strength and training. In contrast, new steel factories, such as that of Falck in *Sesto*, required a reorganization of work. . . . The most important changes were produced by the introduction of the Siemens-Martin furnace, which rendered obsolete the skilled puddler and his labor crew grouped around the open hearth. During the process of metal production, the ovens now remained closed while many forge workers were distributed in various areas of the factory as operators of cranes supplying the ovens with pig iron or as casters who poured molten steel into moulds. Work was no longer carried out in a central location, and the processes of manufacture were broken up into separate departments.[35]

Bell explains how these technological imperatives impacted the experience of work in the metal industry. These new departments were monitored by foremen who were no longer workers but exclusively responsible for supervision; the technical process was completely controlled by engineers, and scientific research took place outside of the factory. The deafening noise intensified with the introduction of new machinery such as steam hammers and made simple communication between workers almost impossible. Furthermore, the possibilities of interaction between different types of workers diminished as production processes were confined to distinct areas of the plant.[36] The factory regulations that forbade leaving one's assigned place provide indirect evidence that this limitation of mobility was a cause of contention.[37]

The spatial layout of the new factories was designed to maximize control while minimizing costs. A report on the silk industry of the late 1800s mentions that there were several new organizational plans invented for the factory. The most prominent was the Delprino system, which was adopted by several establishments. Basically, the factory was set up so that there were special galleries placed above the workers' tables. From there, supervisors could observe whether the workers were attaching the prescribed number of strands to form a regulation thread of silk. The report specified that "some of these galleries were covered in such a way that the supervisors could not be seen by the workers, who, themselves unobserved, could hold the workers' continually under their surveillance." The Delprino system, however, fell into disuse because of the defect that the "supervisors with the task of observing the spinners, being in the gallery, could not themselves be observed by the director," who suspected that they used the time to take a nap.[38] This defect was corrected in the plan for a model factory built in 1897, which was designed so that the manager, literally "above everyone," could maintain continual supervision from a desk situated at the apex of the space.[39]

Although the factory facilitated the expansion of refined methods of surveillance and control, this did not necessarily mean the end of more apparent and direct forms of domination. Physical abuse was among the grievances listed by striking silk weavers in Cremona. An investigation by the mayor in 1896 confirmed that "their ears were twisted in such a way that they bled."[40] Anastasio Rossi, a priest, recorded that similar treatment occurred in the spinning factories in Lomellina.

What conclusions should be drawn from these horrific conditions is far from obvious. There is a long tradition, starting with Adam Smith, that emphasizes the debilitating cognitive effects of the uniform and unceasing motion involved in tending a single machine. Capacity for judgment, imagination, and learning are impaired by the lack of diverse stimuli and meaningful challenges. Ernesto Gallavresi makes a similar argument in his report *Sul lavoro delle donne e dei fanciulli* (On the labor of women and children). He explains, "The tiresome uniformity and privation of interest characteristic of a never ending task, generated by a monotonous mechanical movement which is always the same and limits whatever free activity of the spirit and the body of the worker . . . reduces him very soon to becoming deformed and idiotic."[41] The problem with this analysis is that it reflects the reformers' tendency to slide from a revulsion at the conditions in the factory to contempt for the workers themselves. But the evidence suggests an alternate explanation for workers' passivity. Perhaps it was not only the work but also the authoritarianism and discipline of the factory that had such a strong depoliticizing effect. The mind-numbing exhaustion of the lengthened working day, combined with the extension of social control on the shop floor (constant surveillance, policing of movement, segmentation, hierarchy, and spatialized control) and the threat of drastic punishment for political participation outside the factory gates produced the "docile" workers who had few resources to engage in political activity.

Given these conditions, it is hardly surprising that industrial workers were not initially at the forefront of the struggles for political equality and social change. The factory workers who dared to take visible leadership positions in left-wing politics were simply fired. Militants such as Rinaldo Rigola, the future president of the Confederazione Generale Italiana del Lavoro (CGIL), and Mario Montagnana, the future head of the Communist Youth League, turned to self-employment to support themselves after losing factory jobs.

Impressionistic accounts suggest industrial workers were not at the forefront of the early socialist movement. In his memoirs, Rigola reflected on the absence of industrial workers at the first large May Day celebration in Italy in 1890. He noted that there was much fanfare in the press about the subversive implications of an international workers' day and that industrialists threatened to fire any absent workers, therefore "the factories opened like usual and the industrial workers, with few exceptions, all showed up to work." According to Rigola, the event was still a success because of the strong support on the part of artisans and craftspeople. That night a public meeting took place in the hall of the recreational society affiliated with the mutual aid society Archimede. Three hundred people turned out to listen to speakers representing such political currents as socialism and radical democracy, but again "the factory proletariat was underrepresented."[42]

As we see in chapters 5 and 6, the first sites of resistance in Italy were built by artisans (in the form of mutual aid societies) and landless peasants (in the form of workers' cooperatives). It is not surprising that the first major demonstrations against the capitalist system were attended by the unemployed, that is, those who had the least to lose. Early political upheavals such as the Fatti di Maggio (1898) and the Sicilian Fasci (1893) combined different constituencies by linking the lack of political representation and unfair taxation to the new economic exigencies of the market system.[43] The socialist movement's strength came from its ability to build chains of equivalence between the struggles of peasants, marginal sharecroppers, the unemployed, factory workers, and artisans. These linkages could not be created easily inside the factory. Given the extremely oppressive conditions, it was barely possible to sustain connections among workers at an individual factory. This meant that new sites of aggregation became crucial. (See figs. 3 and 4.) Autonomous sites of workers' sociability—political circles, cooperatives, mutual aid societies, taverns—were the places where individuals came to understand the economic upheavals, to discuss strategies, and to plan political action.

The factory was not simply the antithesis of the nascent popular public sphere. There was a mutually constitutive relationship between the factory and the workers' associations that flourished in its shadows. The discipline and authoritarianism of the factory made the creation of solidaristic, semipublic, and autonomous spaces a political necessity.

Yet one troubling anomaly remains. If the factory was purely the locus of exploitation, how did the image of the factory worker become a positive socialist ideal? A critic could respond that I have painted far too bleak a picture of the factory. She might argue that by emphasizing the particularities of place I have overlooked the importance of time. In other words, by focusing on the abuses of factory discipline at the turn of the century I have ignored the process of transformation that turned the factory into a widely shared dream of power achieved through unity—the proletariat's own dream. By 1920, the factory councils were imagined not only as protection against abuses but also as soviets, the basis of a new form of political power. The idealization of the heroic factory worker was not only a creation of Futurist fantasies, which linked militarism and machinery to the proletariat as revolutionary subject.[44] It was also a strong current that cut across the political spectrum in surprising ways. The most notable representative of this position in socialist circles was Antonio Gramsci; analyzing the tensions in his position will help us understand the ideology of the factory.

The Proletarian Hero and the Factory Councils

In his early writings Gramsci defended the division of labor not only as a crucial way to develop productive forces but also as a powerful way of

Fig. 3. Inside the Breda factory in Milan (ca. 1910). *Source*: Accornero, Luca, and Sapelli, *Storia fotografica del lavoro in Italia*.

Fig. 4. At the Socialist Circle, Imola (1904). *Source*: Accornero, Luca, and Sapelli, *Storia fotografica del lavoro in Italia*.

strengthening working-class solidarity. Factory work was the apex of a producerist ideal rather than a necessary evil. Contrary to Marx, who argued that breaking up production into differentiated, isolated, and routinized tasks was the essence of alienation, Gramsci claimed that specialization engendered a beneficial sense of mutual interdependence on the part of the working class. Rather than lamenting the regimentation of factory routines, Gramsci lauded the discipline learned by the proletariat. He argued:

> The working class, on the other hand, has been developing towards a completely new and unprecedented model of humanity: the factory worker, the proletarian who . . . lives the life of the factory, the life of production—an intense, methodical life. His life may be disorderly and chaotic where his social relations outside the factory are concerned, and his political relations within the system of the distribution of wealth. But, within the factory, it is ordered, precise, and disciplined.[45]

Gramsci resolutely embraced industrial society and technological advance. In a discussion that reflected the dominant ideas of Italian Futurism, Gramsci situated the revolutionary capacity of the working class not in its intrinsic hostility to the factory but instead in its discipline and order. The worker had become an appendage of the machine, but this was not necessarily something to be regretted. Gramsci saw the characteristics of the machine—strength, unity, uniformity, rationality, modernity, productivity—as vital to the successful revolution.

Rather than criticizing the division of labor for causing alienation, Gramsci celebrated it for achieving a higher degree of complexity and unity. For Gramsci, the reality of the factory was not merely a product of capitalism to be transcended. He argued that the greater concentration of workers combined with the specialization of tasks engendered proletarian solidarity:

> The working class has come to be identified with the factory, with production: the proletarian cannot live without working and without working in an orderly, methodological way. The division of labour has unified the proletarian class psychologically: it has fostered within the proletarian world that body of feelings, instincts, thought, customs, habits and attachments that can be summed up in the phrase "class solidarity." Within the factory, every proletarian is led to conceive of himself as inseparable from his work-mates; how could the raw material

piled up in the warehouses come to circulate in the world as an object of use to man in society, if a single link were missing from the system of labour in industrial production? The more the proletarian specializes in a particular professional task, the more conscious he becomes of how indispensable his companions are; the more he feels himself as one cell within a coherent body, possessed of an inner unity and cohesion; the more he feels the need for order, method and precision; the more he feels the need for the whole world to become like a vast factory, organized with the same precision and method and order which he recognizes as vital in the factory where he works; the more he feels the need for the order, precision and method which are the life-blood of the factory to be projected out into the system of relations that links one factory to another, one city to another, one nation to another.[46]

Writing in 1920, Gramsci's position is clear: communist society will be organized as one large factory.

Factory councils played a prominent role in Gramsci's original thinking about the revolution and the eventual socialist state. Proponents of the movement such as Gramsci and Togliatti argued that factory councils could be the basic political unit in the socialist state.[47] The factory councils became prominent because of their role in the occupation of the factories in Turin in September 1920, which involved more than 400,000 workers and seemed to bring Italy to the brink of revolution.[48] The movement was centered in the metal industries in Turin, where employers had threatened to lock out workers in a labor dispute. To prevent the lockout, workers occupied the factories, but production continued, albeit sporadically, under the direction of the factory councils. These organizations differed from unions in that they included all workers in a factory rather than just dues-paying members. Not based on craft distinctions, the factory councils grew out of the internal commissions, consultative bodies with jurisdiction over plant-specific issues such as safety and work rules. Inspired by the peasants', workers', and soldiers' soviets, the factory councils were theorized as a way of overcoming the bifurcation of political and economic life under capitalism. They were an attempt to replace the purely political institutions of the bourgeois state with a form of representation rooted in the core of social and economic life—the process of production.

The occupation of the factories in Turin revealed the limitations of an exclusively factory-based strategy of resistance, which became apparent a few months later when the occupation failed to catalyze a broader political and social revolution. First, the occupation affected only industrial workers and was therefore marginal to the experiences of the overwhelming majority of Italians who labored in small workshops, in the home, or on farms. The structure of the factory council provided no mechanism for forging links between the industrial proletariat and other workers. It is true that the factory councils were not conceived as purely economic instruments but were to serve as soviets, the basic political institutions for a new society. Nevertheless, such a structure excluded workers who were not directly linked to the production process, such as homemakers, the unemployed, students, and retirees. It was also inadequate for representing peasants, the self-employed, and artisans. Second, direct industrial action, the centerpiece of revolutionary syndicalist strategy in general and the factory council movement in particular, exacerbated rather than mitigated the central tension in Italian politics, the rift between the north and the south. The occupied factories were almost exclusively in the industrial triangle of the north. Southerners often perceived northern labor militancy as a defense of an already privileged minority. The occupation of the factories drew attention to the walls that separated the industrial proletariat from the majority of workers. Third, the producerist vision fell far short of its ideal because the desertion of technical and clerical personnel made it difficult to continue production. The division of labor made workers vulnerable and dependent on the skills of white-collar technicians, who were alienated by the strictly proletarian ideology of the movement. Finally, it was difficult to obtain raw materials or credit from the overwhelming majority of capitalist firms and institutions. After one month, the workers voted to end the occupation and return to work in exchange for minor concessions from employers and a government commitment to form a joint management labor committee to draft a law on increased trade union control on the shop floor.

The limited success of the occupation was made possible by prior links that tied the factory councils into a diversified system of preexisting institutions. The Turin Cooperative Alliance provided credit and food for the striking workers. The Turin chamber of labor coordinated exchange between different factories.[49] Where such broad-based organizations did not connect agitation on the shop floor to a more general critique of capitalism, the movement quickly collapsed.

The role of the factory is the controversy at the heart of Italian working-class history. In his pathbreaking book *Proletariato di fabbrica e capi-*

talismo industriale: Il caso italiano, 1880–1900, Stefano Merli vigorously defends the factory as the foremost site of struggle for political change. He juxtaposes two theories—the factory proletariat was a unified, homogeneous, revolutionary avant-garde, or it was a subordinate part of a national bloc, which carried out the incomplete liberal-bourgeois revolution—and defends the former. Although Merli's extremely detailed documentation of the immiseration of factory workers remains unparalleled, his theoretical conclusions have been challenged.[50] The reality is more complex than the two alternatives he offers. Socialism was a broad-based political movement before there was an industrial working class; furthermore, many socialist strongholds such as Emilia-Romagna were in agricultural regions.[51] Clearly, workers were at the forefront of the struggle against their own political exclusion and economic subordination, but this movement included workers who labored in the fields, in small workshops, at home, on loading docks, and on the railways as well as in the factory.[52] Acknowledging the heterogeneous nature of the working class does not mean denying the importance of conflict and struggle. Questioning the leadership of the industrial proletariat is not tantamount to ignoring the role of economic factors in understanding political change. The political inclusion of the subaltern classes was not achieved by elites, nor was it a product of enlightened consensus. It was the result of a war of position in which the fortifications were places such as cooperatives, socialist circles, union halls, and workers' recreational associations.

The walls that separated the factory from society were literal barriers that symbolized important social cleavages. The council movement collapsed primarily because it failed to mobilize those outside the factory gates—southerners, peasants, artisans, unemployed, technical workers, students, and home-based workers, including women. The factory councils could not act as a substitute for territorially based political representation because they excluded those who were linked in complex, indirect ways to the process of production. Gramsci's major theoretical innovations in prison—including the concepts of historical bloc and hegemony—were the result of sustained reflection on the limitations of the factory councils. In the *Prison Notebooks*, Gramsci recognized that fundamental social change in the West would not be the product of a single, definitive assault on the bourgeois state but rather the culmination of a cultural and political struggle to cement alliances between subaltern groups.

The factory in fin-de-siècle Italy could not serve as a privileged site

for the radicalization of democracy. Although the experience of proletarianization mobilized some workers, the factory itself failed as a space
of resistance. Instead it perfected forms of discipline, surveillance, and
coercion that proved effective in disempowering workers. Although the
factory intensified the experience of exploitation, these experiences had
consequences only when they were reinterpreted in endless conversa-
tions, meetings, and debates that took place at autonomous political
sites. The very quality that Marx and Gramsci saw as definitive of the
factory system—the way it embodied the proletariat's distinctiveness
and isolation—proved a hindrance, rather than an aid in the struggle for
change, by reinforcing barriers rather than creating linkages. Especially
in Italy, the highly heterogeneous and fragmented class structure placed
crucial limits on the applicability of a model that assigned the factory
the key role as the nodal point of mobilization. The overwhelming majority of the workers who, then as now, toiled at home, in the fields, offices, or small workshops did not recognize factory councils as a site of
their own empowerment.[53]

This chapter does not deny the important role of industrial workers
and national labor unions in fighting for social and political change but
rather challenges the dominance of the factory as an icon of social democratic politics. The myths of the factory and the proletariat have obscured the transformative role played by other sites of resistance, such
as cooperatives, houses of the people, and joint labor councils, which
have become more rather than less relevant today. History remembers
the Turin factory councils but not the Turin Cooperative Alliance. This
oversight needs to be corrected not only in order to be more true to the
past but also to be more useful to the present. By linking disputes over
the control of production to consumption and leisure, building coalitions between workers and potential allies, and transforming struggles
rooted in daily life into politics, workers created local and regional geographies of power. The sites of resistance analyzed in this book were
the building blocks of popular power at the beginning of the twentieth
century and also the political spaces that are most relevant as models for
the present.

5

THE COOPERATIVE MOVEMENT

The memorable is that which can be dreamed about a place.
Michel de Certeau, *The Practice of Everyday Life*

In the winter of 1919 the Sassari Brigade, a unit of Sardinian soldiers, was sent to Turin, perhaps the most militant working-class city in Europe, heir apparent to the revolutionary passion and discipline of St. Petersburg. This regiment was particularly hated by the Turinese workers because the Sardinian soldiers were famous for their loyalist credentials, which they had acquired in 1917 as a result of their crucial role in crushing labor unrest by firing on strikers. Workers and soldiers, it seemed, were doomed to face each other as enemies. Both sides probably feared the inevitable confrontation. What could have been a violent clash, however, became a transformative encounter.

This time the encounter did not take place on the barricades. At the end of 1919 or the beginning of 1920, the period that Italian historians call the Bienno Rosso, the "two red years," workers and soldiers met on the streets, in the cooperative cafés, and on the margins of neighborhood festivals. Antonio Gramsci spoke in neighborhood socialist circles across the city, emphasizing the history of oppression in his own native Sardinia and underlining the experience of exploitation shared by southern peasants and northern workers. There was a mobilization throughout the city to engage in "socialist and proletariat propaganda"—which involved approaching the soldiers in the street and inviting them for a glass of wine in order to talk about the workers' native region, Turin, how the workers lived, and what they wanted. The results were as follows:

> After a few weeks the mentality of the major part of the Sassari soldiers was already modified. On Sundays there wasn't a neighborhood circle (for example, socialist club, usually organized around a cooperative bar/café) where there weren't a few of these soldiers. In the barracks, the counterrevolutionary speeches of the officers weren't listened to religiously like before. . . . From the same barracks some rifles disappeared and the officers could never figure out where they ended up. During popular demonstrations the sympathy of the soldiers for the people appeared evident. The Sassari Brigade was not the Sassari Brigade anymore. . . . And a few months after its arrival in Turin it was sent away from this dangerous "center of infection."[1]

Encounter

The metaphor of contagion is appropriate in so far as physical contact facilitated the diffusion of new and dangerous ideas. Sociologist Erving Goffman defines an encounter as the "type of social arrangement that occurs when persons are in one another's immediate physical presence."[2] Although Goffman does not emphasize the political implications of encounters, he investigates their unique contribution to the complex process of establishing and maintaining a social order. The concept of the "encounter" suggests a new way to understand the process of building a sense of agency, equality, and citizenship. The ways in which different people encounter one another in particular types of places have implications for their sense of autonomy, identity, and relationship to others.[3] Depending on context, exposure to strangers can establish and reinforce either relations of solidarity between equals or various degrees of subordination. For workers in late-nineteenth-century Europe, sites of encounter included the church, barracks, the bar, and occasionally the local administration that granted permits or assessed taxes. New industrial workers also had contact at the factory. Peasants, homemakers, and shopkeepers sometimes met in the market. Most of these encounters, however, occurred between individuals who held clearly defined roles of leadership and subordination: priest–parishioner, bureaucrat–petitioner, officer–enlisted man, boss (in the guise of landowner or industrialist)–laborer. There was almost no opportunity for either a reversal or transformation of these established roles.

The concept of the encounter also draws attention to the importance of modes of interaction that are not linguistic or even cognitive. An encounter involves the meeting of two bodies in physical space. The site of the encounter might be associated with certain rituals such as an individual removing his cap or making the sign of the cross as well as more general patterns of deference such as a person's posture or silence. There is an irreducible physicality manifest in the individual's gestures and posture as well as the grouping or dispersion of people. The encounter is fundamentally the terrain of the body. At a meeting that includes members of different social classes, the posture, forms of address, and dialect of the dominant class are likely to prevail even in the absence of any conscious or strategic choice. After a lifetime of assuming appropriate postures and demeanor while playing subordinate roles, the habit of deference is embodied in each individual. Foucault's famous insight that the individual subject is the product of the government of bodies applies to contexts well beyond the disciplinary situation.[4]

One of the raisons d'être of the cooperatives created at the beginning of the twentieth century was precisely to facilitate new solidaristic and egalitarian forms of interaction. This goal would be undermined if the gestures, symbols, and practices of subordination could not be temporarily and strategically excluded. The impact of the "visceral register" helps explain the virulence of debates about whether to include honorary members (from the bourgeoisie or aristocracy) in workers' organizations. The advisability of separatism was not merely a theoretical issue. Professionals and elites were always part of the socialist leadership, but their impact in the press and Parliament was distinct from their effect on local organizations. In the context of face-to-face encounters, corporeal intuitions such as the appropriate amount of distance or contact, patterns of seating, and forms of address converge to create a stage on which status hierarchies were displayed. Proximity matters.

A site of encounter, however, cannot be reduced to its physical dimension and architectural properties. A particular site is not a closed system but rather a nexus of intersecting forces. As a nodal point of concentration and transformation it is never fully separate from external contexts and dynamics. In the case of the Sassari Brigade, for example, the soldiers returned to the barracks, yet another archetypical site in the reproduction of power, only to experience it changed, somehow diminished. After their encounters with the Turinese workers' autonomous subculture, the soldiers might have experienced the barracks more as a disciplinary site of external control than as the repository of their own warrior identity.

A site of encounter is not merely a microcosm of larger social structures. The characteristics of the outside world are not merely reflected and reproduced in an encounter, as a metaphor such as "microcosm" might suggest. The patterns of interaction do not correspond exactly to patterns in the world at large. Instead, certain attributes are highlighted while others are obscured. According to a set of either explicit or implicit norms, some characteristics are intensified and others are diminished. This is true of a range of rituals from the religious service, to the sporting competition, to the date. According to Goffman, "A locally realized world of roles and events cuts the participants off from many externally based matters that might have been given relevance but allows a few of these external matters to enter into the interaction world as an official part of it."[5] The transformative potential of encounters lies precisely in the possibility of suspending certain aspects of reality in order to intensify others. Goffman has been criticized for dissecting microprocesses and ignoring their relationship to broader structures; however, juxtaposing the social processes at work in different spaces of varying scales can disrupt what appears to be the homogeneity of the social. The ordering principle of one "other space" can serve to challenge the ordering principle of society at large. Although this alterity may be purely symbolic, it can also have transformative effects by making it possible to temporarily suspend the scripted behaviors and identities that determine interactions.

In the case of the Sardinian soldiers and the Turinese workers, the particular type of encounter was determined by the context of the local cooperative bar, the neighborhood-based center of socialist (and social) life. Conventions of hospitality and camaraderie intrinsic to the "neighborhood circle" conflicted with the identity of "soldier stationed among a hostile foreign population." This tension was resolved in favor of the former in part because the "neighborhood circle" was not something purely local and therefore exclusive and provincial. It took part in a broader ideal, the ideal of socialism, newly interpreted to include solidarity between workers and peasants.[6] Without such a sheltered space for communication and camaraderie, workers and soldiers would have confronted each other on the streets with their prejudices intact. This kind of encounter was made possible by two decades of work building a diverse chain of autonomous, locally rooted, yet loosely linked sites.

Through the encounter, a "we-rationale" can emerge, be acknowledged, and affirmed. Encounters are "world-building" activities, and the new world of mass democracy required new sites of encounter. Emerging elites such as the bourgeoisie met in cafés that were soon formalized into exclusive clubs and salons.[7] These provided models for popular political participation, but they proved inadequate, for reasons discussed in chapter 3. The first important nodal point of popular sociability in Italy was the *circolo;* like the French *chambrée,* this was a cooperative bar where workers met to play cards, drink wine, sing, read newspapers, and discuss politics. In 1919 the Turinese workers and Sardinian soldiers met in these circles, just as new immigrants to northern factories had encountered seasoned workers there for decades. These circles required few resources, demanded little organization, and seemed like a natural extension of informal social life. Nevertheless, even in this nascent form, they played a crucial role in building a solidaristic infrastructure. They often functioned as primitive mutual aid societies in that the profits from card games and wine sales were pooled and saved to pay for funerals or support members in times of misfortune. In the evenings someone would read the newspapers aloud, thereby linking print and oral culture. What Maurice Agulhon wrote of Provence was equally true of Italy: "For the lower classes . . . at the period, to set themselves up as a *chambrée* was, just as much and perhaps even more than learning to read, to become accessible to whatever was new, to change, and to independence."[8]

The Cooperative as a Political Space

The cooperative movement was the largest form of popular organization in Europe at the beginning of the twentieth century. Cooperatives were distinctly modern phenomena that first emerged in nineteenth-century England. They diffused across Europe in response to the new capitalist economy, which disrupted traditional, locally rooted patterns of production and consumption. In Italy in 1902 there were 567,450 members of legally recognized cooperatives. Given that usually only the head of the household was a member, this figure actually represents more than 500,000 families. In England at the turn of the century there were two million members. In France during the same period, the figure was close to three million, but this total includes members of mutual aid societies.[9]

The term *cooperative* designates a nonprofit, democratically managed business that aims to fulfill social needs through collective organization. When I use the term, I am referring to the Rochdale system, designed by a group of skilled workers in England in 1844. The Rochdale pioneers introduced several organizational innovations that are definitive of cooperatives to this day: democratic control based on "one member, one vote," dividends shared in proportion to the amount purchased rather than the capital invested (in the case of consumer cooperatives), an emphasis on education, and despite political and religious neutrality, a commitment to using profits to finance social services collectively. A cooperative can be a grocery store, a bar, a bakery, or a workshop financed by shares purchased by the members (who are either producers or consumers).

Writing in 1903, the Italian socialist leader Antonio Vergnanini defended a theory that he called "integral cooperativism," which emphasized the social and political roles of the cooperative.[10] He argued that the cooperative was a nodal point of the workers' movement; it facilitated communication between workers and between organizations.

> The consumer cooperative ... becomes ... headquarters of the local workers movement, official head of the associations, center of attraction for the population in their days off. It is at the cooperative that the leagues hold meetings, and there that they discuss their interests and [it is at] the cooperative that the chamber of labor diffuses its announcements, its communications, and at the cooperative that it holds conferences, public meetings, etc.

For Vergnanini, the cooperative was both an instrument of struggle and a microcosm of a socialist polity:

> The new life of the proletariat world, in this period of reawakening, is creating a whole series of centers, in which it condenses and from which it irradiates the nascent regenerating force. [The cooperatives] are the seeds of the future social order; the embryo of the organism of the future, that is being shaped under the pressure of facts and that is being prepared in the atmosphere of the class struggle and becomes one of the branches of the chamber of labor.

He emphasized that the transition to cooperative socialism depended on the proliferation of spaces of resistance.

But one difficulty of the free multiplication of the cooperative is the absence of spaces adapted for the goal. Each village—in order to coordinate the various forms of workers' organizations—will have its house of the people with meeting rooms, offices, theaters, public facilities, pharmacy, labor and production cooperatives, storage of agricultural goods. The vision is splendid and there is no reason to doubt its realization. All'opera tutti![11]

Vergnanini saw the cooperative primarily as a sociopolitical space rather than an economic tactic. The cooperative provided a location that served as an informal social center, a nodal point of communication, and a link between different associations. It condensed dispersed individuals' inchoate needs and transformed them into a political force.

Initially it might seem that Vergnanini's description of the cooperative illustrates the familiar claim that grass-roots participation is a critical element of democracy. According to participatory democrats, individuals who take part in voluntary organizations acquire political skills and a sense of efficacy that empower them as citizens.[12] Although sympathetic to this claim, I wonder if this approach obscures the fact that the effectiveness of participation does not automatically generate power. Participation is often orchestrated by elites in order to legitimate previous decisions; alternately, participation in certain grass-roots, local initiatives may distract activists from analyzing and challenging the deeper economic structures that determine existing inequalities. Italian fascism orchestrated a certain kind of mass participation, yet it hardly advanced democracy or redistributed power. Fascist spectacles and public rituals were designed to establish a hierarchical relationship between the people and an exalted leader.[13] The relationship between participation and political power is mediated by economic and political structures.

Social movement theorists use the term *political opportunity structure* to designate moments of disunity or incapacity on the part of governing elites—moments that give outsiders greater leverage.[14] Marxists have long suggested that economic breakdown presents an unparalleled opportunity for radical political change. The next section describes the distinctive structural conditions that facilitated the emergence of the cooperative movement. The economic crisis brought on by globalization was a necessary but not sufficient condition for political change. If political mobilization were simply a product of macroeconomic change, then we would expect that mobilization would be a function of class. We would predict a relatively even distribution of political attitudes across economic and occupational groups, but instead we find clusters of political activity that do not correspond to economic variables. These patterns reveal "centers of contagion" or what we might call geographies of power. Politics is not merely a matter of individuals responding to stimuli such as economic self-interest or exploitation; it is also about people reacting to the presence of other people, their ideas, and their aspirations.

Class, Cooperation, and the World Capitalist System

At the end of the nineteenth century in Italy, the idea of cooperation became a central conceptual framework for approaching the increasingly prominent "social question." Because of the heterogeneous class structure and relative absence of industrial employment in Italy, the consumption-based cooperative movement was a crucial site of political socialization. The nascent process of industrialization, commercialization of agriculture, and especially the effects of competition with more developed countries, led to profound changes in the social and economic conditions in Italy.[15] Increased urbanization, unemployment (especially in the countryside), and the disparity between the high cost of living and stagnant salaries were the background conditions that spurred collective action on the part of both industrial and agricultural workers. Although Italy in the 1890s was by no means an industrialized country with a homogeneous working class, it was nevertheless a society experiencing profound changes. Such changes were less the result of the reorganization of the mode of production and more the result of Italy's subordinate place in an increasingly interlinked capitalist world economy.

During the period from unification until fascism, Italy remained an agrarian economy, despite some expansion of heavy industry that resulted from military expenditures in the Libyan War and World War I. In 1881, 56 percent of Italy's labor force was engaged in agriculture. Out of the 25.2 percent of the population that was categorized as employed in the industrial sector, more than 86 percent were working in the textile and clothing sectors. Although more than one million workers were employed in traditional, low-value-added crafts such as shoe making or carpentry, only 600,000 were working in factories.[16] Even after World War I, the labor force composition did not experience radical shifts. It was not until 1957 that the percentage of the Italian labor force engaged in manufacturing exceeded the percentage employed in agriculture.

Table 2. Labor Force Composition, 1901–36

Year	Agriculture (%)	Industry (%)	Services (%)	Public (%)
1901	59.8	23.8	16.4	Not counted
1911	59.1	23.6	15.3	2
1936	52	25.6	19	3.4

Source: Vera Zamagni, *The Economic History of Italy, 1860–1990* (Oxford: Clarendon Press, 1993).

Table 2 summarizes the occupational statistics provided by the Italian statistical organization ISTAT. For purposes of comparison, it is interesting to note that in 1901 the percentage of the labor force engaged in agriculture was 8.7 percent in Great Britain and 33.1 percent in France.[17]

The broad category of agricultural labor, however, obscures as much as it reveals. Different regions and localities in Italy had very different relations of production in the countryside, ranging from sharecropping to small individual holdings to commercial estates employing day laborers. Even within these groups, social structure depended on the precise type of sharecropping arrangement or labor contracts. The apparent stability in total agricultural employment hides a dramatic increase in the number of landless laborers and a decline in the sharecropping system.[18]

This sketch of labor force composition presents a deceptive image of continuity and stability. Italy was experiencing profound changes during this period as a result of its integration into a world capitalist system. From 1866 to 1913, the annual rate of growth of imports to Italy was 3.1 percent, whereas that of exports was only 2.7 percent.[19] At the same time, Italy's export share of world trade fell from 3.1 percent to 2.6 percent. Italy became more dependent on foreign manufactured goods, and its severe balance-of-payments deficit could only be equalized by remittances from nationals working abroad and tourism. Although Italy was becoming increasingly integrated into a world market, its transition was the product of its subordinate position.[20]

In Italy at the turn of the century, peasants and other workers experienced the dislocations of the transition to capitalism before industrialization. Social upheaval was the result of unemployment, speculation, and inflation more than exploitation through the expropriation of surplus value. Writing in 1880, Engels already saw the possibility of "conflicts not only between the classes begotten of [capitalism], but also between the very productive forces and the forms of exchange created by it."[21] In other words, workers (understood here broadly to include housewives, peasants, day laborers, as well as the industrial proletariat) could experience the dislocations of capitalism as a result of radical changes in the forms of exchange rather than only through exploitation at the site of production. This is a crucial insight; however, Engels failed to consider its implications for the privileged position of class struggle in Marxist theories of social change. Given the structural implications of combined and uneven development, cooperation provided a compelling alternative to the idea of class struggle as a way of both interpreting and confronting the growing social cleavages.

The cooperative movement had a complex relationship to the market; it provided a nonprofit, solidaristic counter-economy, but it was also constrained by laws of supply and demand. The idea of cooperation drew on the values of collectivity that were rooted in traditional, face-to-face social relations, but it was a distinctly modern phenomenon. Cooperation was a way of overcoming the weakness of the individual in the emerging market. It was a response to the increasing commodification of a formerly subsistence-based economy and was often justified as a solution to the rising cost of living brought on by speculation, tariffs, and monopolies. The "Letter to Farmers and Workers," written in 1898 by the Consumer Cooperative at Pontremel, clearly situated cooperation within the logic of a modern economy. It states, "Capitalists unite in banks to serve their interests. . . . why can't a hundred or thousand workers unite themselves together depositing some lire in order to procure bread at a better price as capitalists do to get better interest on their millions."[22] This rhetoric frames cooperation as a way of coping with the new market forces.

Although the idea of cooperation was self-consciously articulated by democratic and radical forces as a solution to capitalist monopoly and competition, it also functioned as an alternative to class analysis. The original Marxist prediction of proletarianization was based on a generalization from the English experience, which was not replicated by other countries that industrialized under very different economic conditions.[23] One cannot understand the economic and political power of cooperation without situating such a strategy in a specific moment and location in the capitalist system. Industrialization did not necessarily lead to increasing homogenization and class consciousness; instead, it often further diversified modes of production (including services, the informal sector, artisanal production of luxury goods, and so forth) in order to fill remaining market niches.[24] Under such conditions, unitary class consciousness did not arise spontaneously from the experience of production.

Unemployment, stagnation, a crisis in agriculture, speculation in land, high taxation, and inflation as the result of tariffs were some of the immediate effects of capitalism in Italy. Cooperatives sought solutions to these negative consequences of economic change. Cooperatives are a tactic appropriate to the reality of combined and uneven development. Not simply an outmoded heritage of preindustrial society, cooperatives were also a response to global integration, a subsequent stage (or different spatial location at the margins) of capitalist development. Although liberals celebrated cooperatives as a form of self-help and Catholics formed cooperatives as an alternative to class conflict, the ideological core of the movement was socialist. Less than 10 percent of the total number of members belonged to cooperatives affiliated with the Catholic political bloc.[25] The reformist socialist leadership of the national umbrella organization, the Lega Nazionale delle Cooperative Italiane (founded 1886), both reflected and consolidated this socialist ethos.

Cooperation, with its diverse constituency, coalitional structure, and territorial roots, was well suited to serve as a basis for political mobilization. In Italy, where peasants and artisans outnumbered industrial workers, a narrow understanding of class struggle would only weaken the movement. As Gramsci came to realize in his *Prison Notebooks*, the only possible resistance to capitalism (whether dressed in the political garb of fascism or liberal democracy) involved building a counterhegemonic bloc made up of diverse subaltern groups. Such solidarity, although always rooted in economic structures, would also need new ideas, institutions, and practices to sustain it.

Marxist and non-Marxist scholars alike have tried to explain political mobilization in terms of class structure. Historians of Italian socialism often credit the *braccianti*, a sort of agricultural proletariat of landless day laborers, with being the key social force behind the socialist movement in Emilia-Romagna.[26] Sociologists such as Carlo Trigilia have explained the continued presence of a red subculture with reference to the stability of sharecropper families.[27] Neither explanation, however, is totally convincing. Any attempt to deduce voting behavior from occupational category fails, because it occludes the critical role of the political process in forging political identity. Orthodox Marxists would predict that socialist activity would be concentrated in industrial areas, but in fact the correlation between industrial employment and support for the Partito Socialista Italiano (PSI) was weak ($r = .494$, $p = .052$).[28] Emilia-Romagna, the region with the highest PSI membership, was among the

Table 3. Regions of Highest Industrial Employment and PSI Membership, 1911 and 1914

Highest Industrial Employment (1911)		Highest PSI Membership (1914)	
Region	Percentage	Region	No. (per 100,000)
Lombardy	35.6	Emilia-Romagna	552
Liguria	31.7	Piedmont–Val d'Aosta	298
Tuscany	27.4	Tuscany	282
Piedmont–Val d'Aosta	26.4	Marches	222
Friuli-Venezia	25.2	Lombardy	200
Emilia-Romagna	21.4	Liguria	190
Veneto	20.1	Umbria	150

Sources: Vera Zamagni, *The Economic History of Italy, 1860–1990* (Oxford: Clarendon Press, 1993), 32; and Maurizio Ridolfi, *Il PSI e la nascita del partito di massa, 1892–1922* (Rome: Laterza, 1992), 36.

least industrialized areas of the north. Table 3 shows that among the regions of north and central Italy, there is no relationship between PSI membership and industrialization.

Similarly, there are no consistent trends linking relations of production in the countryside with support for the PSI. For example, in the province of Forlì, sharecroppers made up 63.3 percent of the electoral district and the PSI (in 1914) received 66 percent of the vote. In Reggio Emilia, where sharecroppers composed only 17.3 percent of the population and landless laborers 60 percent, the PSI received 61 percent of the vote.[29] These data indicate that political mobilization was not the unmediated result of relations of production but the product of a process of forging a political subject around similar but not identical experiences of dislocation as a result of integration into the world capitalist system (see appendix 2).

The absence of a compelling correlation between occupational classification and socialist voting provides preliminary evidence for my suggestion that structural analysis must be complimented by attention to the way sites of resistance create geographies of power. Solidarity was not an automatic expression of the mode of production but rather the result of thinking and acting together. It was created through encounters at the cooperative store, bar, or labor exchange, where previously isolated peasants, Marx's "sack of potatoes,"[30] could recognize and interpret their similar experiences.

Cooperation was a way of generating resources out of the part of surplus value that otherwise went to the merchant or middleman rather than relying on voluntary contributions of workers who barely received subsistence incomes.[31] It became a way in which different peasants and workers could solve social problems and gain resources for political and economic struggles. One such resource was solidarity—the horizontal ties with other individuals who were experiencing analogous dislocations as a result of structural changes in the process of production and consumption.

Mutualism and the Birth of a Workers' Movement

The strength of socialism in rural areas in Italy is surprising from the perspective of Marxist theory. Marx developed his arguments about the reactionary nature of the peasantry in "The Eighteenth Brumaire of Louis Bonaparte," an essay that sought to explain why, given the wide expansion of suffrage, the majority of the French still voted for a reactionary rather than a progressive regime. According to Marx, the peasantry did not have sufficient social intercourse to understand its own interests.

> The small peasants form a vast mass, the members of which live in similar conditions, but without entering into manifold relations with one another. Their mode of production isolates them from one another, instead of bringing them into mutual intercourse. The isolation is increased by France's bad means of communication and by the poverty of the peasant. Their field of production, the small holding, admits no division of labour in its cultivation, no application of science and, therefore, no multiplicity of development, no diversity of talents, no wealth of social relationships. In this way, the great mass of the French nation is formed by simple addition of homologous magnitudes, much as potatoes in a sack form a sackful of potatoes.[32]

Marx emphasizes spatial dispersion over class structure. Rather than arguing that the French peasants, being small property owners, correctly recognized that Louis Napoleon would protect their precarious economic position, he claims that the disaggregation of peasant life—the distinctive combination of sameness and isolation—stifles imagination, making the peasantry incapable of exercising political judgment. Their isolation, dispersion, and lack of social intercourse make them incapable of acting. In subsequent decades, the political patterns that Marx identified changed. As Maurice Agulhon has shown, the rural population in some regions had, by the mid-nineteenth century, already begun to overcome this isolation through mutual aid societies and *chambrées*.[33] These areas in Provence voted "no" in the plebiscite confirming Louis Napoleon as emperor, and in the Third Republic, these same districts elected socialist deputies. Fifty years later, the same transformation from isolation and dependence to solidarity and citizenship was occurring in rural areas and provincial towns in Italy. Although Marx was right that dispersion and isolation limited the diffusion of progressive politics, he was wrong to assume that modern industry was the only way to overcome it. In areas where urbanization and industrialization did not automatically engender more complex social spaces, they had to be created.

Mutual aid societies were democratically administered insurance systems in which members pooled their resources in order to provide a subsidy in times of illness or disability. Workers of a locality or trade agreed to pay regular membership dues, and in the case of illness, they were guaranteed a certain minimal subsistence income. Like cooperatives, mutual aid societies were modern organizations that flourished as the result of political liberalization, improved communication, and economic change at the end of nineteenth century.[34] They were a way of overcoming the peasantry's isolation, creating a nodal point of communication, and maintaining an autonomous space removed from the domination of the traditional elites. Cooperatives and mutual aid societies were important social spaces; they facilitated the social intercourse, "multiplicity of development," and "diversity of talents" that Marx identified as fatally absent from the French peasantry in 1851.

Mutual aid societies used both explicit rules and informal norms to maintain their working-class character. The Associazione di Mutuo Soccorso fra gli Agricolturi e gli Operai di San Lorenzo a Vaccoli, founded in 1896, for example, specified that elite benefactors could speak during meetings and vote but could not hold office. The Società fra gli Operai di Seggiola (commune of Pisa), founded three years later, also accepted honorary members but excluded bosses, factory owners, and their children. Furthermore, the statutes specified that only workers could vote and hold office.[35] Many mutual aid societies originally included members of a single profession, thereby guaranteeing the homogeneity of their social composition. Under the influence of universalistic democratic ideals, working-class associations increasingly emphasized that membership was open to "all citizens of any profession or condition."[36] Nevertheless, there were several ways of reinforcing a distinctly working-class or artisanal identity without necessarily excluding potential allies. The Società Operaia di Mutuo Soccorso Giuseppe Giaribaldi, founded in 1898, for example, stated that its constituency was primarily working class but that it would nevertheless accept anyone. The Cooperative Sociali di Previdenza San Niccolò (founded in 1910) accepted all members "not known to have interests opposed to the goals of the society," in this case the economic improvement of the working class. Thus, the statutes, while emphasizing inclusivity, maintained mechanisms for excluding infiltrators and guaranteed a legal basis for limiting potentially paternalistic control by nonworkers. This reflected the logic of Gramsci's conception of a counterhegemonic bloc; only those political alliances are possible that are not excluded by fundamental economic conflict of interest.

The phenomenal growth of mutual aid societies at the turn of the century indicates their importance as a mechanism of social aggregation. In 1862 there were 443 societies with 111,608 members (not counting employer-sponsored schemes). By 1904 there were 6,347 legally recognized mutual aid societies with just under a million members.[37] They were successful because they integrated three different sorts of needs—economic, social, and political—and linked these different dimensions. In the associations, the basic economic need for support in times of sickness was connected to the desire for sociability. The legal form of the mutual aid society also provided a more instrumental advantage—the mantle of recognition and legality for a host of more controversial political activities. Although the secrecy of such activity makes it hard to gauge its extent, reports of prefects and police spies claimed that many "subversive" groups (for example, socialists and anarchists) used mutualism as a cover for their organizations.

Mutualism and the Counter-Economy

Italian working-class history did not follow a developmental logic whereby populist, heterogeneous, locally rooted organizations matured into more modern, homogenous, class-based unions and parties. Instead, relatively homogeneous, working-class mutual aid societies provided the basis for building a highly diversified web of corollary organizations that brought housewives, artisans, small farmers, and marginally employed agricultural workers into the socialist movement. The national statistics produced by the Ministry of Agriculture, Industry, and Commerce confirm this trend.

In 1878, the census of mutual aid societies asked for the first time whether the societies offered additional services to their members (see table 4).[38] This census reveals the development of a series of initiatives that went beyond the original goals of mutualism. Although the overwhelming majority of corollary activities were in related domains, such as providing small loans to workers in times of crises, a few innovative mutual aid societies began to build consumer, housing, and producer cooperatives in order to combat the high cost of living, speculation, and cyclical employment. By 1904, 8.8 percent of all mutual aid societies had affiliated cooperatives. Rather than narrowing their focus, these workers' organizations were expanding both their field of initiative and potential constituency.

The statutes of mutual aid societies collected in the Biblioteca Nazionale Centrale di Firenze provide further evidence for the interlinked nature of working-class associations. Out of 1,063 mutual aid societies founded in Tuscany, 48 percent had professional/union functions as secondary goals, 19 percent administered cooperatives, and 15 percent explicitly engaged in political work.[39] Rather than a growing differentiation between various types of organizations, we see the emergence of an interlinked set of functionally autonomous yet highly integrated initiatives.

Nor did the development always progress unidirectionally from mutualism to cooperation to trade unionism. The subsequent evolution of the workers' movement, which culminated in nationally organized labor unions, tends to obscure the close ties that originally linked resistance organizations (for example, nascent trade unions) and cooperatives. Many associations stated that their aim was the "economic and moral improvement of the working class" and listed a variety of ways of achieving this goal. The language of moral improvement was necessary at a time when political organizations were still regularly disbanded by the government. Although the term sounds antiquated, it implied more or less what we mean by political education today: the ability to read, write, speak in public, discuss alternatives, and formulate an agenda. Cooperation and trade unionism were also strategies appropriate to different economic conditions. In times of recession when unemployment was high and bargaining power low, producer cooperatives provided an ideal solution for economic survival. During periods of economic growth, however, strikes were more successful.[40]

Such a multilevel strategy was especially common for associations based on occupational identity. The three poles of mutualism, resistance, and cooperation were perceived as related tactics for achieving an

Table 4. Diversification of Mutual Aid Societies

Functions	1878	1885
Total no. of mutual aid societies	2,091	4,896
Loans	243	981
Consumer co-ops	176	287
Libraries	162	161
Unemployment benefits	0	173
Education	578	469[a]
Recreation	0	36
Producer co-ops	0	38
Worker housing	0	6

Source: Ministero di Agricoltura, Industria, e Commercio, *Statistica delle Società di Mutuo Soccorso e delle istitutioni cooperative annesse all medesime* (Rome, 1878, 1885).
[a]The absolute and relative number of mutual aid societies sponsoring education initiatives probably dropped because of the enactment of a law passed in 1877 mandating that the local government finance elementary schools.

underlying goal rather than as different or even antagonistic organizational principles. This is most apparent in the case of producer cooperatives that were often also leagues of resistance (that is, nascent trade unions). For example the Società Cooperative Operai Esercenti dell'Arte Muraria (Cooperative Society of Construction Workers), founded in 1898, was a labor cooperative with the principal goal of engaging in construction projects, including public works, "as a means of emancipation." Twenty percent of the profits were reserved for mutualism, and the statutes also stated explicitly that an auxiliary goal was "the diffusion of the principles of cooperation, saving, and education." Joining a cooperative was also a way of identifying with the socialist subculture without the danger of activism in the party. In 1914 more than one million families were part of the organized cooperative movement.[41] The overwhelming majority belonged to cooperatives affiliated with the Lega Nazionale delle Cooperative Italiane, a coalitional organization affiliated with the reformist wing of the PSI. By contrast, the PSI had 57,274 members in 1914.[42]

Not only did these organizations link economic and political struggle; they also challenged existing class divisions in order to forge a new basis for solidarity. The Associazione Generale fra i Coloni del Pistoiese, formed in 1919, was open to "all heads of families that gain their sustenance from manual agricultural labor, whether on their own land, renting, or sharecropping." The guiding goal was the "improvement of the agricultural working class, without violence, according to the laws, with the force of beneficence and fraternity."[43] To achieve these goals, the association specified three mechanisms: mutualism, joint purchasing and marketing cooperatives, and the provision of legal advice in relations with large landowners. Even in the period after World War I, mutualism, cooperation, and union-type functions were often conceived as integrally related components.

Co-ops provided significant financial support to economic, political, and cultural organizations. Whereas early co-ops distributed all "profits" back to members, increasingly they reserved a percentage for collective endeavors ranging from propaganda to emergency relief.[44] Using the financial resources generated through cooperation in order to sustain labor during industrial conflicts was an important innovation that helped forge a workers' movement out of a set of isolated measures originally formulated for individual benefit. In the province of Parma (in Emilia-Romagna) this logic culminated in the decision taken on December 21, 1907, at the provincial congress, where thirty-three consumer cooperatives agreed that all profits would go to support organizations of resistance.[45]

Società di Mutuo Soccorso di Rifredi

The mutual aid society, initially a nonprofit insurance program, became the foundation of a wide-ranging program of economic empowerment and solidarity. The history of the Società di Mutuo Soccorso di Rifredi illustrates this transformation. Under the influence of the socialist administrators who maintained a majority on the Società di Mutuo Soccorso di Rifredi's council from 1900 until its dissolution under fascism, several important organizational modifications were implemented. First, the council added a clause that the mutual aid society could offer subsidies to workers in "other determinate circumstances" besides illness; this effectively meant that mutualist funds could be used to support strikers, thus significantly strengthening workers' ability to mount a credible challenge to employers. Second, the organization's 1905 statute expanded the existing organizational units (mutual aid, consumer cooperative, reading circle) to include eight more subdivisions. These new initiatives included a cooperative for the construction of workers' housing, a producers' cooperative, a women's section, a savings and loan association, new educational initiatives, and a health clinic.[46] Although not all of these projects were ultimately realized, the goals reflect an important shift in the role of mutualism. Rather than serving merely as a pragmatic strategy for enduring misfortune, it became the center of a series of initiatives for improving working-class life. Another way of thinking about this change is that the Società di Mutuo Soccorso di Rifredi changed from a purely instrumental organization into a multipurpose space. In other words, it became a site of aggregation that provided a context for generating multiple and changing initiatives.

Pragmatic institutions with clear short-term benefits, such as the mutual aid society and consumer cooperative, provided skills and structure for supporting more complex long-term initiatives such as the construction of low-cost housing for workers. This logic was present throughout the cooperative movement, and thus the resources accumulated through the consumer cooperative financed collective goods such as libraries, meeting spaces, and educational programs. A further revision of the Società di Mutuo Soccorso di Rifredi's statutes in 1908 established social funds: 5 percent of the consumer cooperative's profits would be reserved for study and propaganda, 5 percent would subsidize the unemployed, and 10 percent would be devoted to the welfare of the co-op's employees.[47]

What were the political implications of these organizational changes? In the case of the Società di Mutuo Soccorso di Rifredi, located in a working-class suburb of Florence, the society played a key role in representing local interests to the municipal and communal government. In his in-depth institutional case study, Luigi Tomassini argued that the Società di Mutuo Soccorso di Rifredi helped further local interests such as the extension of street lighting, public transportation, and other urban facilities into the working-class suburbs. This reflects the territorial rootedness of such organizations. Unlike the nascent trade unions, which tried to organize individual trades on a national basis, mutual aid societies, cooperatives, and eventually the syndicalist-inspired chambers of labor were rooted in specific localities. Their constituency included industrial and unskilled workers, artisans, housewives, the unemployed, and peasants. Such organizations were also more likely to turn to political strategies because their institutional interests—medical care and health insurance, expanding public works, and fighting the high cost of living—could only be solved through political action.[48]

As the Società di Mutuo Soccorso di Rifredi became increasingly the center of social life and solidarity in the neighborhood, it also became a resource for political organization. The headquarters provided opportunities for encounter, assembly, and aggregation.[49] The café, assembly hall, meeting rooms, cooperative store, and offices facilitated the co-presence of workers beyond the factory and the control of management. I choose the term *co-presence* to indicate a mode of "being there together" that is not oriented toward a specific goal but rather appears as a natural extension of social life.

Traditional Marxist theory assumed a similar logic when it located growing class consciousness in the co-presence of workers facilitated by the factory system. The lived experience of sharing certain locations and routines can engender similar interests and identities. Although such co-presence may appear natural, it is actually a product of other social structures (such as urbanization, the Fordist mode of production, Taylorist strategies for increasing productivity) that may themselves not be apparent. The factory could be the site of either solidarity or isolation; the meaning of these spaces was itself the object of continuous struggle. Several social historians have pointed out that class consciousness only developed when neighborhood solidarities reinforced workplace-based proletarian identities.[50] This is true, although neighborhood solidarities are not the automatic result of the housing market's tendency to advance the segregation of socioeconomic groups. They are a product of the way in which groups mark, interpret, and give meaning to their shared experiences. Sites that were both locally rooted and linked to more broad-based structures played a crucial role in generating solidarity.

Spaces of Hope

The neighborhood *circolo*, the "center of contagion" where Sardinian soldiers encountered Turinese workers, facilitated the three basic social functions of space: encounter, aggregation, and assembly.[51] The ability to aggregate dispersed individuals is the most basic but important effect of any new political space. Bringing a greater number and more diverse assortment of people together encourages communication of ideas, interests, and experiences. The men and women who shopped or drank at cooperatives were more likely to be exposed to political ideas. The cooperative provided opportunities for recognizing or constructing commonalities. It created both formal and informal processes of coordination. The cooperative provided the context for political talk and ultimately the basis for political action.

In any small town, the cooperative usually was the first space controlled by workers that was big enough to hold a group larger than immediate friends or family. Such spaces made it possible to form a group organized around joint interests and ideas rather than immediate personal ties. The spatial and institutional separation from the church and state made it possible for cooperatives and mutual aid societies to shelter oppositional politics and to facilitate the debate, consensus, and planning necessary for sustained collective action. Co-ops also provided meeting rooms where groups could assemble. Assembly is the formalization of aggregation, a self-conscious aggregation for a particular purpose; it is often oriented outward and can take the form of an orchestrated performance for an audience. As Charles Tilly put it, assembly convinces both allies and adversaries of strength and unity.[52] Contemporaneous observers recognized and articulated the decisive importance of place. For example, a report published by the commune of Milan in 1920 argued that the success of the tavern was a result of its role as a site of sociability: "The secret of the grand, incomparable success of the *bettola* [tavern] does not consist in the fact that the workers find wine to drink there, as much as the need—extremely intense in those who labor—to end the day talking with friends in an openly hospitable place [un luogo liberamente ospitale] . . . one drinks the wine in order to pay the bartender for the spot that one occupies in his shop."[53] Workers who toiled in the highly disciplinary environment of the factory had an especially intense need for a place where sociability was infused with autonomy and equality. Although the syntax of the sentence makes it necessary to translate *liberamente* as "openly," a more literal translation of the word is "freely." The *bettola*—the workers' bar-café-snackbar—was a place where it was possible to be human and therefore free.

Not all contexts for aggregation and encounter are politicizing. It is also possible that a group could maintain its precarious sense of community by excluding potential sources of conflict, such as politics. The cooperative, however, was particularly well positioned to link sociability to political action. Because co-ops were formed to deal with broad social and economic problems that individuals could not handle alone, they presupposed some commonality of purpose and interest in collective solutions.

The cooperative movement was beset by contradictions; it tried to build a counter-economy while competing in a capitalist market. It was tied both to the legacy of liberal democracy and the strategy of class struggle. Internally, cooperatives were sites of both conflict and solidarity. They provided spaces for encountering others as equals, comrades, allies, or adversaries rather than dependents or masters. But members also experienced the frustrations of any joint endeavor: the inefficiencies of collective decision making, the rivalries between different visions, the corruption of power, and the constraints of a hostile economy.[54] In other words, cooperatives were spaces distinct from the precarious private home, capitalist market, and authoritarian factory, places where it was possible for the disenfranchised to live publicly. Cooperatives were not salons or gentlemen's clubs but rather sites of a counter-economy. They tied economic interests to social identity and ultimately to political participation. They made it possible to imagine the most banal tasks of daily life, such as shopping, milling bread, or drinking a glass of wine with friends, as an act of identification with socialism. The cooperative experience also defined what socialism meant—not a doctrinaire set of principles but a popular movement for economic change and political inclusion of the working classes.

The socialist-inspired cooperatives became the preeminent spaces of resistance because they were based on democratizing existing sites of encounter and creating new ones. The first cooperatives—stores, workshops, credit associations, bars—had the same basic functions as existing businesses. They fulfilled pressing practical needs, but they did so in a distinctive way. The defining characteristic was the way in which they replaced hierarchical relationships with egalitarian ones. The organizing principle was the elimination of the distinction between capital and labor, creditor and debtor, merchant and customer, boss and employee. The cooperative provided a place where workers could rebuild bonds of solidarity, experience themselves as economic agents, and act as citizens rather than clients. Similarly, the mutual aid societies, evening schools, and libraries helped reconfigure paternalistic charitable endeavors as autonomous sites where policies were collectively controlled by their beneficiaries.

Although it is easy to recognize the strength of the cooperative by looking at the significant number of participants and economic resources, the power of misrecognition is equally important. By misrecognition I mean that the level of identification with the cooperative far exceeded any possible rational or utilitarian calculation on the part of the members. The members did not recognize the limitations of the cooperative. In other words, we can learn something not only by looking at what the cooperative achieved but also by considering what unrealizable hopes it inspired. The cooperative was the embodiment of the workers' dream of collective control over the economy. It was what David Harvey has called a "space of hope."[55]

6

THE HOUSE OF THE PEOPLE

The beauty of the house of the people isn't like that of the church
or communal palace, which obscures and hides the poverty of the
workers. It is not for vanity but for inspiration and education. It
must be a place where we learn to become more demanding, that
is, more civilized.

Giustiza, December 9, 1906

At the end of the nineteenth century, the proliferation of socialist-inspired houses of the people changed the symbolic urban landscape of
towns across Europe. They were sites of sociability that served the pragmatic purpose of providing office space for individual workers' organizations such as peasant leagues, women's groups, mutual aid societies,
and cooperatives. Moreover, houses of the people served an important
role as a point of reference for popular life—both symbolically and
functionally. Yet understanding the social and political resonance of
these spaces requires different conceptual tools than those that are usually employed for approaching written texts. As the French philosopher
Henri Lefebvre points out, the semiological categories of message,
code, reading, and writing can only capture part of the meaning of
space. For Lefebvre, space is also social. Particular places can initiate,
maintain, frame, or interrupt contact between people. Space "permits
fresh actions to occur, while suggesting others and prohibiting yet others."[1] Reading space as a text would privilege the cognitive over the experiential dimension, thereby obscuring the real power of place.

The power of place comes from its ability to link a sense of self and
belonging to broader ideals and institutions.[2] To elucidate this relationship we must distinguish between three levels of analysis: space as a di-

mension of perception (experiential); space as a mechanism for facilitating interaction and forging collective identities (social); and particular places as repositories of condensed meanings (symbolic).[3] Clearly these three dimensions are related.[4] Houses of the people were simultaneously pragmatic solutions to police harassment and surveillance, attempts to embody solidarity, and interventions in the symbolic space of the city. They challenged political and economic structures because they functioned as material and symbolic nodal points for aggregating dispersed people and ideas.

Theories of Space

Reform projects have often emphasized the importance of architectural change. Utopias of both social control and emancipation have tried to restructure the dispersion of bodies in space in order to achieve certain social and political effects. Perhaps the most famous example is Foucault's analysis of Bentham's Panopticon—the prison designed on the principle that the threat of constant visibility would engender the internalization of self-discipline. This archetypical example of the spatialization of control was not only an architectural model but also a principle of individualization that found application in a variety of contexts from the school to the factory.[5] Similarly, the factory system was created not only to benefit from the efficiency of the division of labor but also to expand control. Early factories were simply large spaces rented by merchants, where artisans, who still used their own tools, produced traditional goods. Centralization simplified coordination and facilitated surveillance. Its pedagogic purpose was to break peasants of their traditional work rhythms and inculcate habits more conducive to the intensification of production.[6] The logic of Haussmann's redesign of Paris, a project that involved reorganizing and expanding the boulevards of the capital, was similar. His goal was to facilitate the employment of modern artillery and create an urban terrain unfavorable to the barricades, which had been used so effectively during the Revolution of 1848. This strategic goal, however, was realized in a way that highlighted the state's ability to diffuse the mobilization of the popular quarters. The new urban landscape became an enduring symbol of this control.[7]

For Lefebvre more than Foucault, space has an emancipatory as well as a disciplinary potential. Although spatial configurations, in their monumentality and materiality, can appear to embody a certain rigidity, they are products of human action and therefore are open to transformation. The space we live in is not a natural environment but rather the sedimentation of a social process—what Lefebvre calls the "production of space." Space is not only a modality for producing and disciplining subjects; it is also an expression of human creativity and an element of material life. Lefebvre captures the disciplinary and emancipatory aspects with the distinction between dominated and appropriated spaces. He defines dominated space as the realization of the project of masters, achieved through the manipulation of technology. In contrast, appropriated spaces are those modified to serve human needs.[8]

Lefebvre's distinction between dominated and appropriated places is suggestive but ultimately opaque in that it relies on under-theorized assumptions about the transparency of human needs. To clarify the distinction, he explains that "appropriation cannot be understood apart from the rhythms of time and of life." This statement evokes the distinctive quality of vernacular architecture, the spaces that emerge from an ongoing, collective process of adapting the environment to meet human needs for shelter, privacy, sociality, and beauty. But his archetypical examples of dominated spaces—military fortifications, ramparts, dams—are also produced to satisfy human needs. The difference lies in whose needs are foregrounded and how priorities are determined. Dominated spaces are produced by a particular kind of knowledge, a knowledge that James Scott associates with the state. For Scott, seeing like a state involves creating a domain of legibility, a closed, sterilized emptied-out space that can be replicated, measured, divided into equal units.[9] Dominated spaces are designed to fulfill the needs of citizens and consumers, but these needs are imagined in a particular way. Dominated spaces are created for "standardized citizens who [are] uniform in their needs and interchangeable," totally lacking original ideas, distinctive traditions, and history.[10] These spaces include MacDonald'ses as well as military installations. Such spaces help create the kind of subjects they were built for.

Appropriated spaces subvert this logic. They are produced by ordinary people, using a set of skills adapted to a particular context and acquired gradually through experimentation and revision. Their diversity reflects the conditions under which they were produced—the unique combination of human creativity, inherited experience, and available resources applied to meet immediate goals. Houses of the people were appropriated spaces. They were places created piecemeal by using local knowledge to meet workers' needs for a collective "room of one's own." And although they ultimately became important nodal points of the socialist movement, they were not cells created from above in order to transmit directives and maintain discipline. Instead, their organization was what William Connolly has called rhizomatic, that is, a structure that does not emerge out of a single root but is made up of diverse social formations linked through a web of multiple connections.[11] Such a structure suggests a system of participation that has no center and no hierarchy.

Although the distinction between dominated and appropriated spaces helps account for the way that space contributes to opposing political projects, it is only a partial explanation. The problem is that the approach treats space in isolation from other social and political forces. In addition to looking at the way places fill needs, we have to consider how they reinforce or challenge broader structures. The function of a space emerges from its relationship to other spaces in the way that it reinforces or challenges the dominant concentrations of power. The houses of the people provided a shelter for oppositional ideas and a stage for rehearsing new characters and learning new lines. Although no space can be intrinsically free, it can be liberatory vis-à-vis a particular form of domination.

Foucault's concept of the heterotopia provides a theoretical framework for approaching such a space. He distinguished those sites that "are endowed with the curious property of being in relation with all the others, but in such a way as to suspend, neutralize, or invert the set of relationships designed, reflected, or mirrored by themselves,"[12] and he differentiated two types of such spaces: utopias and heterotopias. For Foucault, utopias are sites with no real place; they express the reversal or radical transformation of society but are essentially mental rather than spatial constructions. He defines *heterotopia* in the following way:

> There also exist, and this is probably true for all cultures and civilizations, real and effective spaces which are outlined in the very institution of society, but which constitute a sort of counter-arrangement, of effectively realized utopia, in which all real arrangements, all the other real arrangements that can be found within society, are at one and the same time represented, challenged, and overturned: a sort of place that lies outside all places and yet is actually localizable.[13]

He employs the term *heterotopia* to express the radical contrast between these sites and the rest of society, which they simultaneously reflect and challenge.

Foucault distinguishes two types: crisis heterotopias and heterotopias of deviation. Crisis heterotopias are places such as the boarding school, military service, the honeymoon trip, that is, privileged or forbidden sites that serve to mark out or mask liminal stages in life. Heterotopias of deviance, places such as the prison, psychiatric hospitals, and rest homes, are a way to embody and patrol the borderline between normality and abnormality.

Foucault did not claim that the heterotopia is a principle of political emancipation, a model of social transformation, or a locus for self-fashioning. He did, however, conclude his lecture with the provocative suggestion that "in civilizations where [heterotopia] is lacking, dreams dry up, adventure is replaced by espionage, and privateers by the police."[14] We are left with the sense that the heterotopia is not just a space of otherness but the basis (or at least the inspiration) for struggle against existing forms of domination. Some of Foucault's followers have been more explicit about drawing this conclusion.[15] They argue that by denaturalizing existing practices, heterotopias contribute to a broader project of social change.

In *Spaces of Hope*, David Harvey challenges this approach to theorizing the relationship between space and politics. He suggests that a position of alterity vis-à-vis the dominant social structure does not, by itself, nurture critique, let alone resistance. According to this perspective, the paradigmatic heterotopias of contemporary America could include shopping malls, gated communities, Disneyland, and militia camps. These too are places where some of our culture's other real sites are represented, inverted, sanitized, or demonized in order to highlight their mythic properties. They are our "effectively enacted utopias." These countersites, however, employ their distinctiveness to perfect rather than to dismantle dominant patterns of consumption.

Heterotopias can be the bases of guerilla struggles against normalization, but they can also perfect more nuanced forms of social control.[16] Thus, we need a more precise concept: the heterotopia of resistance.[17] The heterotopia of resistance is a real countersite that inverts and contests existing economic or social hierarchies. Its function is social transformation rather than escapism, containment, or denial. By challenging the conventions of the dominant society, it can be an important locus of struggle against normalization.

The houses of the people built in Europe at the turn of the century were heterotopias of resistance, real spaces, countersites constructed to materialize an alternate reality. Yet they also made use of, imitated, and transformed preexisting sites or institutions. They reflected preexisting bourgeois forms of sociability such as the Masonic lodge and the reading circle;[18] architecturally, they often incorporated elements of bourgeois styles. They were not closed, isolated units but rather sites in which the dominant reality was represented and contested. They symbolized the socialist belief in a future society in which production and consumption, work and leisure, politics and pageantry, would be reintegrated. Their physical presence served to symbolically challenge the dominance of the repressive apparatus of the state as well as the moral and social monopoly of the church. The groups of workers who constructed such sites tried to design a space that could facilitate solidarity. The houses of the people served to embody the concept of democracy that remained only rhetorical in the polity. These houses of the people, which sprang up in hundreds of small towns and cities across Italy, were the archetypical countersites, real utopias consisting of a fully democratic public life.

Out of the five generalizations that Foucault employs to characterize heterotopias, two are especially germane to the specific form of the heterotopia of resistance. According to Foucault, "The heterotopia has the power of juxtaposing in a single real place different spaces and locations that are incompatible with each other."[19] This principle effectively expresses the logic of the houses of the people, which provided meeting space for a large variety of socialist and democratic associations. Even though organizations such as the reformist cooperatives, mutual aid societies, the inter-classist popular university program, syndicalist producer co-ops, and the Marxist-influenced socialist parties were often ideological adversaries, they were united under one roof. This symbolically communicated that despite serious differences, they were still part of a shared project of furthering the working classes' control over collective life. Physical proximity also had the advantage of facilitating certain joint initiatives such as May Day celebrations or mobilization for election campaigns. The physical structure of the house of the people (also sometimes called house of the socialists, of the union, or of labor) provided a kind of loose coalitional structure that could bring together distinct elements without demanding assimilation.

Another distinguishing feature of the heterotopia is "a system of opening and closing that isolates them and makes them penetrable."[20] According to Foucault, a heterotopia is not freely accessible in the same way that a public space is. Entry may be compulsory, as in the case of the barracks or the prison, or it may be regulated by a ritualized set of exclusions. He claims that even spaces that appear open, in fact, conceal a curious pattern of exclusion. What Foucault emphasizes for heterotopias is true for all allegedly public spaces. The cafés, clubs, and salons that made up the bourgeois public sphere were private. Accessibility was regulated by mechanisms of class segregation such as financial resources and social conventions. Similarly, libraries, journals, reading circles, and the literary salon all had explicit or implicit codes of access such as letters of introduction, peer review, or perhaps the possession of an academic degree. Even the piazza, which since Greek times has been the embodiment of public space, is constantly the locus of police control. By requiring a permit to demonstrate or by enforcing vagrancy laws, access is habitually denied to those who are deemed threatening to public order. Thus, the "public" of the "public sphere" does not refer to a spatial principle, nor even to a procedural ideal of open participation, but rather to the subject matter of discussion, that is, matters related to the state.[21]

The houses of the people also reflected this logic of a quasi-public space. On the one hand, they were conceived as alternatives to the highly exclusionary practices of bourgeois clubs and secret societies. The very name "house of the people" reflected the idea that everyone, regardless of religious or political affiliation, social status or economic resources, could have access. On the other hand, by the late 1800s there was increasing awareness of the need to maintain functional autonomy from existing elites in order to mount an effective challenge. Furthermore, there were pragmatic motivations for creating some ideological criteria for membership. Police surveillance of workers' organizations was common, and the local prefect could arbitrarily disband an association on the basis of an informer's claim that it encouraged subversion. Many houses of the people regulated access on the basis of membership, which was open to anyone who espoused agreement with the association's principles, usually including looking after the economic interests of the members, encouraging mutual assistance, and furthering the intellectual and moral development of the working class through recreational activities.[22] Others reflected more moderate influences and specified the goal of promoting internal and external democracy.[23] Furthermore, membership was often granted only to individuals recommended by two current members. Access to the house of the people was far more open than were preexisting bourgeois societies, but access was still regulated. Membership was usually open to both socialists and republicans, workers and artisans, Catholics and secularists. Yet frequenting the house of the people was still an act that carried symbolic resonance. Part of the political effectiveness of the house of the people was precisely to make the most basic elements of social life, such as drinking a glass of wine in company, into an act of identification with socialism, at least in the broader sense of a popular movement for economic change and political inclusion of the working classes.

Whereas the bourgeois public sphere was based on bracketing economic status, the house of the people was premised on the need for the integration of politics and economics. The diverse forms of working-class mobilization—from theater groups, to political circles, to peasant leagues—would have been impossible to sustain without the financial resources generated through the cooperative. The opportunities for the worker and the bourgeois to participate in politics, even when legally equal, were functionally asymmetrical. Whereas for the bourgeois, the private home, working life, and the economy all generated the skills and resources necessary for full enfranchisement, the worker had to rely on the house of the people to achieve the same result. The bourgeois public sphere was premised on the public conversation of private individuals. This was a conversation between those citizens whose private property and familial intimacy produced the subjectivity that was the constitutive outside of the public sphere.[24] The working classes, of course, had neither property nor an intimate, private sphere for retreat and contemplation. The crowded, unsanitary workers' housing hardly provided "the space [that] was the scene of a psychological emancipation."[25] Given the extreme poverty that workers endured, the private sphere could only be a further source of disempowerment. Only a collective space could serve as the basis of psychological emancipation. Writing in 1901, Mazzinian journalist Giovanni Bacci explained, "Just as the traveler who is tired by the long road . . . dreams of his house where he can find relaxation and repose, similarly the worker dreams of association, the house of the people with its multiple institutions, mutualism, cooperatives, and instruction."[26] Bacci drew an explicit parallel between the function of the individual private home and that of the house of the people. Whereas the elite could afford the luxury of the salon, the billiard room, and the private cook, the workers had the house of the people. The bourgeoisie could obtain financial as well as social/psychological resources in the private sphere, whereas the workers were forced to compensate for individual privation through solidaristic structures.

The House of the People

Houses of the people were built throughout Europe at the end of the late nineteenth and early twentieth centuries. The first record of the term *house of the people* in Italy can be found in 1893, when it was used to describe the initiative of a consumer cooperative in Massenzatico (Reggio Emilia). More than ten thousand workers were in attendance for its inauguration.[27] Most houses of people originally were financed by either cooperatives or mutual aid societies, which were uniquely able to accumulate collective resources from the numerous but economically marginal workers. According to Rochedale principles, most cooperatives sold merchandise at market prices and then distributed profits to the members in proportion to purchases. In addition, a portion of the profits was retained as reserves for the co-op, and a percentage was also devoted to social and political projects. According to the statutes, such projects had to be approved by the majority of members during periodic assemblies. The funds used to construct the houses of the people were the profits that would usually have been distributed to investors as return on capital.

Some houses of the people evolved out of the literacy campaigns that socialists organized in order to expand the working class's representation among the electorate. Because the law restricted the right to vote to those male citizens who possessed a school certificate or were able to pass a literacy exam, participation among the working classes was effectively limited. At first, the socialists rented rooms to organize evening literacy classes. These initiatives soon expanded to include a series of related activities: newspaper reading rooms, libraries, and political discussion groups. The problem was that in small urban and rural centers, the local elite effectively controlled real estate and sometimes refused to rent space to socialists. Alternatively, when political groups tried to meet in bars and cafés, those establishments were often closed by the local prefect, who selectively applied licensing laws to limit socialist groups' access to such supposedly public spaces.[28] Meeting in private homes, however, was not a solution. First, workers almost never had the space to host even moderately large groups. Second, hosting such a meeting increased the risk of police retaliation. Finally, because the socialist movement's goal was inclusiveness, meeting in private homes would be an ineffective mode of increasing broad participation. To overcome these difficulties, socialist activists were forced to build autonomous meeting spaces. Relying on donations of materials and especially of labor, these first houses of the people were usually simple structures reflecting traditional building styles. Yet for their supporters, houses of the people had enormous symbolic and practical significance as the first autonomous sites of popular mobilization.

One example of this trajectory was the *casa del popolo* in Abbadia di Montepulciano (Siena).[29] In the early 1900s, this town of a thousand inhabitants was completely dominated by two large commercial agricultural producers. As a result of the monopolization of economic and political power, socialist organizations were slow to develop. The breakthrough came in 1914 (after the electoral reform granting almost universal male suffrage) when the first socialist municipal councilor was elected. This success, however, precipitated repression by local elites, who refused to rent rooms to the socialist organizations. The local socialists responded by starting a collection that paid for building materials. All work was completed voluntarily by laborers on Sundays and after the normal working day. This house of the people, completed in 1917, included a library, consumer cooperative, meeting rooms for youth and women's groups, as well as the seat of the Partito Socialista Italiano (PSI). The *Almanacco socialista italiano* of 1918 interpreted the construction of this house of the people as an important political victory rather than just a logistical improvement. It wrote, "The red flag [that] waves in one of the towers of our house of the people, pride of this proletariat, nightmare of our adversaries, is our model and stimulus to work, propaganda, and organization."[30] The house of the people was more than just a permanent meeting place for workers' organizations; it was also an important intervention in the symbolic landscape. It was part of a polemical challenge to the authority and dominance of the church, the state,[31] and private capital.

In addition to official repression by the state, socialists had to contend with the church's monopoly on social and spiritual life. For example, the house of the people of Volpiano was built in 1898 to overcome the obstacles created by the priest, who threatened to excommunicate anyone who rented space to socialists.[32] These institutions were perceived by the church as a direct threat, and in fact houses of the people were often explicitly created as an alternative to the conservative force of the Catholic Church, which, in the countryside, was closely allied to wealthy, landowning elites.

The house of the people was a site of recreation, socialization, and the realization of an alternate moral universe. The importance of the symbolic politics of space was not lost on its proponents. After describing the organizational, practical, and pedagogical benefits, the socialist Genuzio Bentini concluded that the house of the people in Bologna was "the germ of the communal future." He continued:

> But the house of the people is more than all that; this imposing structure that arises in the public view, induces those passing by to stop and think of its significance. It is a symbol, but precisely the symbol is the means of propaganda and the most effective affirmation that one can give to the world. In front of our symbol stand those of our enemies—the church, the barracks, and stock market.[33]

This statement underlines the importance of symbolism for politics. To say that politics is about power does not mean that conflict must be resolved with violence. Part of politics is the development, defense, and display of a subculture that nourishes genuine alternatives to the existing distribution of power (see fig. 5).

Journalists and propagandists of the houses of the people employed two metaphors over and over again in their accounts: fortress and church. Typical is Ettore Zanardi's description of the *casa del popolo*, published in *La Squilla:* "the fortress is transformed into a temple given to a great ideal—the economic and intellectual generation of the working class."[34] Certainly, this reflected the imagery most readily available; the church and the barracks were the two spaces that expressed the symbolic (and actual) dominance of religion and the state. The two metaphors also expressed the dual purpose of the house of the people. It was both an organization of resistance and the attempt to institute a universal. It embodied the two alternate conceptions of politics. At first it may appear that these two principles cannot be reconciled. Whereas resistance implies a conflictual and dialectical understanding of change, ethical universalism implies that a rational, consensual solution can conceivably be shared by all. The house of the people was an attempt to incorporate both of these principles: a radical break with existing ideology that tried to redefine the principle of generalizability.

The paradigmatic example of this system was the cooperative Vooruit in Ghent, Belgium. Founded in 1881 on the initiative of a group of textile workers in order to fight the high cost of living, Vooruit, benefiting from the low price of grain after the abolition of import duties, was able to expand its operations at the turn of the century. In 1902 it constructed a major building, Ons Huis (Our House), to serve as a center of working-

Fig. 5. The inauguration of the *casa del popolo*, Bodeno, May 1902. *Source*: Luigi Arbizzani, Saveria Bologna, Lidia Testoni, and Giorgio Triani, eds., *Storie di case del popolo: Saggi documenti e immagini d'Emilia-Romagna* (Bologna: Grafis, 1982).

class political, social, and economic life. In addition to the consumer co-operative, Vooruit included meeting rooms, a restaurant, library, adult education program, theater, café/bar, socialist newspaper, headquarters for the Belgian Workers' Party, and space for eighteen other political and cultural organizations.[35] In 1903 Vooruit entered into production by opening a textile-spinning cooperative. Vooruit also helped found producer cooperatives as a strategy for fighting unemployment, and it provided a livelihood to workers fired during labor conflicts. Vooruit also provided start-up capital, logistical aid, and space to such initiatives. In 1904 it established the first medical clinic, financed out of the social funds of the cooperative. To keep costs down it opened its own bakeries to supply low-cost bread, and in 1910 it constructed a brewery. Thus, the Vooruit complex integrated production, consumption, politics, social services, and recreation under the auspices of Ons Huis.

Unlike the capitalist firm, which was integrated vertically, the affiliated cooperatives and organizations were organized horizontally. Each was managed autonomously by its workers or members, but when possible, Vooruit provided logistical or financial support. Ideological affinity combined with loose organizational links provided a viable context for flexible contractual relations without relying on either market discipline or hierarchical control. During the 1913 general strike, it distributed free bread and "communist soup" to striking workers. The house of the people was more than just a social center; it was also a way of accumulating financial resources and channeling participation. In effect, Vooruit was an institution of economic resistance as well as an alternate social economy within the broader market-based system. By 1913 more than one thousand people worked directly in the socialist sector in Ghent. More than ten thousand families, one-fifth of the city's population, were members.[36]

Nor was Ghent an exception. The number of houses of the people in Belgium grew from 17 in 1890 to 149 by 1914 and reached a high point of 277 in 1935, before being disbanded or transformed under the Nazi occupation.[37] Although each house of the people was administered independently, there were certain features that they all shared. First, there was close coordination with the Belgian Workers' Party, which provided representation in Parliament and local government without sacrificing autonomy to political expediency. Although the party clearly benefited from the resources that the cooperatives provided for propaganda work, the model of Ons Huis also transformed the meaning of the term *resources*. The broad-based popular mobilization, rather than just financial profits, contributed to building the party. The houses of the people also served to create class consciousness and provide an important mechanism for involving unmobilized workers in the socialist world. They served to illustrate the possibility of a labor-managed economy while simultaneously combating the daily problems of the high cost of living and the precariousness of employment. They provided important infrastructure for the genesis of new associations and orchestrated coordination that did not imply subordination. Finally, the Belgian houses of the people were an important intervention in the politics of representation by embodying the growing strength and autonomy of the working class.

The Italian houses of the people, like the Belgian ones, were not subordinated to the national policies of any labor union or political party. They were rooted in local society and therefore took heterogeneous forms, depending on the balance of power between local social forces. Whereas many had an explicitly socialist profile and were active in support of strikers, others were products of democratic-republican initiatives and followed a strategy of building interclass alliances. Despite this heterogeneity, there are four principles that summarize the characteristics of the houses of the people and distinguish them from bourgeois associationalism, clandestine revolutionary organizations, and paternalistic societies for the betterment of the working class. First, they were complex structures for bringing together diverse organizations. Second, they were financed collectively by their members. Third, they were managed democratically by workers themselves. Finally, participation was not limited by economic status or political or religious membership but was based on shared commitment to improving the economic and social life of the subaltern classes.

To what degree was the house of the people an important institution? Unfortunately, written material documenting the everyday life of workers and peasants during this period is limited. Because illiteracy in Italy was extremely high (estimated to be 70 percent as late as 1913),[38] letters and diaries from the period are rare. Published material inevitably reflects not just the propagandistic agenda of the author but also the process of interpreting working-class experience from the outside. Thus, the best documentation on the meaning of the house of the people must be the phenomena itself—the scope, functions, symbolic resonance, and practical effects. Unfortunately, we cannot know exactly how widespread they were or how many there were because no systematic study has been performed at the national level. One survey (based on data from 1919) of a random sample of 164 municipalities distributed across Italy found 29 houses of the people, 15 socialist houses, and 5 miscellaneous sites (cooperatives or leagues of resistance that provided space to other democratic organizations).[39] Given that there are around 8,000 municipalities in Italy, we could estimate that at the beginning of the interwar period there were at least 1,500 houses of the people and many more functional equivalents. Another study looked at the province of Ferrara (which is made up of a total of twenty municipalities); as of 1919 there were 51 houses of the people, and another 14 were founded before they were all declared illegal by the Fascists in 1926.[40]

Because the houses of the people were not merely the headquarters of a political party, it was able to involve people who were not socialists. Palmiro Togliatti explained how during the post–World War I period, a mere twelve hundred party members and a few hundred activists managed to dominate a city as large as Turin.

> In every neighborhood, next to the factory there was a circle, which was different than the party section . . . a place where workers went to discuss possible actions. In the circle in Borgo Vittoria there was a recreational room frequented by women and children and a little theater. . . . Also the Cooperative Alliance involved workers on the margins of socialism, especially women, in a red house which all the bourgeois of the city regarded as a den of subversives.[41]

This statement, however, only emphasizes one side of a mutual relationship. Even as these associational networks provided broader support for the PSI, mass popular participation influenced the programmatic elements of Italian socialism. Under the influence of the mutual aid societies, cooperatives, and circles, the reformist element of the PSI, which advocated parliamentary participation and emphasized the fight for economic improvements, attained internal hegemony. These sites of political discussion provided opportunities to the working class for informal participation.

The structure of the houses of the people embodied the principles of reformist socialism rather than a distinctly Marxist politics. Unlike trade unions, in which membership, identity, and participation were all based on employment, the houses of the people brought together factory workers, peasants, artisans, and the unemployed as well as leftist intellectuals such as journalists, teachers, and lawyers. In the early 1900s, trade unions in the modern sense, that is, industrial-based, national organizations, were increasingly prominent, but membership was still only part of the constituency for socialism. Whereas in 1902, 250,000 industrial workers were organized in socialist national trade-union federations, more than 500,000 were members of the Lega Nazionale delle Cooperative Italiane, the reformist-socialist cooperative federation. The General Confederation of Labor was founded in 1906, and by 1913 almost half of its 327,000 members were agricultural laborers.

The houses of the people were not utopias in Foucault's sense, that is, imaginary sites with no real place. They were very embedded in both rural and urban communities across Italy. According to Foucault, a heterotopia is a countersite that "reflects, subverts, and contests" the dominant culture. The houses of the people reflected the ideal of democracy, which was the basis for constantly challenging the strict limitations to participation maintained by the restricted suffrage and patronage system of the liberal state. By using the democratic procedures of voting, debating, bargaining, campaigning, and festival, they trained hitherto excluded workers in the skills necessary to represent their own concerns. The house of the people is often referred to as a microcosm of the outside world, combining the spheres of consumption, production, and social and political life, but in a more rational, just, and egalitarian form. Although reflecting the outside world, the house of the people was meant to reveal its failings and provide an outline of a better alternative.

Victor Horta's Maison du Peuple

By far the most significant house of the people, from the architectural standpoint, was Victor Horta's Maison du Peuple in Brussels. Commissioned in 1895, the massive building was inaugurated on Easter of 1899, dubbed "red Easter" in the press. In addition to being considered an important example of art nouveau, the structure also presented several innovative ways of realizing the unique function of the building. Horta summarized the challenge as follows: "to construct a palace that wouldn't be a palace but rather a 'house' in which the air and light would be the luxury so long excluded from the workers' hovels."[42] In fact, Horta created the effect of grandeur by using light and air rather than the finery and ornamentation of bourgeois palaces. Also, he expressed power through the innovative use of a skeletal frame of iron and steel, which created an impression of stability and massiveness without the heaviness characteristic of the concrete employed in most monumental architecture. Furthermore, his use of new industrial materials such as steel symbolized the progress, achieved through labor and industrialization, that would culminate in a new society.[43]

The two central spaces of the Maison du Peuple were the bar-café-restaurant on the first floor and the 1,500-seat auditorium on the top floor. The building was organized in a way that allowed the greatest possible opportunity for communal life. Whereas the restaurant was designed primarily for social life, the auditorium emphasized the exigencies of political life. Both spaces, however, undermined the rigidity of such a distinction. Daily newspapers were available in the bar-café, which was also the setting of informal political discussions. The auditorium provided a state-of-the-art space for musical and theatrical performances by employing new acoustical principles.[44] The auditorium was located on the top floor so that it could make the greatest possible use of natural light. In the bar-café, Horta pioneered the technique of employing removable panels that allowed the space to be adjusted to accommodate a variety of uses.

The design of Horta's Maison du Peuple is the inverse of Bentham's Panopticon (see figs. 6 and 7). Whereas the Panopticon was structured on the principle of individualization, the Maison du Peuple served to build solidarity. At the center of the Panopticon was the economical use of power, the solitary or even absent guard whose imagined presence would guarantee self-discipline. In contrast, at the center of Horta's construction was the diversity and polyvalence of the crowd, involved in a potentially subversive combination of drinking and debate, entertainment and education. At the periphery of the Panopticon were rows of transparent cells, which rendered each individual fully visible. The spaces at the periphery of the Maison du Peuple were offices and cooperatives that were separated from the communal space, thereby expressing the need for privacy, difference, and diversity. Nevertheless these spaces were an organic part of the larger construction, embodying the constant need for continued interaction, coordination, and alliance. Essentially, power emanated from the spatial margins, from the diverse institutions such as unions, cooperatives, and recreational groups, which made up the structure. The blueprints formalized principles that were developed over a decade by users of similar sites. The opposite was true of the Panopticon, where power emanated from the center and the periphery was the object of parsimonious control. The Panopticon and the Maison du Peuple were two heterotopias on opposite ends of the continuum of domination and appropriation. These two designs were archetypical models that were imitated to various degrees, adapted in response to new constraints, and sometimes appropriated for opposite purposes.[45] Nevertheless, they represent two opposite ways of analyzing the relationship between politics and space.

Because we are investigating the issue of space and politics in the context of early-twentieth-century Europe, a crucial question to ask is

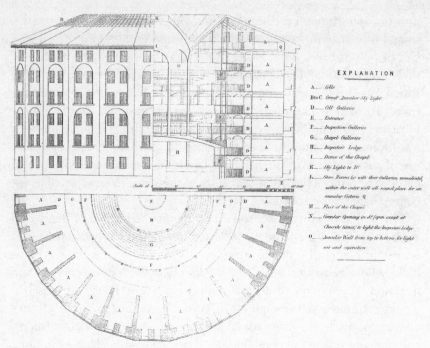

Fig. 6. Jeremy Bentham's Panopticon.

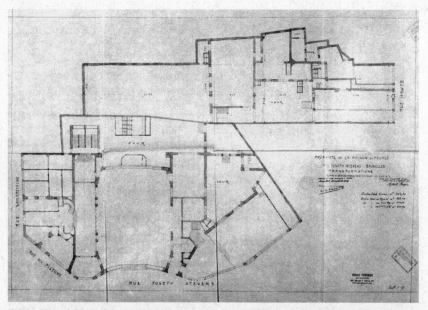

Fig. 7. Victor Horta's Maison du Peuple. *Source*: Jean Delhaye, *La Maison du Peuple de Victor Horta* (Brussels: Atelier Vokaer, 1987).

whether the fascists had "safe spaces." Fascism was also a form of resistance to the compromises reached by the liberal parliamentarian regime. And it too had its sites. This objection is one particular form of a larger challenge posed by Francesca Polletta, in her article "'Free Spaces' in Collective Action," in which she claims that the growing body of scholarship on "free spaces" (or its many equivalents, such as havens, spheres of cultural autonomy, and spatial preserves) has two basic flaws. First, the metaphor *free spaces* substitutes a structural property for a cultural characteristic. She claims that often it is not structural isolation (the "spaces") but ideological content that provides the basis for counter-hegemonic challenges.[46] Second, she argues that much of the literature in this tradition fails to offer the necessary specificity about the characteristics of free spaces.

To restate this challenge in terms of our own subject, fascism and socialism may both have built heterotopic sites, but what distinguished them was the opposing content of their ideology. This claim, however, rests on the debatable assumption that ideology has no effect on spatial practices. Although it is true that one cannot deduce politics from spatial arrangements (or vice versa), certain spatial arrangements are more or less suited to particular goals. Because fascism and socialism had different political purposes, they used space in different ways. Fascist spaces were often built on a monumental scale to evoke authoritarian power; even their "houses of fascism" were structured to subordinate the masses to the leader. As we will see below, the *casa del fascio* differed from the *casa del popolo* in significant ways.[47] Because there is nothing intrinsically democratic or emancipatory about "protected spaces," it is necessary to engage in careful historical analysis in order to understand how the built environment either promotes or inhibits particular identities, solidarities, and orientations toward the state. Theorizing space contributes to (but does not replace) such work.

The Casa del Fascio

How did the houses of fascism differ from the houses of the people? Before answering that question, a caveat is in order. Any simple equation between formal architectural elements and specific political effects would be an oversimplification. Many of the elements associated with fascist architecture were equally common in Stalin's Russia and FDR's America. The reverse is also true. Giuseppe Terragni's exemplary Casa del Fascio in Como exhibits some formal similarities with Victor Horta's Maison du Peuple in Brussels. Both structures were built around a central atrium, which functioned to encourage the aggregation of the masses; both provided spaces for a series of offices and social services at the perimeter; both buildings emphasized the use of glass and light to create an effect that was monumental yet transparent and open. Yet the Casa del Fascio, designed as the party headquarters of the Partito Fascista Nazionale (PFN) and a symbol of monolithic state power, was meant to play an important role in strengthening the cultic elements of fascism by housing a shrine to fallen fascists and providing the backdrop for carefully orchestrated displays of participation by acclamation.[48]

Do these similarities imply that there is no connection between formal architectural elements and political effects? This question suggests an important dilemma for the project of theorizing the relationship between space and politics. If similar spatial forms can be appropriated to serve such opposed projects, how can we make any compelling argument about the power of place? Although such a question draws attention to an important issue, it nevertheless needs to be reformulated, because it is based on the problematic assumption that we can isolate formal properties from other dimensions of space. Highlighting certain structural similarities is deceptive because it takes formal elements and isolates them both from other elements of the overall design and from the production of space.

The formal similarities between Victor Horta's Maison du Peuple and Giuseppe Terragni's Casa del Fascio are partially the product of the logic of competition and mimesis by which artistic models circulate and are cited in subsequent designs. Horta's innovative combination of steel and glass was widely admired and incorporated in different styles, including Terragni's rationalism. There was also a certain similarity between the functions of the two buildings. The house of fascism was meant to replace the social and cultural services that previously had been a source of power and solidarity for the socialist movement. The goal of fascism was not to destroy all social life but rather to integrate it into the framework of the monolithic state. Mussolini encapsulated this logic in his statement "Everything in the State, nothing outside the State, nothing against the State." Certain formal elements reflected genuine functional similarities, but these functions were incorporated into the framework of a very different structure.

A close reading of the semiotics of the two buildings reveals signs of such difference. For the sake of brevity, I highlight only two. First, even a casual observer immediately notices the curvilinear facade of Victor Horta's building (see fig. 8). This is one of the emblems of art nouveau, an attempt to incorporate references to nature, which created a feeling of organicity.[49] This effect stands in marked contrast to the geometric regularity of Terragni's rationalism. The contrast between the two facades, however, was not merely a stylistic choice; it also reflected the very different conditions of the two buildings' production. For both political and logistical reasons, the Belgian Workers' Party had trouble getting land in the center of town to build their headquarters and had to settle for an irregularly shaped building lot; Horta's design was a creative way of conforming to the very real material constraints.[50] The Casa del Fascio, in contrast, was built on an ideal site centrally located next to the cathedral. Under the direction of Attilio Terragni, vice president of the fascist party organization and subsequently mayor (*podesta*) of Como, the city donated the land.[51] The collusion with power made possible a certain "rationalist" use of space; the architect, supported by the local and national authorities, was able to control all aspects of the project. Victor Horta, however, executed a design constrained from the outset by its implication in a strategy of resistance to the existing powers that controlled urban space.

A second element worth noting is the differing relationship established between the two buildings and the space outside. Terragni's structure included a glass wall between the atrium and the piazza in front of the building. This wall was made up of eighteen doors that both symbolically and literally opened it up to the piazza, facilitating the integration of interior and exterior space for mass assemblies. Such permeability was not possible for socialist organizations that existed under conditions of tenuous legality. Although the houses of the people were organized on the principle of genuine inclusivity, they had to face the real problem of surveillance and repression by police. They had to negotiate the tension between their role as a strategic space, a sort of red "fortress" for sheltering opposition, and their function as a public space for facilitating political inclusion. The houses of fascism, which were extensions and symbolic embodiments of the dominant social structures, did not have to negotiate this tension.

To understand the significance of the houses of people, we cannot separate the formal architectural analysis of space from the way it is appropriated and experienced. Despite such a prominent exception as Victor Horta's Maison du Peuple in Brussels, what is significant about the houses of the people is less the exemplary influence of architectural in-

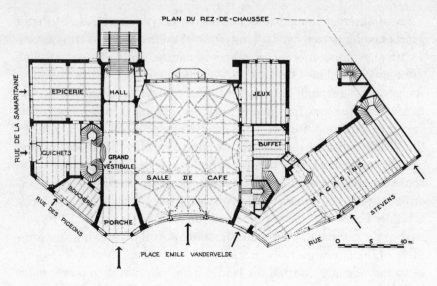

PLAN I.

Fig. 8. Victor Horta's Maison du Peuple. *Source*: Delhaye, *Maison du Peuple de Victor Horta*.

novators than the production of space by those who lived in it. The un-named architects of the houses of the people were the workers who built spaces to meet their needs and thereby collectively expressed what those needs were. When charitable institutions or government agencies tried to construct social centers modeled on the house of the people but with-out the active participation of unions and co-operatives, they failed.[52] The houses of the people were products of the interaction between utopian theorists, engaged activists, architects, and most of all, partici-pants. Marco De Michelis argues that the error of architects, urbanists, and planners in the 1920s was that they tried to introduce an institution without its vital organs. They forgot that a house of the people was not just for, but by, the people. It was the fruit of solidarity generated through struggle and sustained through democratic self-management, and therefore it could not be generated or replaced by even the most in-spired philanthropic endeavors.[53]

The Longing for Home

The house of the people was a particular historical phenomenon, but the phenomenon suggests the outline of an ideal type—one that reflects the unlikely convergence of public sphere and home. The term *home* is perhaps a little suspect in political theory. Postcolonial cultural theorists such as Homi Bhabha emphasize the *unheimlich*, the "unhomely," as the condition of the (post)modern world. Bhabha argues that the disorientation and historical trauma of displacement can provide an opening for critical theorizing.[54] For many progressives, the term *home* also carries the volkish connotation of its Heideggerian heritage. It seems to imply a natural retreat from conflict and contention, an unquestioned basis for identity and action. But it is precisely this naturalization of the existing spatial configuration that the house of the people drew attention to and contested. It revealed how the bifurcation into private and public served to mask the dominant principles of control based on the military, the police, and the market. The house of the people was an intervention with the aim of denaturalizing the existing boundary between economic life and political power. But this unmasking would be insufficient if it did not also imply a corollary project of reconstruction. The house of the people also functioned as a space of resistance, a protected space in which to explore and develop an alternate set of values, policies, and institutions. In "Difference, Dilemmas, and the Politics of Home," Bonnie Honig has written, "If home is to be a positive force in politics it must be recast in coalitional terms as a site of necessary nurturing, but also strategic, conflicted, and temporary alliances."[55] Not recast but rediscovered.

7

THE CHAMBER OF LABOR

If the snake sheds his skin before a new skin is ready, naked he will
be in the world, prey to the forces of chaos. Without his skin he
will be dismantled, lose coherence and die. Have you, my little ser-
pents, a new skin?

—Tony Kushner, *Angels in America*

Vasco Pratolini's neorealist novel *Metello* (1955) tells the story of the political and personal coming-of-age of a Florentine youth from the
lumpenproletariat. The narrative takes place in the late nineteenth century, and Metello's maturation parallels the growth of the Italian workers' movement. The novel describes the city of Florence, the poverty of
the workers, and the tension between individualism and responsibility.
The climax of the plot, Metello's pivotal role in the construction workers' victory, was based on the famous strike of 1902. The theme of solidarity, however, emerges early in the novel. Metello is orphaned when
his father drowns while working in the Arno. His wet nurse in the country reluctantly agrees to raise him. When his adopted family seeks work
in the coal mines in Belgium, however, visa restrictions forbid Metello
from accompanying them. In anguish, he goes back to the city, and a
former friend of his father's helps find him a trade. Although Metello
initially focuses on his own immediate self-interest and sensual pleasure,
avoiding involvement in politics, he eventually finds that he cannot
avoid his responsibility to other people.

The initial step in his politicization involves going to the chamber of
labor. At first "it was enough for him to be on [the socialists'] side and to
show it: to go to meetings, read the *Class Struggle*, sign up at the Labor

Centre [chamber of labor], though not with the Party."[1] Unwilling to make the sacrifices required of a militant, Metello is still exposed to new ideas and new interpretations of his own experiences. Enduring police brutality and poverty, however, slowly changes him and draws him closer to the workers' movement. He begins to go to the chamber of labor regularly after work to help by dusting or sweeping the little room, where "if as many as twenty people turned up the room was packed, [and] they'd be arguing in the doorway and down the stairs."[2] As the conflict with the construction bosses intensifies, the chamber of labor becomes more prominent as a site of aggregation and a symbol of the workers' unity.[3] The strikers assemble there to plot strategy, win allies, and resolve tensions, such as the one that arises when the most impoverished workers are tempted to break the strike. The workers pass their time at the chamber of labor because physical togetherness helps strengthen their resolve. Metello's optimism was sustained by the realization that the workers "were no longer isolated persons, individualists, libertarians." According to Metello,

> These were people who owned nothing, but from now on intended to use that nothing. The doctrine they professed, even if the majority of them continued to be ignorant of its dialectic and its precise exposition, established a clear relationship between giving and taking, between the sweat that drips and the stomach that grows empty, between, as they put it, the exploiters and the exploited. They were people, perhaps still illiterate—like Il Niccheri who recounted history by singing it in stanzas—who knew they understood only a few things, but those quite clearly. And they believed in them. They believed in their stomachs and their sweat. Instinct was more to be trusted than intelligence; a brutal but explicit truth sustained them by its reason.[4]

This passage reminds us how the popular public sphere, the world of the chamber of labor, differed from the bourgeois public sphere. The popular public sphere was based on a rationality that involved fidelity to the world of things and skepticism toward truths produced exclusively by argumentation and speech. Linguistic competence and persuasiveness are skills acquired through formal education and are therefore disproportionately the province of elites. They are a sign of class privilege as much as a mechanism for achieving moral insight and resolving political conflict.[5] Communicative rationality can lead to rationalization as well as to truth. In a society that defines the bosses' interests as normative, workers' arguments are easily dismissed as a defense of special privilege. Questioning the discursive foundations of ethics, however, does not imply a rejection of rationality. Italian neorealist films and novels such as *Metello* suggest a materialist-humanist alternative to the deliberative ideal of the bourgeois public sphere. Pratolini challenges the assumption that speech is the most important human capacity. The alternative is reminiscent of the early Marx: the idea that labor—the vision and skill necessary to transform the world according to the desires and imagination—is fundamental to human nature and that the person who labors should be able to satisfy the other basic human needs, including nourishment, shelter, and social life.

Osvaldo Gnocchi-Viani, a Milanese socialist representative and labor organizer, explained the difference between the goals of the bourgeoisie and the workers more explicitly: "The first would like to win greater development and freedom of thought; the second, forced to spend twelve or fourteen hours of the day in almost exclusively manual labor, would like to win the possibility of thought. The first needs a political revolution, the second, a change in the social order."[6] According to Gnocchi-Viani, as long as political ideals such as freedom and equality are theorized de jure and not de facto, their universalistic aspirations are ideological and the language of rights becomes a defense of privilege. For the inclusive and egalitarian aspirations of the bourgeois public sphere to be realized, its bourgeois character had to be repudiated. In essence this meant that economic and social concerns could no longer be excluded from politics.

The chambers of labor, local coalitions of existing workers' organizations, were founded to represent economic and political interests. They also provided a place for workers to meet, organize, discuss their interests, and coordinate tactics. The chambers overcame the isolation of the producers' cooperatives and leagues of resistance, which were exclusively made up of workers from a single workplace or industry. They provided an alternate place for workers to come together that, unlike the factory or the bourgeois public sphere, was not already dominated by existing elites. In 1895, the *Gazzetta di Venezia* called the chamber of labor "a place where workers acquire consciousness of their own rights and their own interests and honor them with liberty and in legality."[7] According to Gnocchi-Viani, the chamber of labor, "just like the chamber of commerce, [is] . . . a covered place where workers meet to take care of and defend their interests."[8]

In contrast to the smaller, more homogeneous groups organized by occupational classification or neighborhood, the chamber of labor was a public space of contestation and acrimonious debate. The chamber mediated conflicts between primary economic or social groups and government institutions. It provided a place for leaders to speak to their constituents and to listen to them. The chamber of labor also represented the interests of workers in other forums, such as the municipal government.

Writing during the early phase of fascism, labor leader Rinaldo Rigola reflected, "The chamber of labor was the most wonderful and original creation of our epoch. . . . In Italy [it] was the center of all local proletarian life and gave life to a large number of integrative institutions of resistance. It really was, for the proletariat, that which the [medieval] commune was for the bourgeoisie."[9] The commune (a self-governing municipality) was the symbolic expression of the ascendancy of the rising commercial bourgeoisie in late medieval Italy. A nodal point that linked together economic and political power,[10] the commune, organized on principles of both inclusion and exclusion, was a center of trade and a military fortification. The commune was a concentration of economic power and the inscription of this power in stone, a symbol that was legible to foreign sailors, local craftspeople, visiting tradesman, and provincial peasants. These various groups' relationships to each other were reflected and reinforced in urban space.[11] Processions were an important part of public life because they made the principles of power legible for all to see. By publicly displaying hierarchy, they also strengthened it, encouraging each individual to identify with the social order. The piazzas and palazzos of the bourgeoisie reflected and established its domination. The chamber of labor functioned in a similar way for the working classes; it was a nodal point and symbolic expression of workers' growing power.

The pragmatic dimension is most readily apparent; the chamber of labor was a center of coordination that mediated (and later organized) strikes, studied social problems, advocated solutions, and tried to regulate employment. It linked heterogeneous, isolated workers' organizations into effective coalitions. To participants and observers alike, the chamber was a symbol of the growing visibility and political power of the working class. Workers had always taken part in public life; for example, in the eighteenth century, artisanal corporations had participated in highly ordered processions headed by the ecclesiastical authorities and local elites. But now the mode of participation was different. Workers' organizations were no longer subordinate to the church or the

Fig. 9. Nuns in a workshop in Monza: "In truth I tell you the moment has come to choose between the chamber of labor and the reign of the heavens" (caption in original; my translation). *Source*: *L'uomo di pietra*, 1901.

notables but instead formed lateral ties with each other (see fig. 9). This was visible in the new way in which the lower classes inhabited public space. No longer at the back of a hierarchical ritual procession led by clerics and nobles, workers entered into the streets en masse for May Day celebrations and demonstrations.[12] The chamber of labor was the symbol of this "right to the city."[13]

My account of the chamber of labor draws on a range of sources, including militants' memoirs, local histories, the socialist press, and literary accounts. One of the most important documents on the early history of the chamber of labor is Osvaldo Gnocchi-Viani's *Dieci anni di camere del lavoro*, published in 1899. Gnocchi-Viani, a prominent socialist intellectual and activist, helped found some of the first labor unions and was elected on the left-wing slate to the Milan Chamber of Deputies. A critic of the Second International, he articulated a detailed defense of the necessary link between democracy and socialism. Although his writings range broadly from the theoretical to the polemical, he is best remembered for his defense of the chambers of labor.[14] A second source of the material presented in this chapter is the socialist press, especially the biweekly Milanese journal *Critica Sociale*, which was founded in 1891 by reformist leader Filippo Turati and Anna Kuliscioff. Along with the more popular *Lotta di Classe*, this intellectual journal provided an important forum for debates about strategy and ideology. A third way of approaching the chamber of labor is indirectly, by looking at references such as Pratolini's neorealist novel, which illustrates how the chamber of labor functioned as the backdrop for political mobilization. Finally, I draw on the detailed accounts of individual chambers of labor and social histories of particular towns in order to evaluate the relationship between these microspaces and the local political context that they transformed.

The Milan Chamber of Labor

It is winter 1889 in Milan. The seasonal unemployment in the building trades aggravates an already tense conflict between contractors and construction workers. Subcontractors have been hiring workers from rural areas outside the city. In the early months of 1890, the crisis deepens as hundreds of workers in the metal and engineering industries are laid off because of low demand. Meanwhile, tension builds among rural workers who have to pay a special bread tax (*dazio di consumo*) on their sandwiches when they enter the confines of the city. Under these conditions, talk of a chamber of labor begins to circulate.

The idea was inspired by international models. In 1889 a delegation of Milanese workers had gone to the International Exposition in Paris, where they saw the famous Parisian *bourse du travail* firsthand and were impressed by its ability to ease labor market tensions. Giuseppe Croce and Constantino Lazzari (both militants of the Partito Operaio, a forerunner of the PSI) proposed founding something similar in Milan, "a place where workers could meet, discuss their interests, and apply for jobs through a system that put their needs first."[15]

The initiative also benefited from the support of Gnocchi-Viani, who published a pamphlet titled *Le borse del lavoro*, which traced the history of similar institutions in Europe and explained the need for a chamber of labor in Italy. Gnocchi-Viani also visited workers' circles throughout the neighborhoods of Milan, speaking in favor of the chamber of labor. Given the growing conflicts not only between workers and bosses but also among workers, he recognized the need for a place where they could consult and coordinate with one another. Because conflict was inevitable, it was preferable to have a forum in which the workers themselves could try to reconcile their differences. The chamber of labor could be a way to represent workers' concerns to the municipal government and to mitigate the worst effects of industrialization, such as unemployment, dangerous factory conditions, and overcrowded urban slums.

Both the Partito Operaio and the typesetters' union sponsored proposals for a chamber of labor. The two initiatives were consolidated and, in 1890, a citywide conference was called. Seventy-three associations from Milan, including mutual aid societies, cooperatives, and unions, sent representatives and elected a committee of fifteen workers. More than three thousand workers were present at the founding meeting.[16] After several weeks of discussion they published a report stating that new forms of organization were needed to cope with changing social and economic circumstances, that charity and efforts to combat unemployment were inadequate "to confront the growing social disorder."[17]

In 1891, with a small subsidy and a space allocated by the Milanese city administration, the chamber of labor was formed to serve as an intermediary between buyers and sellers of labor and to promote workers' interests in all aspects of life. Over time, what started out as a slightly glorified unemployment agency became a center of working-class power and social change in Milan. In addition to serving as an unemployment agency, the chamber of labor organized strikes and celebrations, helped regulate working hours, bargained over holidays and wage rates, ran literacy classes, formed producers cooperatives to fight unemployment, founded a library, and organized popular university classes. Through the chamber of labor, workers fought for the extension of municipal services, abolition of the tax on grain, and introduction of a progressive property tax. According to proponents such as Gnocchi-Viani, the Milan chamber of labor played a role as a defender of civil rights, built democracy through coalition politics, functioned as an agent of municipal reform, and helped stabilize the labor market.

Form and Function of the Chamber of Labor

The socialist militants at the end of the nineteenth century were acutely aware of the way in which power relations were structured by space. For groups trying to organize strikes or political meetings that were considered illegal, it was apparent that space constrained the types of assemblies that could take place. Sergei Eisenstein's landmark film *Strike* (1925) depicted how workers in czarist Russia futilely tried to find a meeting place to coordinate and concentrate their forces. Constantly followed by police spies and forcibly dispersed by a series of government agents (first the police, then the fire brigade, and finally soldiers), they are ultimately driven onto a field and slaughtered. In the film, safety is a by-product of physical proximity and dispersion results in slaughter. In the Italian context, the workers' struggle for a "room of their own" is also a recurrent motif. In a more comic vein, one socialist activist in Biella recounted the strategy of socialists who wanted to found a new newspaper. To avoid the harassment of the police, the editorial board had to climb high into the mountains—where the overweight police officers could not easily follow.[18]

Gnocchi-Viani explicitly recognized the need for a "privileged, central place in which consciousness is produced." He argued that the "autonomous consciousness of the working class is not an immediate reflection of the conditions of work and of life (and even less the result of an external force elaborated by intellectuals and spread among workers)" but instead is the product of "the experience of voluntary association, independently fashioned and lived."[19] Gnocchi-Viani rejected both the extreme structuralist and extreme idealist approaches to socialism. To truly become citizens, workers must inhabit, at least some of the time, a place in which they experience themselves as the bearers of rights and responsibilities, with the capacity to make decisions collectively. For Gnocchi-Viani, this place was the chamber of labor. Positioning himself between economic determinists on the one hand and utopian socialists on the other, he called for the construction of a "concrete utopia," a place where workers could come together to discuss their interests, formulate strategy, and act collectively (see fig. 10). It would be a place where participation was not a mere ritual but a way to

Fig. 10. A dinner at the chamber of labor, Piacenza (founded in 1891). *Source*: Arbizzani et al., *Storie di case del popolo*.

resolve the most immediate and pressing concerns of economic and social life.

Chambers of labor were formed across Italy in the late 1880s and early 1890s. Although the legal form varied, there were several general characteristics that defined the chambers. First, their primary function was to build an enduring coalition between existing cooperatives, mutual aid societies, and leagues of resistance (nascent trade unions) and to encourage the proliferation of these workers' organizations. In other words, the goal was to increase the organization and unity of the working class. Membership was institutional, not individual, but there were provisions to allow unorganized workers to affiliate with the chamber in order to facilitate the process of forming new sections. Usually the chamber provided services to all workers, regardless of membership. There was an employment office and a mediation service to help resolve labor conflicts. The employment office tried to limit the exploitative effects of subcontracting by providing direct links between employers and laborers. The goal of mediation was to resolve labor disputes through consensual means whenever possible. Both of these functions were strengthened by the information gathered by the chambers of labor, which conducted surveys, compiled statistics, and researched the labor market and wage rates. Reliable information about cost-of-living increases and wage rates across an industry or region (things we take for granted today) provided important leverage for isolated and uneducated workers beginning to engage in collective bargaining.

The chamber of labor's structure took advantage of preexisting organizational ties. One reason that the chamber quickly became an important political force was that it did not have to build from scratch and then sustain a membership base. Each member organization paid dues to the chamber of labor but continued to maintain a high degree of autonomy in internal matters. Furthermore, a diverse range of organizations was included. Unlike the national labor federations that were organized by craft or industry, the chamber was a very heterogeneous coalition. Member organizations included mutual aid societies of various political orientations, leagues of resistance, producer cooperatives, and consumer cooperatives. The exact rules governing which organizations could affiliate was a topic of heated controversy. The problem, especially in the early phases, was whether to allow the affiliation of mutual aid societies or craft guilds that included employers (which were almost exclusively artisans with one or two employees) as members.[20] This issue was especially controversial in Florence, where a republican organization of Mazzinian inspiration, the Fratellanza Artigiana, played a crucial role in the initial formation of the chamber of labor; the Fratellanza was ultimately excluded on the grounds that a cross-class coalition could be paralyzed by conflicts of interest. Nevertheless, the chambers remained internally variegated popular institutions. They included skilled and unskilled workers, men as well as women, factory workers, artisans, the unemployed, and the self-employed. They also included workers in their roles as producers as well as consumers. Large numbers of consumer cooperatives joined the chamber of labor in Florence, and many neighborhood-based organizations affiliated with it in Turin.[21]

The funding and organization of the chambers took different forms. In Florence, the chamber of labor was the product of an initiative by the local chamber of commerce, which believed that an institution representing a broad cross-section of the working class could help ensure social peace. The promoters hoped that the chamber of labor could help build channels of negotiation and mediation as alternatives to disruptive strikes. Other chambers of labor were formed under the sponsorship of the municipality.[22] This was especially true in cases in which the chamber was originally conceived of as a labor exchange (*borsa del lavoro*) whose primary task was exerting a rationalizing function on the labor market. In Turin, for example, the *borsa del lavoro*, founded in 1891 with a subsidy of five thousand lire from the commune, was a semipublic entity with "primary ties" to the local administration. It had a statutory obligation to offer services to nonmembers and to maintain political neutrality.[23] In Piombino, where the local administration had been dominated by socialists since 1902, the chamber of labor was formed as an alternative to the power base of the PSI. Initially composed of twenty-six organizations, it was founded by revolutionary syndicalists after the break with the PSI at the Rome Party Congress in 1906.[24]

Is there any way to evaluate whether the chambers achieved their goals? One preliminary piece of evidence is the high level of membership. By 1901, membership in Milan had grown to 40,000,[25] with more than 500,000 members in seventy-six similar organizations across Italy (see appendix 3). By 1897 the Milan chamber of labor had found work for 2,622 unemployed laborers and mediated forty-seven potential strikes. Also, the influence of the chambers of labor was recognized by local authorities; even the police (*questore*), by no means the natural ally of workers' organizations, acknowledged the positive impact. A report presented to the Ministry of Agriculture, Industry, and Commerce in December 1898 summarized the positive evaluations of the chamber of labor by local officials in Milan, Bologna, Catanzaro, Parma, and Cremona, noting in particular a statement that the "police chief of Milan recognizes that after the institution of the chamber of labor there weren't any more disorders; public disturbances for economic reasons have disappeared." A report of the Office of Public Security said that with the influence of the chamber, "conflicts have become less strident, mediation more possible without either side having to renounce or subordinate its own personality or dignity."[26] The press praised the chamber for its "public usefulness" in fighting unemployment and promoting the responsibility of the working class.[27] After the demonstrations, strikes, and upheavals known as the Fatti di Maggio in May 1898 and subsequent violent government repression, the chambers of labor, along with all workers' organizations, were disbanded. But this setback was short-lived, in part because moderates recognized the chambers' useful role in ensuring that class struggle did not turn into class hatred.[28]

In many localities both minimalists and abstentionists participated in the chamber of labor.[29] The various informal discussions, meetings, conferences, and demonstrations that took place in the chambers were the mechanisms through which these positions crystalized and through which the members publicized their respective visions and competed for support.

The twentieth century saw the role of the chamber of labor transformed. With the legalization of strikes in 1900, the chambers played a larger role in supporting and promoting militant tactics, and they began collecting funds to maintain strikers. They also lobbied municipal government to provide relief through public works projects and to support cooperatives through contracts or loans. The success of the chambers of labor came from their ability to link direct economic interest to political identity, class consciousness, and action. The chambers of labor, rather than unions or political parties, provided leadership for the general strike of September 1904. They also continued to expand their reformist functions, including regulating apprenticeships and providing adult education. In 1911, the Turin chamber of labor opened a special office to provide medical care and legal aid to workers who were injured on the job. According to its statutes, the chamber offered services to everyone, not only members.[30] In the prewar period, "the most important labour organizations in Italy were still the chambers of labor."[31] The chambers maintained their autonomy as workers' organizations, but they came to pursue agendas that were much broader than the immediate corporate interests of a specific profession or group. They focused on both the expansion of public education and the municipalization of public services. They published newspapers and organized festivals, such as the popular May Day processions. According to Martin Clark, they were "above all centres of a Socialist popular culture and a Socialist morality."[32]

What exactly was "socialist morality"? Although it is unusual to see contemporary historians use the term, it was very common at the turn of the century. For example, the statute of the Partito dei Lavoratori, a forerunner to the PSI, stated that one of its goals was to help "the working class escape from the state of oppression and of moral and material inferiority in which it is held." Because some version of this provision was incorporated into the statutes of many organizations, unraveling the meaning of the term could provide important insight into the goals of these organizations. I suggest that the term *moral* came to mean what would today be called "cultural." Reformers from diverse ideological positions saw workers' organizations as a way to combat the improvidence and alcoholism that they associated with lower-class life; however, socialists interpreted these "moral" improvements as ways to increase autonomy and power. Many socialist-oriented associations that strove for "moral improvement" were not primarily temperance societies or religious groups; there is nothing in their statutes about sexuality or piety (although many emphasize the need to follow parliamentary procedures and remain within the bounds of legality). For the Fratellanza di Greve in Chianti (founded in 1890), the means to achieve the goal of "moral improvement" included founding a library and teaching general education courses. The chamber of labor of Scandicci (founded in 1896) planned to work for moral improvement by organizing conferences, classes, and reading rooms for the development of "individual intellectual facilities" and the practice of solidarity.[33]

The concept of socialist morality also raises the question of the relationship between such sites of resistance as the chambers of labor and the PSI. Is the popular public sphere a synonym for socialist subculture? Not exactly. Participation in the workers' movement was much more extensive than membership in the socialist party. In fact, activists writing at the turn of the century insisted on the distinction. In his famous essay "Should the Chambers of Labor Become Socialist?" (1901), Claudio Treves argued that the separation between economic and political organizations is the essence of the socialist strategy. He emphatically rejected the resolution of the Congress of Laborers of the Land that called for the chambers to become explicitly socialist in orientation. He made two arguments against "hoisting the red flag over the chambers of labor." First, he claimed that the experience of resistance (for example, through economic organizations such as unions or cooperatives) played a crucial role in initially exposing workers to the basic reality of exploitation. Explicitly socialist agitation was unnecessary because "the *place* and opportunity" created by economic organizations would be enough to introduce workers to an initial sense of solidarity and understanding of the need for struggle.[34] The second reason for maintaining the distinction was strategic. Treves argued that the economic institutions would lose credibility if there were any suspicion that they were being instrumentalized for sectarian political purposes. He claimed that "all of the great successes in mediation and the provision of employment were possible only in so far as the chamber of labor did not present itself clothed in political garb but was recognized as an apolitical entity."[35] He predicted that "flying the red flag" would lead to an exodus of nonsocialists, which made up the majority of the members of the chamber. Given that the socialist party in Milan only had 1,500 members and 12,000 voters, it was clear that the majority of the 40,000 members of the chamber of labor were not socialists.[36] Losing these members would destroy the Milan chamber, eviscerating a crucial institution for the politicization of the masses. To maintain a chamber of labor made up exclusively of socialists would be ludicrous because its membership would effectively be the same as that of the existing socialist party organization.

For Treves, the term *politics* was synonymous with what we would today call partisanship. He argued that the chambers should not be partisan; in other words, they should not be subordinate to the electoral agenda of the socialist party. This does not mean, however, that they should not be political, in the broader sense of developing the capacity for citizenship. Politics involves collective decisions about the distribution of resources and authority. The chambers of labor were clearly political in so far as they were one way in which previously excluded groups came to define, defend, and attain recognition of their collective interests.

There are essentially two opposing ways of carrying out the struggle for power under conditions of unequal access. One, associated with Leninism, involves training a cadre of highly committed, unified revolutionaries who are subordinate to a hierarchical leadership. The second strategy, associated with Gramsci's work in prison, emphasizes the need to build a mass movement that is rooted in and transforms existing patterns and meanings of daily life. The chambers of labor were an example of the latter, because they coordinated the mass movement. They made use of existing economic organizations in the cities and built on traditional forms of association in the countryside in order to forge a meaningful force for social change. They were based on the premise that unity did not require uniformity. Gnocchi-Viani, the key protagonist in the movement for their establishment, emphasized that "socialist theory benefits from pluralism and contestation."[37] He advocated for the chambers because he thought their participatory culture was a way to prevent the socialist movement from becoming political, in so far as *political* connoted careerism and a tendency to focus on electoral maneuvers that had little relevance outside Parliament. The chambers were a way of maintaining the connection to the constituents' concerns and needs. According to Gnocchi-Viani, the chambers could prevent the spiral of "knowledge-power" that guarantees the dominance of intellectuals and blocks the workers' own process of political and cultural self-emancipation.[38]

If emancipation had to be the project of the workers themselves, what contribution could theorists and intellectuals make? Gnocchi-Viani envisioned the role of the intellectual as that of an architect rather than a general or teacher. The role of intellectuals was not to supply answers but to help build and fortify a place where workers could create their own solutions. The intellectual could not provide privileged truths. According to Gnocchi-Viani, theoretical sophistication or scientific rigor could not substitute for the capacities of the masses to identify and act on their interests. This meant that the appropriate contribution of the intellectual would be limited to helping construct spaces in which political education and economic advancement could take place. For someone who took seriously the idea of "rule of the people," the outcome of political participation could not be guaranteed, but the opportunity for criticism, debate, and collective action had to be provided. The chambers of labor could achieve this objective primarily by serving as a "practical and idealistic" reference point for dispersed workers. The role of the "architect" would be to build this space.

The chamber of labor was the spatialization of Gramsci's idea of the historic bloc—an alliance between anticapitalist forces. Whereas the factory brought together members of one trade or production process, the chamber of labor created commonalities between cigar girls and construction workers, metal workers and weavers. Given the heterogeneous class structure in Italy, a narrow definition of worker was not viable. In his essay "L'organizzazione dei lavoratori improduttivi," Gnocchi-Viani recognized that the primary danger of the producerist ideology was the exclusion not only of potential allies such as technical personnel but also of the weakest, most precarious workers: the unemployed, women, children, and apprentices.[39] In contrast to Marx, who dismissed the *lumpenproletariat* as a counterrevolutionary force, Gnocchi-Viani emphasized the political salience of what he called the "fifth estate." He argued that a successful democratic-transformative movement must include not only the industrial working class (the fourth estate) but also allied subaltern groups (the fifth estate). Rather than being a source of disunity and weakness, this robust coalition should be a source of strength.[40]

Memoirs of a Turinese Worker

In his memoirs, Mario Montagnana recalled his first May Day celebration, which took place at the chamber of labor.

> In 1912 I participated for the first time in the extremely crowded public meeting held in the courtyard of the chamber of labor, my only memory is that Claudio Treves spoke, but I completely forgot the content of his speech. What remains impressed in my memory of the meeting—other than its immensity—is that along with the "Hymn of the Workers" . . . the "Hymn of Garibaldi" was also sung. . . . My interest in the socialist movement was still very superficial.[41]

Montagnana's recollections provide insight into the way individuals experienced the sociopolitical spaces that linked urban life in Turin. The memoir spans the period from the beginning of his apprenticeship as a mechanic in 1912 to 1926 when, fleeing fascist repression in Italy, he went into exile in France. Montagnana first became actively involved in politics during his apprenticeship in Turin in 1912. His first contact with the socialist youth group, of which he eventually became a leader, occurred during the electoral campaign of October 1913, when a speaker at Borgo San Paolo asked the young people present to help the socialist electoral committee by getting out the vote in the neighborhood. Montagnana recounts how the youth group broke with the parent organization ("the old drunkards") to establish their own meeting place. He remembers that "the new site, in via Fréjus, included a little room for the office, including a relatively extensive library with an independent entrance, a vast courtyard with a bocce ball court, and then a sort of bar, a room with six or seven tables and a few chairs, a little room for dancing." The nascent youth center's first controversy was not ideological but spatial. Mario Montagnana reflected, "But as for me, who was really a bit puritanical in the era, I would have liked to see in the youth group nothing other than a 'Temple to the Ideal'; the dancing room especially did not work for me at all . . . so I came out against putting together in the same place Terpsichore and Karl Marx, dancing and socialism."[42] Montagnana was eventually convinced by the others that the bar and dancing were necessary not only to cover the cost of the rent but also to attract the young workers of the neighborhood, with the goal of involving them in politics.

In the early stages of the narrative, political events are oriented around two sites: the youth group's headquarters and the chamber of labor in the center of Turin. Camaraderie, propaganda, debates, agitation, and leisure take place at the youth group's headquarters, which becomes a neighborhood center of working-class life. But the chamber of labor appears throughout the memoir as the most important site of coordination and initiative, the site that serves to unify various primary groups. Demonstrations and marches begin and end at the chamber. Important speeches and decisions are made there. The references to the chamber are not systematic or conclusive, however; *Ricordi di un operaio torinese* is a first-person narrative, not a work of political science, let alone one that focuses on sites of resistance. The memoir conveys the significance of the chamber of labor effectively because the chamber itself is not the object of analysis but appears most commonly as a site of aggregation ("thousands of workers gathered at the *camera del lavoro* to listen to . . .") or a locus of decision making ("the *camera del lavoro* proclaimed a general strike to protest . . ."). In the aftermath of World War I, the chamber of labor even functioned as a sort of alternate municipal government, taking on the responsibility for maintaining civil peace and ensuring the distribution of food. Montagnana recalls that during the food riots (which broke out in response to hyperinflation after the end of the war), "the government and municipality were terrified. . . . the shopkeepers, in mass, throughout Italy, could do nothing other than close their shops and bring the key to the chamber of labor, putting themselves under its protection."[43]

At the end of the memoir, which takes places during the onset of fascism, Montagnana tries to convey the sense of discouragement produced by the failure of the national leadership of the workers' movement. The primary events are no longer strikes, meetings, and discussions but rather tales of fascist violence, arrests, and the unique combination of boredom and terror that arises from the experience of living with illegality. He writes with sadness and disappointment as he witnesses the destruction of the cooperatives, chambers of labor, meeting halls, and community centers that workers had built so painstakingly and with such pride and perseverance over the previous decades. Most chillingly, Montagnana recounts the night of December 18, 1922, the night of the fascist onslaught in Turin. On the pretext of avenging the death of a fascist killed by a worker acting in self-defense, the Turinese fascists prepared to attack the opposition's forces. Fearing for their safety, Montagnana and two fellow militants decided to sleep in hotels; they split up to avoid detection more effectively. He recalls:

> Monday evening after having left, Pietro Ferrero, instead of going to a hotel, must have approached the chamber of labor. Probably it was already surrounded by fascists that were planning to set fire to it, and someone recognized the head of the metal workers' union. They seized him and tied him to a truck that was then driven, at high speed, along Galileo Ferraris Street, toward the monument to Victor Emmanuel, at the intersection with Victor Emmanuel Street. The next morning along the vast road, there were shreds of the flesh of Pietro Ferrero and stains of his blood to discover. . . . In that tragic night he had wanted to give one last glance at the house of the people, at his house. That act cost him his life—the most horrible of deaths.[44]

The rise of fascism brought with it the destruction of the spaces of resistance such as co-ops, chambers of labor, and houses of the people. The fascists understood the extreme importance of these "safe spaces" and did everything possible to ensure their destruction. Where complete physical destruction was not yet possible, symbolic attacks turned refuges into places of heightened vulnerability. Where the fascists could not destroy the concrete site, they made every possible effort to disrupt the spatial practice by turning a "home" into a battleground. For example, in Sesto San Giovanni where a strong working class had slowed the rise of fascism, the fascist squads did not dare burn the house of the people but instead destroyed the furniture, records, flags, and symbols.[45]

The fascists' strategy was to target the autonomous spaces rather than the organizations. Even after Mussolini became prime minister in 1922, workers' organizations were not immediately banned; however, the cooperatives, chambers of labor, and houses of the people, the nodal points of the movement, were physically destroyed. The reason seems to stem from the recognition that it was these places that nourished democratic culture and solidarity. In a sense, the spaces of resistance were the roots from which the organizations grew, and the fascists were determined to destroy these anchors. One of the distinctive features of legality is the right to appear in public and retreat in private. Both of these were effectively denied to anti-fascist forces. The fascists assumed that without the necessary roots, the already emasculated organizations would be relatively easy to disband; they proved correct in this assumption. Nevertheless, thousands of workers were killed defending the cooperatives, chambers of labor, and houses of the people—their houses.

Fascist Spaces

If our goal is to theorize the relationship between space and politics, a crucial question is whether the fascists themselves had "safe spaces." Fascism was also a form of resistance to the compromises reached by the liberal parliamentarian regime. And it too had its sites.[46] In *The Culture of Consent* Victoria de Grazia documents the growth of fascist recreational spaces such as the Dopolavoro; although most workers initially refused to take part in the fascist organization, participation became widespread in the 1930s. The question of how to treat fascist spaces is one aspect of a larger challenge posed by Francesca Polletta in her article " 'Free Spaces' in Collective Action," in which she claims that the growing body of scholarship on "free spaces" (or the many equivalents, such as "havens," "spheres of cultural autonomy," and "spatial preserves") has two basic flaws. First, the metaphor of free spaces substitutes a structural property for a cultural characteristic. She claims that often it is not structural isolation (the "spaces") but the specific ideological content that provides the basis for counterhegemonic challenges.[47] Second, she argues that much of the literature in this tradition fails to offer the necessary specificity about the characteristics of free spaces.

To restate this challenge in terms of our own subject, fascism and socialism may both have built heterotopic sites, but what distinguished them was the opposing content of their ideology. This statement, however, rests on the debatable assumption that ideology has no affect on spatial practices. Although it is true that one cannot deduce politics from spatial arrangements (or vice versa), certain spatial arrangements are more or less suited to particular goals. Because fascism and socialism had different political purposes, they used space in different ways. Fascist spaces were often built on a monumental scale to evoke an authoritarian power; even its houses of fascism were structured to subordinate the masses to the leader. As we saw in chapter 6, the *case del fascio* differed from the *case del popolo* in significant ways. It is beyond the scope of this work to tell a larger story of the spatial practices of fascism, but there is excellent scholarly work in this area. For example, in *Making of the Fascist Self*, Mabel Berezin traces how the fascist regime became adept at using public space and political rituals such as commemoration, celebration, demonstration, and symposia to forge a link between the individual and the state. The characteristic fascist spaces were the famous sports stadiums and plazas that facilitated mass fascist spectacles rather than self-managed clubhouses. Still, it is true that there is nothing intrinsically democratic or emancipatory about "protected spaces"; therefore, it is necessary to engage in careful historical analysis to understand how the built environment either promotes or inhibits particular identities, solidarities, and orientations toward the state.

Spaces of Resistance

So far I have distinguished five elements that accounted for the power of places such as the cooperatives, chambers of labor, and houses of the people. First, at the most general level, they provided a site of encounter where "insiders" and "outsiders" could come together and possibly discover commonalities. Such an encounter brackets certain types of social relations and intensifies others. Individuals encountering each other in places marked as sites of resistance were more likely to bracket factional identities (as clients of certain patrons or workers in particular trades) and intensify solidarity. Second, these sites fostered oppositional practices by sheltering counterhegemonic ideas and identities. Third, the chambers of labor and houses of the people were coalitional structures. This distinguished them from other places such as the tavern or factory, and it allowed them to overcome isolation and aggregate dispersed forces. It made it possible to mobilize participants for political projects that transcended parochial concerns while still maintaining accountability to the base. Fourth, they were democratic; their statutes and by-laws established rules to guarantee both voting and deliberation; they set up procedures to ensure that everyone could speak and to prevent anyone from dominating the conversation. Finally, they were able to sustain enduring commitments because the density of ties (social and economic) provided a pragmatic anchor for political activity. In addition to supplying material benefits, shopping in the cooperative or drinking in the *casa del popolo* linked one's daily routine to a political project.

These sites mediated individuals' identification with an oppositional political project—a political project motivated by diverse experiences such as the discipline of the factory and the economic disruptions brought on by the penetration of the world market. Focusing on the properties of sites of resistance does not mean denying the relevance of ideology. But there has never been a lack of interest in high socialist theory. For reasons that are bound up with the structure of academia, intellectual history is a most appealing genre. Yet if we are to remain true to the original goal of theory, searching for insight, we must try to see in new ways. The fecundity of the spatial orientation is that it might provide a new set of glasses.

MUNICIPALISM: THE LEGACY OF LOCALISM

At the turn of the century, Sesto San Giovanni was an agricultural town with a small silk-weaving industry. Sesto was located near Milan and therefore was well situated to profit from the industrial expansion that was taking place in Italy in the early 1900s. Several major manufacturing plants moved to the town during a drive for modernization, so that in twenty years the population almost tripled to 19,000 and the labor force became dominated by industrial workers.[1] The resulting social and political transformations are captured in social historian Donald Bell's richly detailed account *San Giovanni: Workers, Culture, and Politics in an Italian Town, 1880–1922*.[2]

One of the questions that frames Bell's study is whether working-class solidarity and political consciousness were formed primarily in the factory. Bell finds that institutions such as the mutual aid society, which antedated the foundation of the factory, assumed an important role in the formation of working-class identity and mobilization. The factory proved a difficult place to organize consensus for several reasons: the large plants were balkanized into separate divisions; modern machinery made conversation impossible; foremen could effectively police and discipline workers; and production processes originally maintained or exacerbated the distinction between skilled and unskilled labor. Bell concludes that "political militancy often grew more directly from problems arising from the local community than from those rooted mainly in the context of factory labor. Workers . . . focused their efforts on creating a 'proletarian public sphere,' a distinct network of activities, beliefs, and institutions which eventually provided a basis for political activism."[3]

The printing cooperative and the mutual aid society, both founded in 1880, were the first experiments with self-administration in Sesto San Giovanni. In 1898 the hundred-member mutual aid society inaugurated a central hall, complete with a library and an evening school for apprentices. At first the space did not appear too controversial—a meeting room, some offices, a bar—but it was a place that would shelter the growing opposition to the elite's domination of politics. The mutual aid society was hardly a hotbed of radicalism, yet it was banned in 1898, along with other workers' organizations. According to Bell, this experience helped politicize the mutual aid society, transforming an "ethos of mutuality" into an "ethic of opposition."[4]

The major political challenge in the early part of the nineteenth century was to build links between skilled workers, unskilled operatives, and artisans. The library, evening school, and bar helped by providing places to meet and build social ties that did not reflect the hierarchies inside the factory. Although the socialists had limited success at involving local peasants, who turned to the Catholic organizations founded to challenge the socialist influence, workers' organizations began to overcome residential and skill-based divisions. This was difficult because class divisions were intensified by residential differences. The longtime town residents, peasants and artisans as well as the bourgeoisie, lived in Old Sesto, which was located east of the railroad tracks and was characterized by narrow streets, small shops, and buildings dating back to medieval times. The more recent immigrants, mostly the town's industrial working class, were concentrated in New Sesto. This area, located west of the railway line, had new housing on a grid pattern, which had been built by developers and occasionally factory owners. Thus, architecture and physical layout highlighted deep-rooted social and political differences.

A crucial turning point came in 1905 with the formation of the Circolo Avvenire, a sociopolitical group that became the nerve center of the democratic opposition to the ruling clique. The Circolo Avvenire played a crucial role in bringing together Old and New Sesto, artisans and industrial workers.[5] Bell writes that it "provided a place where [workers] could meet over a glass of wine to discuss the events of the day, and it afforded a sense of physical solidarity." Members appeared together at rallies and demonstrations, distinguishing themselves with red berets. By the First World War the Circolo Avvenire had fifteen hundred members and served as the "organizational umbrella" for a wide range of groups, including a local newspaper, a band and choral society, a consumer cooperative, a section of the popular university, and a housing cooperative formed to provide low-cost housing to workers.

What was the electoral impact of the diffusion of socialist subculture? Carlo Borromeo, a member of the printers' cooperative, was elected to the communal (and eventually provincial) council. Whereas in 1863 all identifiable members of the town council were either landowners or silk manufacturers, by 1915 one-quarter were laborers or skilled workers (a mason, carpenter, and so forth), half were white-collar professionals (an attorney, architect, shopkeeper), and the remaining handful included an industrialist and a tenant farmer.[6] The election of July 1914, the first local election after the expansion of suffrage, was a three-way battle between traditional conservatives (elites and Catholics), moderates (anticlericals, mainly shopkeepers), and socialists (artisans and workers).[7] The PSI obtained a plurality (43.9 percent of the total), the conservatives came in second (42.4 percent), and the moderates third (13.7 percent). Because the moderates and socialists were unable to form a coalition government, the prefect (the non-elected local representative of the central government) put the city under trusteeship. A new round of elections took place on December 13. The conservative list, made up primarily of industrialists and large landowners, was expanded to include some of the small manufacturers and shopkeepers from the moderate formation. With the support of the Milan prefect and the Catholic Church, this new "constitutional alliance" of moderates and conservatives won the election with 55 percent of the vote.

The lesson from this experience was the importance of redoubling efforts to build sites of aggregation to overcome the lingering tensions between artisans and industrial workers. After World War I, several neighborhood-based groups such as the Circle of New Sesto, the Little Circle, and Circle Edison (near the Falk plant) emerged and involved the growing proletariat in the left subculture. Membership in the workers' political and cultural associations rose to three thousand. At the same time, trade union strength grew, especially in the Federazione Impiegati Operai Metallurgici (FIOM), the metal workers' union. At first these trends seemed to point toward greater balkanization into specialized organizations. But simultaneously, new coalitional sites were founded as a means to link the different elements of the movement. A chamber of labor was organized to coordinate union activity. Its offices were located alongside the FIOM headquarters, the building cooperative, the PSI section, and the Circolo Avvenire in the new *casa del popolo*.[8]

World War I expanded both the level of industrial employment and the amount of discontent in the town. In the municipal elections of 1918, socialists gained 66.2 percent of the vote and administered Sesto until the fascist violence made open political activity by the left impossible. Bell credits this victory to the impact of the Circolo Avvenire, the chamber of labor, and "the network of community and cultural institutions which continued to expand with the growth of Sesto's laboring population."[9] In other words, the development of a broad network of new spaces of resistance was the precondition of electoral victory. This configuration was characteristic of municipalism: a dense network of associations that linked economic needs and neighborhood-based solidarities to a political program. The power of the local government was "capillary," that is, it arose out of a series of semiautonomous workers' organizations that were linked together in overlapping sites of integration and coordination.

Once in power, the socialist administration focused on modest reforms: administrative hiring on the basis of a merit system, urban planning, the building of new water and sewage disposal systems. It put forth proposals for workers' housing (*case popolari*) and a town hospital. To fulfill these relatively modest goals, it increased the taxes on large properties. These relatively modest achievements, however, were not viewed as ends in themselves: "Capturing a city hall meant enlarging the domain of resistance to capitalism and creating a protected enclave within which resistance might be organized."[10] Although Joan Scott's assessment was referring to late-nineteenth-century France, it is equally applicable to Italy a decade later. Capturing a city hall was a way of expanding the scope of existing experiments in popular participation. Part tactic and part outcome, socialist municipalities were the nodal points of the uneven geographies of power in Italian politics.

The Practice of Municipalism

The socialist party's emphasis on local politics was initially a pragmatic response to its exclusion from governing in Parliament. The PSI always stressed the importance of attaining power at the national level, but this goal was elusive, and the party found that playing the role of permanent parliamentary opposition was paralyzing. Even though the socialists had a plurality of seats in Parliament as of 1913, they were excluded from governing at the national level. The center and right-wing parties were able to maintain a precarious coalition of southern *latifundisti*, northern industrialists, and small proprietors, all united around the desire to keep the socialist forces out of government. Thus more by necessity than by choice, the socialists focused on municipal government, and local politics became their arena for experimentation and policy initiatives.[11] Given the strong local cultural organizations, municipal government became a logical focus for initiating political change.

After the electoral reform that granted near universal male suffrage in 1913, the PSI won control of 450 municipalities and entered into coalitions in others.[12] In 1914 socialists lead the administrations of most of the major cities in central and northern Italy, including Massa, Reggio Emilia, Verona, Novara, Alessandria, Cremona, Milan, and Bologna. They also won victories in four provinces: Bologna, Reggio Emilia, Ferrara, and Mantova. In 1920 the socialists attained power in 2,115 communes, slightly more than 25 percent of the total number. Although there were socialist administrations in every region in Italy, they were concentrated most heavily in Tuscany and Emilia-Romagna, the only two regions in which more than half of the communes were governed by socialists (see appendix 4).

In his book *Il PSI e la nascita di una partita di massa, 1892–1922*, Maurizio Ridolfi argues that the commune became the privileged point in the emancipatory project of the socialists because it presented the possibility for achieving economic and political democracy.[13] The main elements of municipal socialism were public education, the municipalization of services (transport, electricity, water, and sewage), and the promotion of workers organizations such as chambers of labor and cooperatives. Cooperatives were seen as the ideal partner for public works projects such as low-cost housing.

Experiments in municipal reform were particularly well suited to the Italian context. Writing in 1901, Bolton King and Thomas Okey insisted that "local government has a more than usual importance in Italy."[14] A history of local autonomy and late national unification intensified the importance of local political structures.

In post-unification Italy, the communes (municipalities) were administered by a council of fifteen to eighty members, depending on population. Members held office for six years, with elections for half of the seats every three years. The mayor, elected by the council, held a three-year term. The duties of the communal councils included maintaining roads and lighting; organizing markets; providing elementary education, poor relief, and sanitation; and managing local police and prisons. The communes formed the basic unit of administration, with responsibility for matters such as the registration of births and deaths. Beyond these compulsory duties, they could engage in other initiatives, such as subsidizing cultural or recreational activities like theater and festivals. Communes had a great deal of freedom, with the crucial caveat that these discretionary "services or offices of public utility" were subject to veto by the prefect—an outsider appointed by the king. Local government had the potential to serve as a locus of experimentation and initiative, but it was also highly constrained by this dual structure of power. Like the French town, the Italian commune was the site of struggle between local democracy at the periphery and attempts at political control exerted from the center.[15] The prefect could—and did—dissolve democratically elected local administrations.[16] Also, the prefect and the provincial government had the power to oversee finances and could effectively veto the commune's budget, which presented a serious obstacle to municipal reform. In fact, there were many examples of the prefect intervening to undermine progressive agendas. At Novara the prefect cut out eight-ninths of the funding designated to provide meals for poor schoolchildren. Two mayors were suspended for sanctioning official May Day celebrations. At Reggio-Emilia the council was forbidden from renting communal land to an agricultural cooperative.[17]

Despite these constraints, some communes made significant progress in reforming municipal government. The extremely repressive force of the central government was lessened under the "liberal" regime of Giovanni Giolitti, who became minister of the interior in 1901 and prime minister in 1903. Combined with the growing influence of socialists in Parliament, the arbitrary action of the prefects abated somewhat and municipalities became important sites of policy innovation and expanded participation. The main achievements of the socialist municipalities were in the areas of tax policy, social policy, public works, education, and the provision of municipal services. They also enforced laws on factory safety, schooling, and public health—laws that had been passed by the national government but were ignored by previous administrations. To finance local initiatives, however, the commune had to increase revenue. These local taxes took two forms: property tax and consumption tax (*dazio consumo*).[18] The tax burden had traditionally fallen on the poor through a high duty on staple items such as bread. However, one result of the socialist administrations' power was a shift from the onerous consumption duty to increased taxation on property. Another major initiative was in the area of primary education. Although there was an 1878 law mandating that communes support public elementary schools, it was regularly ignored. Up to seventy pupils in a classroom was not uncommon. Often the socialists formed electoral coalitions with the moderates on pledges to fill statutory obligations to provide adequate schools.[19] Other typical measures included expanding municipal services such as water, sewage, and electricity, which until then had been often unavailable, especially in the new working-class neighborhoods.

Throughout northern and central Italy, the municipalities that became the epicenters of the socialist universe often included elements of direct democracy, such as the referendum. For example, in 1904 in Sesto Fiorentino, the socialist-republican town council used a referendum to decide whether to build a municipal electric facility. It passed, with 1,101 in favor and 214 against the initiative.[20] Citizens did more than decide to accept or reject the communal council's proposals. Policies were often initiated and executed by groups of citizens, under the guidance and with the financial support of local government. Much-needed public housing (*case popolari*) was built not by a central housing authority but by local cooperatives, which were administered by members, co-financed by the state, and overseen by the municipal administration. In effect, there developed a form of local corporatism that linked together an organized civil society and an accountable local administration.

The commune's initiatives were not restricted exclusively to local issues. Although the commune's power was limited, it would be erroneous to understand municipal socialism as a kind of myopic provincialism. The commune connected local concerns to deep-rooted issues of power and equality. The popular communal council reconceptualized its role as an organ of representation rather than just administration.[21] The full scope of its activities included the following: proposing laws to the national government (especially reform of the taxation system), issuing declarations on political controversies (such as support for the Russian Revolution), and intervening in labor disputes. One historian of the pre-fascist period concluded that the commune "became for the popular masses a reference point in relation to the major domestic and international events to which they were directly or indirectly tied."[22]

Theory of Municipalism

The success of municipal socialism inspired reflection on the role of the municipality in socialist theory. Although some worried about "socialism in one province," others suggested that local government could be the lever for achieving broader economic advances. In the pages of the *Critica Sociale*, Alessandro Schiavi claimed that a socialist-led coalition could have important economic effects at the local level. The commune could overturn the destructive character of capitalist competition that undermined the economic position of workers.[23] According to this reasoning, the municipality had the capacity to serve as a break on the downward spiral of wages. Although the individual firm could not unilaterally raise wages without itself succumbing to the pressures of competition, the commune was not constrained by this same dynamic. The wages of public workers were paid from tax revenues and could be set based on alternate criteria, such as community consensus about an appropriate standard of living. This increase could initiate a cycle of competition to attract employees, which would raise the overall wages. If the commune was paying the highest wages and thereby attracting the best workers, other private employers might be forced to follow suit. This argument, which was made by British Fabians and guild socialists, was one way of linking the mundane function of the municipality as an administrative unit to the more ambitious goal of radical economic transformation.[24]

According to Giuseppe Zibordi in his article "Primavera di vita municipale" (Springtime of municipal life), municipal politics "is about little struggles, humble battles that would make an outside observer laugh. But still, there where socialism vanquished the stupid competition of personalistic parties, there where a conflict, even in a nascent and protean form, takes place between interests and principles and true political parties, which become organized around the Commune, there are in these immediate struggles an immense moral value."[25]

The reformist socialist leader Filippo Turati's vision of the municipality was similar. He saw the commune as a way to aggregate popular forces around the issues of immediate, direct relevance to the people, thereby challenging the power of the state. In anticipation of the administrative elections in Milan in 1910, Turati wrote an essay contrasting the "moderate commune" and the "popular commune," in which he argued that the former is the traditional type of local politics in Italy; the commune is used to consolidate the personal interests of the leaders and functions primarily as a slave of the central state. The popular commune, in contrast, is accountable to the people rather than to the king. According to Turati,

> The Commune is the truer *patrie*: here we are born, we suffer, we are aided, here is the cemetery where our remains rest; here are our affections and memories. In short here is life . . . which can and should be under our control. . . . The popular commune . . . is the house and the thing of everyone, but especially, you understand, of the poorest, the most troubled, of those who have most need of it.[26]

Turati's essay articulates the defining vision of municipal socialism. The commune should not be the administrative unit of a distant state. Instead, the local government should use social ties to build consensus around solidaristic initiatives.

Turati's way of depicting the commune is suggestive. He marshals the powerful emotive and affective resonance of locality to a transformative political project. He does not deduce democratic values such as participation, accountability, and accessibility from universal principles or natural law. Instead, he sees them as rooted in the lifeworld. Turati implies that living in a place engenders a type of proprietorship that is based not on abstract rights but on what we might call use value. Birth, suffering, work, celebration, solidarity, strife—these life processes leave traces on the natural environment and on people themselves. To emphasize the connection between people and their lifeworld is not to subordinate individuals to a mythic rendering of their collective past. In fact, it would be a mistake to see municipal socialism as a form of nostalgia for conflict-free communal life. Turati explicitly contrasts the popular commune with the traditional clientelistic type of local politics. Municipalism mobilizes the resources of locality for an explicitly political agenda.

History has not been particularly kind to Turati. The founder of PSI, the Italian Socialist Party, leader of the reformist wing of the party until his death in 1932, and editor of such influential journals as *Critica Sociale* and *Lotta di Classe*, Turati has been overshadowed by his fellow Italian, Antonio Gramsci. Turati's reputation in socialist circles is similar to that of the much-reviled German revisionist Eduard Bernstein, who shared many of his views. Both men emphasized the ethical core of socialism and the gradual nature of social change. Both opposed the extremes of quietism and violence, pushing for alliances with the middle classes, social legislation, electoral power, and the self-organization of the masses in associations.[27]

Turati's theory of municipalism was part of a broader vision of social (or what I would call radical) democracy.[28] He was the main proponent of the socialist Minimum Program, which called for universal suffrage, freedom of the press and association, regional and municipal autonomy, tax reform, democratization of the army, nationalization of railroads, and land reform. He also endorsed the three key components of radical democracy: a program of alliances between subaltern groups, the democratization of sites of power outside the state, and citizen involvement in governing through associations. In his early pieces in *Lotta di Classe* ("the voice of the democratic socialist workers' associations of Milan"), he encouraged small businessmen and white-collar workers to vote socialist, arguing that all exploited classes should join together. In "The Modern Class Struggle" he insisted that violence was powerless because it could never fundamentally change the economic structure. According to Turati, only by capturing the sites of bourgeois power—the state, the municipality, the court, the school—could the socialist movement gain power.[29] Turati was the first theorist of the war of position, and the first positions captured were municipal governments in places like Milan.

Municipalism Today

The concept of "municipalism" is a theoretical elaboration based on the experience of local government, which began in the pre-fascist period and reemerged in the aftermath of World War II. It is a politics of everyday life concerned with the issues that immediately affect citizens, including education, policing, jobs, culture, and services. Municipalism is a political approach to community. This means that political cleavages are based on opposing interests and ideals rather than ascriptive status or traditional hierarchical relations. Municipalism involves citizens in governing through participation in associations such as the chamber of labor that blur the line between state and civil society. Simply representing interests, however, is not democratic if existing institutions are themselves exclusionary and/or elitist. This means that one role of the municipality is to foster associations like trade unions that disperse concentrated power and political spaces like houses of the people that build alternate linkages.

Initially, the concept of municipalism may seem similar to communitarianism. Both share an emphasis on locality and solidarity. Both approaches assume that politics cannot simply be reduced to the aggregation of individual interests. Yet municipalism is distinct from, and in certain ways opposed to, the conventional understanding of communitarianism. The neologism *municipalism* comes from the Latin term *municipalis*, meaning "free city," via *municeps*, or "citizen with privileges." It emphasizes the city as a political space not an organic entity. Its localism is not a rejection of the outside world but a way of mediating between local interests, federal structures, and international contexts. A municipality is made up of citizens, who are linked together by a shared physical world. This shared world, however, is not passively inherited but actively (re)created through practices of citizenship. This political conception of community is implied in the term *municipalism*, which does not suggest a natural or mythic origin but rather a distinct domain constituted through political action.

The problem with the term *communitarianism* is that it can refer to several different ways of theorizing community: municipalism, communalism, association, and *homonoia*.[30] Communalism is similar to what Ferdinand Toennies called *Gemeinschaft*; it is based on organic bonds developed gradually over long periods of time in a given locality. This traditional formation is what critics have in mind when they attack communitarianism as stifling individuality and progress. But this is only one of several possible modes of sociality. Toennies famously juxtaposed *Gemeinschaft* with *Gesellschaft*. Association, another form of community, is the product of deliberate choice. It is the aggregation of autonomous individuals who choose to pursue some joint end. The third possibility is what I call *homonoia*, based on the Greek word for unanimity or like-mindedness. Unlike communalism, *homonoia* does not assume an organic unity created through a shared history; instead, it recognizes that unity is created through a political project. This political project, however, is one of dissimulation. Rather than emphasizing its own constructed character, it creates unity through elaborate founding myths and ritualistic reconstruction of shared culture. Rousseau's *On the Government of Poland* provides a paradigmatic example of this alternative.[31]

The liberal-communitarian debate is a sustained consideration of the strengths and weaknesses of these three modes of sociality. According to poststructuralist critics, communalism is a nostalgic desire for an imagined past rather than a viable political formation. Even if it were a real possibility, it would share the flaws of homonoia. An ethos of like-mindedness could risk stifling the dissent necessary for good personal and collective judgment. It might also fail to provide the conditions for individuality and creativity that are part of many visions of human flourishing. An overemphasis on unity easily turns into conformity or exclusion. But association is not necessarily a viable alternative. A purely instrumental view of collective behavior opens up all of the problems associated with free riding.[32] It is doubtful whether such an association could inspire the commitment needed to achieve long-term or transformative goals. Its instrumentalist ethos would not provide the motivation for including those without resources; therefore it would not function effectively as a mechanism for the social integration of heterogeneous groups.

One thing that distinguishes association (or what Michael Sandel calls "instrumental community")[33] from communalism is its characteristic understanding of the individual; the "idea of social union" is "based on conventional individualist assumptions which take for granted the self-interested motivations of the agents." In contrast, communalists "conceive of their identity—the subject and not just the object of their feelings and aspirations—as defined to some extent by the community of which they are a part."[34] In other words, community is constitutive of the self. The crucial caveat, of course, is the phrase "to some extent." The dispute between communitarians and poststructuralists comes down to whether the subject is (and perhaps more importantly, should be) constituted by a relatively stable, conflict-free context or whether it is formed at the intersection of multiple and sometimes opposed subject positions. Municipalism also has a distinctive understanding of (inter-) subjectivity. According to municipalism, the subject is constructed at the intersection of economic, social, and psychic forces. Politics itself also constitutes the subject.

Municipalism is a distinctly political and democratic mode of adjudicating conflict. It recognizes community as constructed through politics and motivated by proximity. Proximity means that people who live and work adjacent to each other will inevitably be tied together through interdependent interests and shared experiences. Even conflict is one of the experiences that can link citizens together, at least when there is a shared context for resolving it. Municipalism alternates between two modes of adjudication: negotiating consensus (local corporatism) and electoral competition. In its corporate function, it links together different groups that are constituted by interest or affinity. Electoral competition ensures that alternate frameworks for mediating local interests can emerge and triumph. Electoral competition guarantees that the principles guiding corporate bargaining can be revised to reflect changes in the balance of power or normative goals. Municipalism is not a particular vision of what constitutes a community but an inclusive forum for debating, applying, and revising such visions. It is the arena in which the citizen "has to acquire a perspective of commonality, to think integrally and comprehensively rather than exclusively."[35] Municipalism exists at the intersection of the solidaristic orientations of preexisting groups, the mediating influence of parties or coalitions, and the transformative power of contact with challengers. In pre-fascist Italy, municipalism was the achievement of a mobilized socialist subculture.

Municipalism and Ideology

The problem with the theory of municipalism is that it seems to conflate a nonpartisan context for political struggle with a particular ideological orientation. It opens up the question of whether municipalism could generate a conservative, elitist, and exclusionary politics. Without a general theory of universal rationality, human nature, or historical progress, no particular procedure, no matter how democratic, can guarantee justice and equality. Citizens may be shortsighted or selfish, disinterested or deceived, or they may even have irreconcilable notions of the good life. No purely procedural mechanism can erase this possibility.

The relationship between municipalism, democracy, and socialism is especially complex in the case of Italy. Italian political sociologists have identified not one but two territorial political subcultures: white and red, Catholic and Communist, respectively. According to Carlo Trigilia, both the Catholic areas of northern Italy and the Communist regions of central Italy created local political systems capable of mediating conflict, building consensus, and involving citizens. Both the Communist and Catholic subcultures contributed to the success of democracy by forging institutional and ideological ties between citizens and government. The territorial, political "subculture" thesis emphasizes the political effects of shared ideology, regardless of its particular content. According to this position, both socialist ideology and Catholic theology could serve as the basis of principled policies, long-term strategies, and consensual solutions. Carlo Trigilia suggested that red and white subcultures were "characterized by a high degree of consensus," which facilitated "an elevated capacity of aggregation and mediation of diverse interests at the local level."[36] The political subcultures helped generate popular support for the local administration and increased the government's accountability to the people. The web that linked associations, political parties, and local government also provided a stable context for enacting and implementing policies.

The parallels between the red and white local political systems were first drawn in the context of a study seeking to explain the high levels of economic growth in those two very different parts of Italy. Both red and white subcultures may have provided a way to facilitate economic growth by coordinating local interests, but they were not equally effective at dispersing power. Participation in associations affiliated with the Catholic Church—labor unions, cooperatives, voluntary groups, and the Catholic political party—did not lead to fundamental shifts in the bases of local power. White municipalities were democratic. The Catholic coalition achieved electoral victory in those areas where it effectively organized its largely peasant constituency. But white municipalities did not democratize the sources of power. The constitutive associations remained largely hierarchical. The leadership of the priest, usually in alliance with large landowners, was the basis of Catholic subculture. The church, with its pulpit and pews, was its spatialization of community.

Catholic subculture, like Communist subculture, provided the high level of consent necessary to achieve effective administration. But popular legitimacy is not radical democracy. Radical democracy implies not passive consent but active participation; it involves attentiveness to the way power is constituted in civil society, bureaucracies, and the state. Radical democratic practices such as municipalism democratize these diverse sites of power.

Now we are in a position to understand the final component of Zibordi's statement quoted earlier, his claim that municipalism exists "there where socialism vanquished the stupid competition of personalistic parties." At first it seems paradoxical that a particular ideology like socialism could have a privileged relationship to municipalism, which provides a context for competition between "interests, principles, and true political parties." But interests, ideas, and institutions will only matter if citizens' choices are not already constrained by relations of dependence. Socialism, understood broadly as the struggle against economic subordination, played an important role in breaking these relations of dependence. A particular movement stands in a privileged relationship to democracy only in so far as it challenges the prepolitical bases of exclusion.[37] In Italy at the turn of the century, the diffusion of socialist-inspired sites of resistance in places such as Sesto San Giovanni challenged the local monopoly on political and economic power.

The Legacy of Localism

At first it might appear paradoxical that regions such as Tuscany and Emilia-Romagna with the greatest traditions of municipalism were also the areas of fascist strength. Fascism did not arise in the traditionally conservative regions of the south but in precisely those areas like Milan and rural Padania where municipal socialism had made the most significant inroads. The most plausible explanation is that the more radical initiatives of political reform also inspired the most virulent reaction. In the south and in some rural Catholic areas of the north, the traditional relations of patronage and clientelism were never broken; therefore more vigorous forms of repression and policing were unnecessary.[38] In these areas, the vertical ties that connected local elites to their constituents (through the selective distribution of "pork," charity, government jobs, and priests' influential letters of recommendation, which provided access to employment) remained relatively unchanged not only under fascism but also into the period of Christian Democratic hegemony after World War II. In the red areas of central Italy, however, these ties were irrevocably broken. The fascist reaction was largely an attempt to reassert control through a new combination of violence and mass mobilization around an authoritarian center. The democratic spaces and practices were destroyed under fascist rule, but their impact was not entirely eradicated. The horizontal ties that were achieved among social groups, the experience with self-government, and the capacity for autonomous collective action proved to be lasting legacies of that era; they were also preconditions to building successful democratic institutions in the post–World War II period.[39]

It is one of the truisms of Italian politics that the red areas of central Italy have experienced an enviable degree of political stability, social cohesion, and economic success in the post–World War II period.[40] Not beset by the corruption and clientelism that seems to undermine government initiatives in the south, these areas managed to build schools and hospitals, provide services, and manage economic growth. These achievements are particularly surprising given that these areas voted overwhelmingly communist in the post–World War II period, thereby passing up the patronage available from the Christian Democrats, who governed nationally for forty years. Perhaps the explanation of this anomaly lies in the legacy of municipal socialism.

Testing this hypothesis poses several difficulties. The first of the many hurdles is how to measure the success of subnational government institutions. This problem, however, has largely been solved by the techniques developed by Robert Putnam in his research on the Italian regions. Putnam and his collaborators studied the Italian regions from the mid-1970s, when regional autonomy was implemented, to the late 1980s.[41] The strength of Putnam's *Making Democracy Work* is that it establishes a nuanced way of comparing the success of subnational government units.[42] Putnam rejects a purely proceduralist understanding of democracy and includes bureaucratic responsiveness, efficiency, social policy, and legislative innovation in his criteria for success. He argues that democratic institutions must be responsive to constituents concerns and they must have the capacity to implement collective decisions. The "index of institutional performance" used to compare the twenty Italian regions includes the following components: social policy (daycare centers, housing and urban development, family clinics, health spending), efficiency (budget promptness, cabinet stability, information and statistical services, development of industrial policy instruments), and responsiveness (reform legislation, bureaucratic responsiveness).

According to Putnam, the success of regional government in the 1980s was the product of the strength and intensity of civic life. He argues that "choral societies, soccer clubs, and bird watching groups" build the capacity for trust and cooperation that are a necessary precondition of meaningful citizenship and responsive government. At first this suggestion sounds plausible, but Putnam's vision of civic life is strangely apolitical and conflict free. His measures of civic community include sites of sociability but not sites of resistance. He excludes all groups affiliated with the Catholic Church, unions, or political parties, thus effectively eliminating the overwhelming majority of associations in Italy. This approach ignores the relationship between successful regional democracy, political associations, and their affiliated cultural networks. Italian scholars have long emphasized the political salience of the Catholic and Communist subcultures, which have linked ideology, party membership, and participation in a wide range of associations such as labor unions, recreational groups, cooperatives, and women's leagues.[43] Putnam's approach overlooks this work on the importance of cultural and social groups aligned with either the Catholics (white) or Communists (red), the two ideological blocks in Italy.

To understand the political impact of municipalism, I studied the relationship between institutional performance and political subcultures.[44] The guiding question was which of the following better explained the success of democratic institutions: the trust engendered in conflict-free domains of social life, such as bird-watching societies and choral groups, or the popular power generated in political spaces such as the cooperatives and houses of the people. In this research I used regression analysis to test the relationship between red subculture, white subculture, apolitical associations, and Putnam's index of regional government performance. In addition, to evaluate whether current political patterns were indeed the legacy of pre-fascist practices, I traced these subcultures back to their genesis at the turn of the century.[45] A full description of the methodology employed in this study can be found in my "Civic Republicanism versus Social Struggle: A Gramscian Approach to Associationalism in Italy."[46] Here I summarize the main conclusions:

- The relationship between the density of apolitical associations and institutional performance (for example, whether democracy works) is weak.[47] In other words, those regions with a high concentration of sports clubs and recreational groups are only marginally more likely to have effective and responsive regional governments.
- The density of white (Catholic) associations is not linked to strong democracy. In fact, Catholic associations do not really form a coherent political subculture. The concept of political subculture implies that there are certain geographical areas where political identity is reinforced through participation in related cultural activities and institutions. My research showed that the strength of the Christian Democratic Party was not tightly linked to the density of Catholic associations. One possible reason is that Christian Democratic membership was often motivated by patronage rather than active participation in a Catholic-affiliated organization. Christian Democratic membership was high in areas of the south where Catholic associations were absent.
- Red subculture is highly correlated with the success of democratic institutions. The measure of red subculture included membership in both the PCI (Italian Communist Party) and the organizations that are loosely affiliated with it: ARCI (includes groups focused on cultural, athletic, recreational, political, and identity issues), the CGIL

(trade union), and the Lega Nazionale delle Cooperative (includes consumer cooperatives and producer cooperatives). This finding supports the Gramscian thesis that mass-based cultural organizations allied with a political party are most likely to break the hegemony of the economic and political elites.

- Looking back to the period between unification and fascism, we find similar results. The density of Catholic associations has no effect on current democratic practices, whereas the density of membership in the PSI and its affiliated mutual aid societies and cooperatives in the same period is a strong predictor of good government almost sixty years later. The regions of Italy with the highest density of socialist membership in 1914 and 1920 are the ones with successful democratic practices today (see fig. 11).

- Earlier we suggested that successful democracy might be the long-term legacy of a politics that broke existing ties of clientelism and dependence. In the period between unification and fascism, socialism was a democratic force because it created new horizontal ties between the diverse elements of the subaltern classes and helped integrate them into political life. Whereas Catholic and bourgeois organizations also provided important social and cultural services, they reflected an interclassist ideology and remained subordinate to the local church and elites. At the turn of the century in Italy, the church was not a site of resistance but rather a nodal point for reinforcing the traditional hierarchy. Given its long-standing links to landowners, the church's resources for challenging entrenched powers were limited.

A municipality is not a space of resistance in the same way that a church or a chamber of labor is. The term *space* can refer to vastly different scales from a pinpoint to a galaxy. It is useful to distinguish three different dimensions. At one end of the continuum is the site; this term refers to the location at which a particular activity takes place. Although many of our sites, such as the chamber of labor and the house of the people, host multiple activities, they still can be identified with a precise location and a particular set of practices. At the other end of the continuum are political geographies such as the nation, which we know through electoral results, aggregate data, and imagined communities. These are vast territories where heterogeneous groups interact and highly varied activities take place. In between these two extremes is the scale of the municipality. It does not have the simple structure of a site

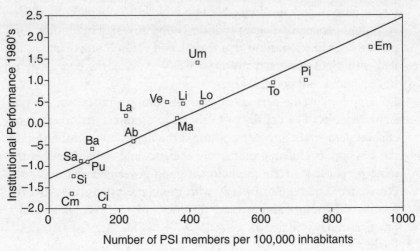

Fig. 11. Institutional performance (1980s) and PSI strength (1914 and 1920). *Note*: Ab, Abruzzi; Ba, Basilicata; Cl, Calabria; Cm, Campania; Em, Emilia-Romagna; La, Latium; Li, Liguria; Lo, Lombardy; Ma, Marches; Pi, Piedmont; Pu, Puglia; Sa, Sardinia; Si, Sicily; To, Tuscany; Um, Umbria; Ve, Veneto. *Sources*: Robert Putnam, *Making Democracy Work: Civic Traditions in Modern Italy* (Princeton: Princeton University Press, 1993); Carlo Trigilia, *Grandi partiti e piccole imprese: Comunisti e democristiani nelle regioni a economia diffusa* (Bologna: Il Mulino, 1986).

or the level of complexity and differentiation of a territory. Like other sites, it can facilitate encounter. Like a nation or province or empire, a municipality encompasses the entire panoply of processes that produce and reproduce life. Therefore, it cannot be reduced to any unitary aim let alone a political project. The municipality is one of the modes of connectivity that transforms micropractices of political socialization into enduring political outcomes.

The distinctive geographies of popular power in pre-fascist Italy correspond highly to ones that endure today. It is not associational life in general that "makes democracy work" but rather the capacity to challenge the monopoly on power held by economic elites. The causal mechanism is not trust but the capacity for resistance. This capacity can only be built in places that are strategically sheltered from the influence of dominant elites. It is heightened at sites that link together the struggle for economic improvement, social solidarity, and political leadership.

In the preceding four chapters I have focused on the rapid changes that took place in Italy between national unification and fascism, a time of ferment and transformation. These changes in power relations were

reflected in the geography of the municipality. Before 1900 the hegemony of the church and clerics was inscribed in the built environment.
It was legible on a map of the town. The historian Ernesto Ragionieri
wrote, "The agricultural villages that constitute the commune [Sesto
Fiorentino] are grouped around the church. In that spot the inhabitants
receive the first official recognition, marry, and die; around the church,
the Sunday market takes place."[48] The church was a nodal point that
seemed to link immutably the eternal and the temporal, the local and
the universal, the self and the community. It was a place that tied the
material world of sensation—incense, candles, songs, images—to the
social and spiritual worlds.

In alleyways and back rooms, however, a new geography of power was
emerging. New gathering places such as the chambers of labor and
houses of the people were built (see fig. 12). The dynamism of these sites
emboldened the commune, which began to challenge rather than reinforce the hegemony of the church, local landowners, and central government. The municipality became a nodal point of power. The map of
the city had to be redrawn. According to Ragionieri,

> The extension of the tasks of the commune, the construction itself of
> the new headquarters of the municipality, the transfer to the new pi-
> azza of the festivals and markets that were held for so many years at the
> piazza of the church, were all facts that gradually and almost insensibly,
> began to give life to a certain center of autonomous civil life distinct
> from and opposed to the one of the church.[49]

Place is the anchor of meaning and memory. Power relations are inscribed in places and reproduced through the experiences of people who
inhabit them. Spatial formations are not like opinions that can be
changed at will. They are relatively enduring structures and symbols of
the social world. But they are not neutral, static, or silent. In a period of
less than twenty years, the lived geography of Sesto Fiorentino changed
fundamentally. The original order was disrupted by new sites of power
at the margins of accepted practice. Once established, these new places
were constant reminders of the new citizens' aspiration for a different
distribution of power.

The built environment is one kind of text that reveals the past, but
reading it requires much care and attention. The millions of tourists
who pass through Florence and Rome see the magnificent Renaissance
churches and palaces that document the centrality of religion and mer-

Fig. 12. A postcard of the central piazza of Cavriago. The building on the right is the house of the people (built in 1906). *Source*: Arbizzani et al., *Storie di case del popolo*.

cantile might. The church's temporal power was inscribed on the skyline and the cityscapes that endure to this day. But the more intrepid traveler who wanders beyond the tourist destinations into industrial suburbs and working-class neighborhoods will discover more modest monuments such as the houses of the people. These sites of resistance are also landmarks of urban life. They are not traditional monumental sites. They are seldom set apart from the life of the street to be gazed on as remote markers of power. They are usually built in vernacular styles and integrated into the tapestry of the street. They are also markers of an important moment in history—what we might somewhat grandiosely call the transformation from subject to citizen and the birth of modern democratic politics.

CONCLUSION

Give me a place to stand, and I will move the world.

Archimedes

On April 1, 1899, a poem celebrating the completion of the house of the people in Brussels was published in the special edition of the socialist newspaper *Le Peuple*. The poem has no literary merit, and its folkloristic charm is lost in translation. It is interesting because, for me, it captures the dream if not the reality of the *maison du peuple*. It is a testimony to the fact that the term *house of the people* is not simply shorthand for referring to the member organizations. Political space does not merely aggregate people; it also becomes a symbol of their aspirations and a motivation for political activity.

Several of the thirteen stanzas of the poem celebrate the pragmatic functions of the new *maison du peuple*:

> It is here, in this marvelous place
> That we will raise the battle cry
> It is here that ardor will awaken us
> And will make us remember fecund debates
>
> It is here that with words aflame
> Our representatives will come to speak to us
> Here that our souls will be sparked
> Here that we will find consolation

It is here at the source of our study
Full of ardor, we [illegible word]
And it is here, connected to custom
That we will come to fraternize

The house of the people was a place for study, socializing, and debate. But it was more than that. The poem calls the house of the people "the source of our study." It is not merely a place where books, teachers, and students come together; rather, something in the site itself provides a motivation for study. It is a microcosm of a world where it has become meaningful to study and to learn political skills. There is a reason to understand the workings of the social world because it is possible to change it.

The poem also emphasizes the importance of place in encouraging emotional identification and motivating action. Words such as "aflame," "pride," "ardor," "soul," and "spark" suggest that politics is about passion, and passion is more effectively captured by a material place than an abstract concept. In his seminal work *The Collective Memory*, Maurice Halbwachs explained that we capture the past by understanding how it is preserved in our physical surroundings.[1] The house of the people was a way of locating memories. The poem states that it "will make us remember fecund debates." The house of the people is a reminder of the contestation and the solidarity that built the movement; it is a locus of memory for those who participated in its construction. It is also a reminder for the future. One of the purposes of the building is to "evoke for history the memory" of the people's struggles and achievement.[2]

The members of the house of the people understood it as a thing of grandeur, an oeuvre created by the weakest members of society without the tutelage of the government or the elites. It encapsulated the logic of the society that workers wanted to create. The new building embodied the social power and political dominance of the common people, which they called socialism. It served as a physical manifestation of the conviction that such an ambitious goal was achievable.

From Microspaces of Resistance to Geographies of Power

The theme that links together the different historical and theoretical threads of this narrative is the claim that place plays a role in transformative politics. At the margins of Europe, at the beginning of the twentieth century, traditional forms of co-presence and encounter were imaginatively reconfigured as resources for resisting authoritarian relations. These new political sites were not oases of consensus; they were themselves constantly reinvented through power, struggle, and debate. Although space clearly contributed to political practice, it has not been recognized in contemporary political theory. There is still a widespread suspicion that a political appeal to place is conservative, essentialist, or anachronistic.

Throughout this project, I have shown space as a terrain of struggle for control over bodies, movement, labor, meaning, and sociability. Chapters 3 and 4 emphasized the contested nature of political space. Both chapters revealed a tension between the way space was lived and how it was theorized. Chapter 3 looked at the sites that constituted the bourgeois public sphere in order to reveal their implicit exclusion and hierarchy. This sphere was a site of resistance that created a social milieu for new alliances and identities that undermined the power structure of the old regime; however, the salons and secret societies were marked by traditions and practices that limited their ability to incorporate new challenges from the outside. Chapter 4 investigated another crucial site of struggle between the bourgeoisie and the popular classes. It showed that the factory was an attempt to increase surveillance, discipline, and control over workers. The factory gathered workers together but also separated them from potential allies. The nascent proletariat had to reconstitute horizontal ties outside of the factory gates.

Chapters 5–7 recounted details of particular radical democratic sites that flourished in Italy between the time of national unification and the rise of fascism. These sites provided an opportunity to encounter new people and ideas, to communicate controversial theories under conditions of relative security, and to experiment with new identities. During the day, workers were quite literally "objects," inputs in the production process with only an instrumental value. At the cooperative or the house of the people they could finally be subjects, co-creators of an alternate world. Given the high degree of surveillance at work and the isolation of home, it was crucial for them to create a place where it was possible to view the world in new ways. Studying these sites allows us to answer the question "Given the imperfect world into which we are thrown, how can we make it into a place where we can flourish?"

In chapter 8 I introduced the concept of municipalism, a theoretical elaboration based on these experiences of radical democracy at the local level. Derived from *municipalis* meaning "free city," the term describes a distinctly political approach to community. In the areas of Italy where municipalism flourished, clientelistic ties of dependence were permanently broken. Even though many sites of resistance were destroyed under fascism, they created geographies of popular power that endure in the present.

Although the more radical dream of collective control over the economy was not realized, incremental reforms were won and nodal points of popular power were established. Microspaces of resistance were important not only for their direct contribution to mobilization; they were also read by both workers and their adversaries as reference points in a struggle over the possible meaning of democracy, an intervention in the debate over popular control. Places such as the chambers of labor played a crucial role in the process of building a sense of political agency among the masses. In his autobiography, the carpenter and labor leader Rinaldo Rigola (1868–1954) emphasized this change. He argued that by the 1920s there were both pro- and anti-socialist parties but that there were no longer pre-socialist parties. He explained that after the rise of socialism, it would be impossible to return to the elite politics of the nineteenth century, a time when workers agreed that "Politics is the business of gentlemen."[3] In effect, the mobilization achieved through cooperatives, mutual aid societies, labor unions, socialist circles, and peasant leagues was critical to democratization, that is, the process of working out counterprojects and forcing decision makers to take such projects into account.[4] The workers' movement radicalized democracy by insisting that only the self-organization of society can provide a constant challenge to the explicit and implicit exclusions reified in the state. Far from abandoning the state, these groups not only tried to act collectively to gain leverage over existing institutions but they also created new hybrid institutions. A loosely linked chain of popular political spaces was crucial in rooting a sustained challenge to the elite dominance of political life. A red (socialist and later communist) subculture came to mark the political map of Italy. The new politics that emerged in municipalities in the pre-fascist period is important for understanding the high levels of political participation and innovative government in certain Italian regions to this day.[5]

Theorizing Space

One of the puzzles that initially motivated this study was the realization that class position alone could not explain progressive politics in Italy.

As we saw in chapter 5, neither the distribution of agricultural versus industrial employment nor relations of production in the countryside (sharecropping, day labor, and so forth) could account for concentrations of socialist voting and activism. Political participation seemed to exhibit distinctive geographic patterns. This made me curious about the political properties of space. Economic factors such as poverty, unemployment, or factory work may lead to disenfranchisement and subordination without encouraging resistance. Recognizing these experiences as similar requires more than just a theory explaining their connection. It also requires opportunities for contact and discussion that seldom emerge in everyday life. Spaces of resistance provide a context for political speech, reflection, and action. Although some political theorists and activists have emphasized the power of place, many others have taken it for granted as part of a broad concept like "society," "institution," or "discourse." Spatial analysis is not opposed to these alternatives; instead it enriches them by exploring how oppositional social identities are constituted and where new discourses germinate.

Several properties of space have emerged from this study. Particular spaces function to initiate, maintain, or interrupt interaction. They aggregate or exclude; they encourage or inhibit contact between people; and they determine the form and scope of the contact. The spaces discussed in this study initiated contact between a variety of workers by providing traditional services—low-priced food, entertainment, wine. Locating these traditional activities in the cooperative or house of the people transformed the nature of these encounters by physically linking them to other activities of the socialist subculture.

The power of place also results from the way it serves as the backdrop of a shared world. The experience of this shared world constitutes how we know ourselves not only as individuals but also in relation to others; it is the basis of intersubjectivity. The general concept of intersubjectivity, however, does not fully capture the affective, gestural, and symbolic dimensions that emerge when people come together in the same place.[6] The visceral register is conveyed through the precognitive impact of things such as greeting, focus, tone, posture, inflection, recognition. We see evidence of this in the statutes of mutual aid societies, which often specified that "honorary" upper-class members could not speak at meetings (or sometimes could not even attend them). Although honorary members were not excluded from the organization, they were prevented from being physically present and thereby determining its character.

Spaces are not simply physical; they are also social. There are different "scripts" or repertoires appropriate for different places. We could call this spatial coding. The patterns of interaction typical of particular places such as the school, church, or barracks do not correspond exactly to patterns in the world at large. As we saw in chapter 5, the way soldiers and workers interacted in the *circolo* was different from their behavior on the street. Solidarity does not arise directly from contact between people; rather, it depends on how the interactions are framed. This framing is achieved by space. Physical spaces mark off a context in which certain attributes are highlighted and others are obscured. According to a set of either explicit or implicit norms, some characteristics are intensified and others are diminished. Sociologist Erving Goffman uses the term *encounter* to convey how "a locally realized world of roles and events cuts the participants off from many externally based matters that might have been given relevance but allows a few of these external matters to enter into the interaction world as an official part of it."[7] The transformative potential of space lies precisely in the possibility of suspending certain aspects of reality in order to intensify others.

Particular uses of space aggregate people and resources to facilitate communication, coordination, and control. By overcoming dispersion, nodal points persuade both adversaries and allies of unity, strength, and power.[8] In a political movement, these spaces facilitate and deepen the connection between militants and supporters of the cause as well as between times of mobilization and normal periods. Sites of resistance are a microcosm of the polity itself, and therefore they provide important political training and experience that is otherwise unavailable to the disenfranchised. Many political leaders, like Carlo Borromeo of Sesto San Giovanni, emerged out of the cooperative movement because there they learned important skills such as running a meeting, speaking in public, and building consensus.

The previous four points are general characteristics of the relationship between space and politics. They could describe fascist clubhouses just as easily as houses of the people. To understand the political function of a space, one must consider its position in relation to the dominant powers and its particular values. Although architectural form cannot be deduced from ideology, democratic spaces often exhibit certain shared characteristics that reflect their inclusive and pluralistic character. As we saw in the comparison between the house of the people and the house of fascism, different principles are reflected in their spatial practices. The sites that made up the popular public sphere cultivated room for reflection and judgment. In contrast, the archetypical fascist spaces such as sports stadiums and plazas provided settings for orchestrated mass rituals that minimized a feeling of individuality and intensified identification with the leader and the state.

It is an error to conceive of deterritorialization as something intrinsically progressive. The national may be mobilized against the local or the local against the (inter)national, depending on where an authoritarian system is more susceptible to challenge. As we saw in chapter 8, the socialist party concentrated on municipal politics when it was effectively excluded from the national government. This had the fortuitous, if unintended consequence of encouraging a dense network of local social sites and economic institutions with political experience. It is no more possible to escape the logic of territoriality than it is to escape politics. As engaged activist-theoreticians such as Gramsci recognized, politics is about creating fortifications, assuming positions, knowing the terrain of struggle, and taking advantage of scale. But these tempting military metaphors are by themselves insufficient. More important than fighting wars of position or maneuver is building a popular public sphere. The popular public sphere is made up of places, like the chambers of labor and the houses of the people, that lay the groundwork for conventional political activity. It is this lifeworld that I have tried to uncover in this project.[9]

Creating spaces of resistance is an example of world-building activity. World building, however, is not like system building. It is beset by contradictions, setbacks, unintended consequences, and all the other messy facets of social life. World building is not the work of God the father, the omniscient narrator, or other great men. It is achieved by men and women as they try to adapt their material and social environments to meet their needs. Buying bread and drinking wine at the socialist cooperative, studying and discussing politics at the chamber of labor—these are the activities through which people try to build a world in which humanity and dignity are possible.

Such activities dissolve Hannah Arendt's influential opposition between work and labor.[10] For Arendt, work involves the creation of unique and meaningful words or deeds. She contrasts this with the repetitive, Sisyphean struggle to sustain life. Work is recognized in the public sphere, whereas labor is hidden in the private domain of the household. I have argued that a politics of everyday life encompasses both the private domain of reproduction, nature, unproductive labor (a redundancy for Arendt), and the public domain in which the enduring achievements of action, appearance, and recognition are possible.

Works such as the cooperative, the neighborhood, the house of the people, and the city itself belie this distinction between the social (private) and political (public) domains. The cooperative is built when the profits garnered by people buying bread and wine are used collectively to build something they can share: a library, a summer camp, a newspaper. The lifeworld is produced by people pursuing banal concerns of everyday life: work, pleasure, creativity, reproduction. The landscape of the countryside, with its characteristic arrangements of paths, fields, trees, and vineyards, and that of the city, with its plazas, houses, and streets, are both examples of how the most repetitive labor incidentally creates the most enduring monuments.[11] The places analyzed in this book—the cooperatives, the chambers of labor, and the houses of the people—were rooted in social needs, yet they provided the space for the human aspirations for a shared public life. Studying these spaces reveals that the distinction between labor and work, or, more broadly, the distinction between the social, economic, and political, is illusory.

In this study I turned to history to learn about the popular public sphere—the places, practices, and modes of sociality that sustained a tenuous balance between liberty and equality, autonomy and solidarity, unity and plurality, consensus and conflict. I found a series of sites of resistance that linked a politics of personal transformation to a collective project for acquiring power. Recognition was not accomplished by changing individuals' minds but by changing social structures.[12] This recognition was not something ephemeral, achieved by temporarily bracketing status differences. Relations of personal dependence were dismantled by economic struggles waged by mutual aid societies, cooperatives, leagues of resistance, and chambers of labor. Participation was not an end in itself but a means of achieving control over government.

Peasants, artisans, day laborers, the unemployed, women in textile mills, and new arrivals from the countryside reimagined themselves as workers and built a series of sites of resistance: houses of the people, chambers of labor, union halls, political circles, mutual aid societies, cooperatives. They won the right to vote and to organize. They built the first mass political party in Italy, won a plurality in Parliament, governed numerous municipalities, and passed social legislation. Nevertheless, their movements were weakened by acrimonious ideological splits, rivalries, and failed strategies (both extremism and paralysis), all of which contributed to the eventual fascist takeover. Pietro Ferrero, the head of Turin's metal workers' union, cast one last glance at the chamber of labor before he was dragged to his death and the building was burned by fascists. Mario Montagnana, his chronicler, fled into exile; later he returned to fight for the partisans and lived to see the chamber of labor rebuilt.

The sites discussed in this study were cathexes of heterotopic desires. They captured peoples' contradictory longings for a place that is at once a home, an agora, and a fortress. Today, these sites are artifacts from a forgotten time and place. In their irreducible particularity, these sites serve as reminders of the precarious nature of our generalities, our interpretations, our conclusions. The physical spaces are traces that serve to mark practices which otherwise might be forgotten. We study artifacts—texts, ruins, cultural fragments—because they are "made up of processes," compress history, and mark social antagonisms.[13] These struggles, which are now at best hazy memories, are forgotten parts of who we have become. Why disturb the past, forcing that which is reluctant to speak to us? Walter Benjamin wrote of the cognitive and political power of "involuntary remembering of a redeemed humanity."[14] This strategy is based on the conviction that momentarily disrupting the certainties of the past may open up the possibility of reconfiguring the future. Perhaps achieving this goal requires the voluntary remembering of an unredeemed humanity.

POSTSCRIPT:
THE LOCAL IN AN AGE OF GLOBALIZATION

The beginning of the twenty-first century seems a particularly unpropitious moment to reflect on the power of place. If there is a single word that best encapsulates the political, economic, and cultural challenges of the present it would be *globalization*.[1] Academics and other elites enamored of the possibilities of new information technologies write paeans to virtual reality and cyberspace.[2] The frenetic pace of late capitalism, combined with accelerated circulation of images, words, and data, seems to reflect the loosening of ties to any particular physical location, a logic of deterritorialization. Goods and capital especially, but also people and ideas, flow across boundaries with ease. Furthermore, such flows seem to defy national sovereignty and elude traditional forms of political control. Reactions to this process are concentrated in two camps. Some see globalization primarily as the expansion of the power of capitalism, a largely negative but inevitable phenomenon that renders local strategies ineffective and necessitates increasingly global responses. Others valorize the cultural aspect of globalization and see its hybridity, fragmentation, and fluidity as a liberation from the hierarchies and fixed identities of the community or nation.[3]

Does it make sense to study the political effects of place in a global society where attachments to locality are becoming more and more precarious? Are spaces of resistance such as the cooperative and the house of the people at best quaint anachronisms? Should we support a more cosmopolitan democracy that "distributes democratic energies across disparate spaces"?[4] These questions are motivated by the influential work of Deleuze and Guattari, which celebrates the fluidity, multiplicity, and flux of deterritorialization. In *A Thousand Plateaus*, Deleuze and Guattari invoke the figure of the nomad, who spurns the security of a fixed abode and rejects a sedentary existence. Is there something intrinsically emancipatory about the lack of fixity and rootlessness associated with the nomad? Are they suggesting that in a global age, the only meaningful orientation is one that embraces deterritorialization?

A careful reading of *A Thousand Plateaus* suggests that any simple opposition between territorialization and deterritorialization breaks down. Deleuze and Guattari warn at the outset: "Every rhizome contains lines of segmentarity according to which it is stratified, territorialized, organized, signified, attributed, etc. as well as lines of deterritorialization down which it constantly flees. . . . That is why one can never posit a dualism or a dichotomy, even in the rudimentary form of the good and the bad."[5] They insist that there is always something that escapes the binary organization, that flows or flees, subverts rationality and distorts reality. The relationship between territory and deterritorialization is not one of absolute externality, transcendence, or opposition. Instead, the two elements are different moments of the process of politics. Throughout *A Thousand Plateaus* they insist that "the territory is inseparable from certain coefficients of deterritorialization."[6] The production of space involves both processes.

The celebration of deterritorialization is especially problematic when we consider that capitalism is the deterritorializing force par excellence. Capital is almost by definition a means of circulation, that which accelerates the flow of goods, capital, people, and ideas across borders, cultures, and economies. It weakens other roots, such as those linking the individual to family and fatherland. The factors of production (including people) are distributed according to the criteria of profitability rather than traditional affinities. Yet capitalism is also a form of reterritorialization. It breaks traditional ties asunder in order to create other, perhaps less explicit and stable but nevertheless ultimately enduring relations of dependence. Analyses of the global market confirm that rather than furthering equality, investment in developing countries is motivated by the enormous disparities in the cost of production. It is precisely these differences that it profits from and that it sustains. And this involves the support, either explicitly or through appropriate proxies, of institutions (the International Monetary Fund, the World Bank, the World Trade Organization, states, multinational corporations) that reinforce the conditions of profitability. The dispersion of production increases rather than decreases the importance of the core global cities as axes of command, control, and coordination.[7] The process that deterritorializes certain patterns and nodes of power serves to reestablish other ones. Rather than thinking of globalization as deterritorializing, it is more useful to consider what sorts of stabilities it undermines and which ones it reinforces.

Globalization is itself a kind of space. It is located in airports, hotel conference centers, computer networks, interchangeable beach resorts. The global encompasses both exclusive locations of privilege and places, such as the maquiladoras, which refine a strict hierarchy of subordination. These spaces combine relative isolation with complete dependence. The identical hotel conference centers, located at the periphery of the city, are often linked directly to the airport. These connections do not bring together different places but instead link other, more dense points of intersection. Such nodal points seem to be a world apart, with almost no recognizable connection to the cultural and historical uniqueness of the location. Yet their function is based on locally rooted service providers, the practically invisible armies of maids, gate agents, data entry clerks, waiters, baggage handlers, reservation agents, and the local economy that they create. It proves more useful to think of globalization not as a unidirectional process of deterritorialization but rather as a new way of linking territories together.

Both nomads and sedentary peoples need markers. Nomads in particular need markers to serve as reference points that create implicit pathways through vast territories. This same logic holds true for the broader question of the role of localities under conditions of globalization. The vaster the uncertainties produced by capitalism, the more important it becomes to act collectively to create spaces (such as cooperatives) that are not directly subordinate to the logic of the market and to build places that reinforce and explore other sources of value and meaning. We should be careful about juxtaposing locality and cosmopolitanism. Spaces such as the chambers of labor actually challenged the political logic of territoriality (the nation state) and fostered identification with the international workers' movement. As Leslie Sklair points out, "Although capitalism is global, the only possible disruptions are local," that is, bound to a place.[8] Only utopian ideas do not have a locus because the term literally means "no place." Resistance necessarily occurs in the form of local guerrilla struggles that can sometimes attain global significance. It is unclear what it would mean to suggest that local struggles rooted in specific places could somehow be definitively superseded. Any meaningful challenge must contest a specific manifestation of the general structures of domination; only then can it transcend its context by serving as an inspiration, a model, a resource, or a link in a chain of similar struggles, which proliferate in response to broader structures of domination.

Fredric Jameson makes a similar argument in more abstract terms when he points to the dialectical relationship between the global and the local. He emphasizes that the very concepts of global and local are intrinsically linked through the structure of opposition. For Jameson it is impossible to even conceive of one except in relation to the other. The global makes no sense except as the convergence of different localities.[9] Jameson argues that this is another variation of Hegel's position in *The Encyclopaedia Logic*, where Hegel insists that the very concept of "identity" is meaningful only in so far as it is distinguished from "difference." Thus, the true nature of the dyad identity-difference is a totality expressed through conceptual interdependence.[10] The same is true of the global and local. One only makes sense as the limitation or boundary of the other.

It is important to note that the global and the local are not natural scales but theoretical constructs that emphasize different dimensions of the distribution of people and power into places. Globalization suggests the shifting of relations between different localities. It involves mitigating the degree of isolation, separation, and distinctiveness. This is not a reason to overlook the power of place. Instead, it is a reason for intensifying the search for new kinds of connections other than market relations. Acknowledging that globalization tears asunder traditional communities intensifies the need for investigating what kinds of spaces can serve as alternatives. Politics consists of the struggles to build replacements for disintegrating solidarities. The question is not whether reterritorialization will take place but who will decide what form it should take.

Today some of the favored "sites" for building new connections— e-mail, the Web, chat rooms, and list serves—are not spatial in the physical sense highlighted in this book. The importance of virtual communities and wired (or wireless) communication raises the question whether co-presence is really necessary in the Internet age. By 2003, however, the initial enthusiasm for the democratic and solidaristic possibilities of the Web has already cooled. Despite some prominent exceptions such as the Zapatistas' successful use of the Web to garner international visibility and support, the Web has become increasingly commercial and fragmented.[11] Even leaving aside the enormous digital divide, domestically and internationally, there are good reasons why the Internet will probably not fulfill the more optimistic prognostications. The anonymity of the Internet occludes accountability. Cass Sunstein worries that the hyperspecialization that computer technology facilitates will impoverish the diverse experiences that sustain a pluralistic culture. The Internet provides extensive choice but little direction; it offers exhaustive information but little synthesis. By making it easier to read news and analysis produced by like-minded people instead of subscribing to general interest forums such as the daily paper, the Internet reinforces rather than challenges our parochial worldviews.[12] A similar logic applies to social interactions. The Internet, with its chat rooms and list serves devoted to particular dog breeds or car makes, promotes this kind of hyperspecialization. By increasing our ability to filter out unchosen interactions with other people and ideas, the Internet approximates the logic of the private sphere more than that of the public. The possibility of involuntary exposure to new and surprising experiences declines when we interact exclusively with those who are like us. The effect of encountering a homeless person on the street, for example, cannot be approximated through an e-mail. In the presence of another human being we cannot simply press delete and make her go away. A pluralistic democracy requires experiences dealing with difference.

Although the Internet is useful for sharing information with members of a particular group, it is less effective at involving the unaffiliated and engaging those with different viewpoints. The Internet makes seductive advertising and detailed information more accessible, but it encourages the role of consumer rather than that of citizen. Although it is beyond the scope of this postscript to offer a complete analysis of the potential and limitations of the Internet, I think it is fair to conclude that virtual communities will not replace "bricks and mortar" community centers. The Internet will function admirably as a new form of linkage, but it will not replace the basic units of political and social life.

Are there places—similar to the chambers of labor, the houses of the people, and the cooperatives—that facilitate political education and engagement today? My intuition is that the answer is yes. This intuition is motivated not by research but by an experience that wakened my interest in political space several years before beginning this project. While living in Germany in the mid-1990s, I discovered a community center called the Alte Feuerwache (an old fire station). I went there for the first time when I had to repair my bike; a neighbor had told me that I could use tools from the workshop for free. There were also German classes, art studios, and seminars. The old brick building was surrounded by a huge courtyard, filled with salvaged café tables and sculptures. The first floor contained a room with high ceilings that was used as a bar and restaurant. Upstairs there were meeting rooms for community organizations, cultural groups, offices, and a theater. After fixing the bike I went back often, usually for a drink, but sometimes for a political meeting or concert. In the entrance, groups set up exhibitions or provided information about local events or issues such as German arms sales to Turkey. At the Alte Feuerwache, neighborhood residents, including the many foreigners, were all citizens in the etymological if not the legal sense of the term: free people with a right to the city.

Appendix 1
Sources

For the historical material in this volume, I relied primarily on the extensive secondary literature in Italian on associationalism, cooperation, municipal socialism, and working-class mobilization. This project is what historians would call a synthetic essay because it draws on the police reports, factory regulations, internal documents, and newspaper accounts uncovered by social historians.

In my research, I made use of two sources to supplement the secondary literature. First, I explored the collection of materials on working-class associationalism housed in the minor documents department of the Biblioteca Nazionale Centrale di Firenze. This archive, made up of 1,821 documents, includes statutes, legal papers, inaugural addresses, and other materials produced by cooperatives, mutual aid societies, chambers of labor, and resistance organizations. The collection focuses on materials printed between 1882 and 1922. Although records from northern Italy and Tuscany are overrepresented, the archive includes statutes from around the country. My analysis is based on a close reading of a randomly chosen sample of the documents available from sixty-five associations. I also looked at the contemporary accounts of socialist activists and intellectuals who both documented and interpreted the political mobilization of the pre-fascist period. These materials were published in the pages of socialist journals such as the *Critica Sociale* as well as in memoirs, pamphlets, and treatises.

The historical material in this project comes from Italy, with occasional discussions of developments in other countries that were important for understanding events in Italy. There are several reasons for focusing on Italy. First, the historiography of the Italian working-class movement has received little attention in English; therefore this lacuna provided an opportunity to bring the practices of pre-fascist Italy to a broader audience. Second, associationalism and cooperation have played a very visible role in Italy from the founding of the republic up to the present; therefore, Italian political theory and historiography provide resources for analyzing the popular public sphere. Finally, I believe the dynamics and practices considered in this book are not unique to Italy but are relevant to many countries on the margins of Europe and in the developing world, where capitalism is experienced as the effect of the penetration of the world market rather than the growth of industrialization.

The following is a list of the archival materials, primarily statutes, that I analyzed for this project. The materials are located in the Fonti Minori collection of the Biblioteca Nazionale Centrale di Firenze. The more accessible sources (newspapers, pamphlets, census figures, and published memoirs) are cited in footnotes.

Cooperatives (20)

Includes associations which list both mutualism and cooperation as their primary purpose.

Cooperative "Nazario Sauro" fra Carciatori, Scaricatori, e Marittimi (1922)
Società Cooperativa di Consumo e Soccorso Porta à Mare—Pisa (1911)
La Preservanza—Sezione Cooperativa delle Panche (1919)
Cooperative Sociale di Previdenza di San Niccolò (1910)
Fratellanza Artigiana d'Italia: Magazzino Cooperativo di Consumo di Peretola e Petriolo (1887)
Fratellanza Cooperativa di Consumo in Prato (1904)
Società Anonima di Cooperazione Economica di Granaiolo—Empoli (1910)
Società Anonima Cooperativa di Consumo fra gli Impiegati Ferroviari—Cecina (1886)
Cooperative di Produzione e Lavoro—Cooperative Sociale Costruttori Idraulici (1903)

Società Cooperativa Santa Croce al Pino e Dintorni (1900)
Società Cooperativa San Martino alla Palma (1889, revised 1909)
Società Operaia le Cure (1915)
La Fratellanza e Magazzino Cooperativo San Lorenzo à Vaccoli (1911)
Circolo Operaio Cooperativo della Unione in San Salvi (1890)
Unione Cooperativa Sestese—Sesto Fiorentino (1909)
Unione Operaia Cooperativa di Consumo di Firenze (1892)
Società fra gli Operai Seggiola, Pisa (1899)
Unione Cooperativa di Consumo Pontremoli (1898)
Associazione Generale fra i Coloni del Pistoiese (1919)
Società Cooperativa Consumo Scansano (1911)

Mutual Aid Societies (10)

Associazione di Mutua Assistenze Colletiva Fra i Soci Fascio Ferroviario—
    Pisa (1894)
La Previdente Operai Braccianti—Vicarello Pisano (1896)
Società Operaia di Mutuo Soccorso G. Garibaldi (1898)
Società Democratica Operaia di Mutuo Soccorso, Pisa (1887)
Associazione Operaia di Mutuo Soccorso Democratica—Vicopisano (1890)
Associazione di Mutuo Soccorso fra gli Agricolturi e gli Operai di San
    Lorenzo à Vaccoli (1896)
Fratellanza Artigiana—Gracciano (1915)
Società Operaia di Mutuo Soccorso—Scandicci (1894)
Circolo Operaio delle Nunziata—Società di Mutuo Soccorso (1885)
Fratellanza di Greve in Chianti (1890)

Chambers of Labor and Affiliated Sections (18)

Lega di Miglioramento Pasticcieri, Confettieri, e Affini—Livorno (1902)
Camera del Lavoro—Piombino (1910)
Lega di Resistenza fra Cuochi, Camerieri, Caffettieri e Affini—Pisa (1901)
Sezione Addetti alle Macchine—Livorno (1901)
Lega di Resistenza fra le Filatrici in Seta—Pistoia (1906)
Lega di Resistenza fra Operai Stoviglai (1901)
Sezione Cuochi, Camerieri, Cafferrieri—Firenze
Sezione Commessi e Impiegati d'Aziende Private—Firenze (1901)
Sezione Vetrai e Lavoratanti in Vetro—Firenze (1894)
Società Cooperativa Operai Esercenti l'Arte Muraria (1898)
Federazione Italiana dei Lavoranti in Legno (1901)

Cooperative fra Classificatori e Classificatrici di Stracci—Prato (1909)
Cooperative fra Lavoranti Sarti (1917)
Camera del Lavoro—Scandicci (1896)
Camera del Lavoro—Pistoia (1901)
Camera del Lavoro—Firenze, Sezione Intagliatori (1896)
Lega di Resistenza fra i Lavoranti in Granate—Larciano (1911)
Associazione tra i Lavoranti Trasporti e Communicazioni—Empoli (1893)

Miscellaneous and Political Associations (17)

Includes working-class, mixed, and bourgeois organizations.

Società Umanitaria Milano
Cassa di Sussidio alla Disoccupazione (1909)
Casa del Lavoro (1908)
General statutes (1893, revised 1910)
"Origine e Significato del Primo Maggio" (1925)
Federazione dei Circoli Operai della Regione Lombardia (1912)
Circolo Pensiero e Azione di Genova (1887)
Associazione Democratica Torie-Pellice (1909)
Circolo Politico Nazionale (1848)
Associazione Democratica Tortona (1903)
Circolo Studio e Lavoro—Luno (1896)
Federazione Provinciale Republicana Lucchese (1921)
Circolo Ricreativo Socialista—Livorno (1903)
Associazione Democratica Costituzionale "Italia e Casa Savoia"—Livorno
    (1908)
Associazione Liberale Monarchica (1891)
Associazione Patriottica Liberale Torinese (1876)
Casa dei Socialisti Massa (1901)
Circolo Socialista di Maschito Patenza (1903)
Circolo Socialista Massa Maritima (1896)
Circolo Operaio Piombino (1892)
Partito Socialista Anarchico—Federazione Carrarese (1902)

Appendix 2
Relations of Production in the Countryside

Province	Peasants (*contadini*)	Sharecroppers (*mezzadria*)	Renters (*affittuari*)	Laborers	
				Regular	Irregular
Bologna	2,886	41,387	3,595	8,039	39,852
Ferrara	915	1,433	595	9,122	24,746
Forlí	606	14,423	403	4,005	3,339
Modena	1,852	11,796	2,990	7,099	11,458
Parma	7,138	4,220	1,915	16,137	10,846
Piacenza	8,080	1,757	3,498	33,816	12,334
Ravenna	674	8,073	491	4,965	4,477
Reggio Emilia	8,915	10,386	4,509	24,052	12,218
Mantova	6,356	2,293	5,375	34,132	32,637
Bergamo	8,550	26,608	1,101	13,484	8,733
Brescia	7,740	8,245	2,310	17,649	23,677
Arezzo	6,464	61,421	143	11,062	13,791
Florence	3,488	54,649	1,386	23,553	14,469
Grosseto	7,297	1,590	177	13,662	11,328
Livorno	943	517	160	2,663	1,694
Lucca	16,150	14,605	6,248	29,115	15,064
Massa	8,634	3,398	241	10,541	6,366
Pisa	3,034	28,659	979	3,584	18,130
Siena	1,574	25,755	83	2,663	9,173
Ancona	3,866	58,418	781	14,254	16,949
Ascoli	4,412	17,512	102	5,565	4,141
Macerata	5,863	42,469	682	17,974	13,575
Pesaro	1,257	17,319	193	6,098	18,329
Perugia	4,776	29,627	285	33,977	14,357
Belluno	16,215	9,376	852	17,898	19,672

Province	Peasants (*contadini*)	Share croppers (*mezzadria*)	Renters (*affittuari*)	Laborers	
				Regular	Irregular
Urbino	4,848	17,024	165	8.808	5,237
Padova	6,488	1,192	24,945	48,397	35,025
Treviso	10,618	26,025	23,284	35,612	29,430
Udine	44,277	11,608	18,958	64,737	60,054
Venice	1,913	4,862	13,276	28,509	22,399
Verona	11,550	7,503	3,490	36,943	31,790
Vicenza	22,347	5,392	8,665	27,447	36,100
Rovigo	5,580	346	2,110	28,714	21,470

Source: Ministero di Agricoltura, Industria, e Commercio, *Censimento della populazione del regno d'Italia: Populazione classificata per condizioni e professioni* (Rome: Tipografica Bodoniana).

Appendix 3
Membership in the Chamber of Labor, 1907 and 1909

Region	1907			1909		
	Chambers	Sections	Members	Chambers	Sections	Members
Piedmont	14	277	31,746	13	271	37,219
Liguria	6	156	32,423	6	181	22,229
Lombardy	13	441	48,423	17	645	83,430
Veneto	5	74	11,340	8	143	14,036
Emilia-Romagna	13	1,247	143,888	16	1,549	186,551
Tuscany	14	322	27,034	14	400	31,193
Marches	2	50	5,241	3	71	7,321
Umbria	2	44	4,616	1	23	4,997
Latium	2	86	8,361	2	132	10,986
Abruzzi	—	—	—	2	22	2,631
Campania	5	120	19,348	7	137	22,724
Puglia	3	61	16,419	5	95	34,381
Basilicata	—	—	—	—	—	—
Calabria	2	17	1,403	1	13	768
Sicily	3	137	36,738	2	145	42,266
Sardinia	—	—	—	1	7	506

Source: Richard Bachi, *L'Italia economica nell'anno 1909* (Turin: Società Tipografico Editrice Nazionale, 1910).
Note: The dashes indicate that there were no chambers of labor in the region at the time.

Appendix 4
Socialist Administrations by Region, 1914 and 1920

Region	Socialist Communes		Socialist Provinces
	1914	1920	1920
Piedmont	100	463	2
Liguria	10	54	0
Lombardy	150	651	5
Veneto	31	220	3
Emilia-Romagna	86	217	7
Tuscany	12	154	6
Marches	1	62	1
Umbria	5	54	1
Latium	4	40	0
Abruzzi and Molise	3	55	0
Campania	2	22	0
Puglia	18	44	0
Basilicata	6	5	0
Calabria	6	41	0
Sicily	4	21	0
Sardinia	5	12	0
TOTAL	451	2,115	25
Percentage Socialist (%)	5.44	25.34	36.23

Source: Marizio Ridolfi, *Il PSI e la nascita del partito di massa, 1892–1922*
(Rome: Laterza, 1992), 72–76.

NOTES

Chapter 1. Introduction

1. See Marcel Henoff and Tracy B. Strong, eds., *Public Space and Democracy* (Minneapolis: University of Minnesota Press, 2001).

2. Setha M. Low, "Cultural Meaning of the Plaza: The History of the Spanish-American Gridplan-Plaza in Urban Design," in *The Cultural Meaning of Urban Space*, ed. Robert Rotenberg and Gary McDonogh (Westport, Conn.: Bergin and Garvey, 1993), 75.

3. Maurice Halbwachs, *The Collective Memory* (New York: Harper and Row, 1980).

4. Richard Sennett, *The Conscience of the Eye: The Design and Social Life of Cities* (New York: Norton, 1990).

5. As Pierre Bourdieu argues, learning does not necessarily pass through discourse in order to become part of knowledge. Bourdieu used an extensive discussion of the Kabyle home to illustrate how spatial configuration serves social reproduction. Through spatialization, social distinctions appear as part of the natural world. Pierre Bourdieu, *Outline of a Theory of Practice* (Cambridge: Cambridge University Press, 1977); idem, *The Logic of Practice*, trans. R. Nice (Cambridge: Polity Press, 1990).

6. In this book, space signifies an internally structured domain of experience, flexibly demarcated from the outside. Place is a synonym for space, connoting a slightly greater degree of particularity. This formulation is influenced by the definition of the term *field* offered in Bernhard Waldenfels, *Order in the Twilight* (Athens: Ohio University Press, 1996), 29.

7. See especially Bourdieu, *Theory of Practice*. For a more general philosophical discussion of the phenomenology of space, I found Maurice Merleau-Ponty, *Phenomenology of Perception*, trans. Colin Smith (London: Routledge and Kegan Paul, 1962), very useful.

8. Henri Lefebvre, *The Production of Space*, trans. Donald Nicholson-Smith (London: Basil Blackwell), 137.

9. Michel de Certeau, *The Practice of Everyday Life* (Berkeley: University of California, 1988), 99.

10. Peter Katz, *The New Urbanism: Toward an Architecture of Community* (New York: Mc-Graw-Hill, 1994). For a more critical view, see Keally McBride, "Consuming Community," *Socialist Review* 28 (2001): 3, 4.

11. Cited in Fred Dallmayr, *Twilight of Subjectivity: Contributions to a Post-Individualist Theory of Politics* (Amherst: University of Massachusetts Press, 1981), 51.

12. William Connolly, *Why I Am Not a Secularist* (Minneapolis: University of Minnesota Press, 1999).

13. Bourdieu, *Logic of Practice*, 66–76.

14. Michel Foucault, in *Archeology of Knowledge* (New York: Pantheon, 1972), identifies discourse as a level between the formal principles of language and the abstract realm of ideas. Discourse denotes particular rules that regulate the production of meaningful statements in a given context. See also Thomas Dumm, *Michel Foucault and the Politics of Freedom* (Thousand Oaks, Calif.: Sage, 1996).

15. For example, Foucault wrote, "But as the establishment of a relation, in medical discourse, between a number of distinct elements, some of which concerned the status of doctors, others the institutional and technical site from which they spoke, others their position as subjects perceiving, observing, describing, teaching, etc. It can be said that this relation between different elements is effected by clinical discourse: it is this, as a practice, that established between them all a system of relations that is not 'really' given or constituted *a priori* . . . not verbal phenomenon of expression, but condition for emergence; not product of speaker but condition of possibility of speech" (*Archeology of Knowledge*, 52).

16. For an excellent discussion of the different types of democratic effects, see Mark Warren, *Democracy and Association* (Princeton: Princeton University Press, 2001).

17. This definition differs slightly from the one offered in Mark Warren, "What Should We Expect from More Democracy: Radically Democratic Responses to Politics," *Political Theory* 24, no. 2 (1996): 241–70. Warren agrees that radical democrats seek empowerment "in the institutions that most directly affect their everyday lives." My definition, however, emphasizes the acquisition of political power over personal transformation.

18. C. Douglas Lummis, *Radical Democracy* (Ithaca: Cornell University Press, 1996).

19. Chantal Mouffe, *The Return of the Political* (London: Verso, 1993), 18.

20. Benjamin Barber, *Strong Democracy: Participation Politics for a New Age* (Berkeley: University of California Press, 1984).

21. Robert Dahl, *A Preface to Economic Democracy* (Berkeley: University of California Press, 1985); Samuel Bowles and Herbert Gintis, *Democracy and Capitalism* (New York: Basic Books, 1986); Carol Pateman, *Participation and Democratic Theory* (Cambridge: Cambridge University Press, 1970); David Miller, *Market, State, and Community: Theoretical Foundations of Market Socialism* (Oxford: Clarendon Press, 1989).

22. Anna Marie Smith, *Laclau and Mouffe: The Radical Democratic Imaginary* (London and New York: Routledge, 1998).

23. Ernesto Laclau and Chantal Mouffe, *Hegemony and Socialist Strategy: Towards a Radical Democracy Politics* (London: Verso, 1985), 152–59. On the humanist language used by nineteenth-century French workers, see Jacques Rancière, *The Nights of Labor: The Workers' Dream in Nineteenth-Century France* (Philadelphia: Temple University Press, 1989).

24. The term *radicalism* was used more frequently in the early 1800s. Gareth Stedman Jones argues that a central tenet of English radicalism in the eighteenth and nineteenth centuries was the attribution of evil and misery to political sources. Radicals identified the salient political cleavage as the line dividing the represented from the unrepresented rather than the capitalist from the worker; Jones, "Rethinking Chartism," in *Languages of Class: Studies in English Working Class History, 1832–1982* (Cambridge: Cambridge University Press, 1983), 105.

25. Roberto Unger makes a similar point in *False Necessity: Anti-Necessitarian Social Theory in the Service of Radical Democracy* (Cambridge: Cambridge University Press, 1987).

26. In a later essay, Ernesto Laclau argues that it is possible to build "chains of equiva-

lence" through struggles over the terms of universals such as democracy or citizenship. See Laclau, *Emancipation(s)* (London and New York: Verso, 1996).

27. In this study I use Gramsci's term "subaltern classes" and the plural "working classes" interchangeably. Although I want to evoke the centrality of economic position for political identity and power, I also want to emphasize the heterogeneity and diversity of workers.

28. For a concise overview of the different influential strands of democratic theory, see David Held, *Models of Democracy* (New York: Polity, 1986).

29. Because the goal of this project is to understand how space serves a progressive or democratic political project, I do not focus on the fascist period, a period characterized by the violent and absolute repression of the entire spectrum of democratic practices from social movements to free elections. For an interesting study of the relationship between public space, mass spectacle, and fascist ideology, see Mabel Berezin, *Making the Fascist Self: The Political Culture of Interwar Italy* (Ithaca: Cornell University Press, 1997).

30. See Robert Putnam, *Making Democracy Work: Civic Traditions in Modern Italy* (Princeton: Princeton University Press, 1993); Margaret Kohn, "Civic Republicanism versus Social Struggle: A Gramscian Approach to Associationalism in Italy," *Political Power and Social Theory* 13 (1999): 201–35; Tamara Simoni, "Il rendimento istituzionale delle regioni, 1990–1994," *Polis* 11, no. 3 (1997): 417–36.

31. Antonio Gramsci, "The Study of Philosophy," in *Selections from the Prison Notebooks*, ed. and trans. Quintin Hoare and Geoffrey Nowell Smith (New York: International Publishers, 1971), 341: "Mass adhesion or non-adhesion to an ideology is the real critical test of the rationality and historicity of modes of thinking. Any arbitrary constructions are pretty rapidly eliminated by historical competition, even if sometimes, through a combination of immediately favorable circumstances, they manage to enjoy a popularity of a kind."

32. Walter Benjamin, "Theses on the Philosophy of History," in *Illuminations*, ed. Hannah Arendt (New York: Schocken Books, 1968), 254–55.

33. Martin Jay, *The Dialectical Imagination: A History of the Frankfurt School and the Institute of Social Research, 1923–1950* (Boston: Little, Brown, 1973).

34. For a good introduction, see David Couzens Hoy and Thomas McCarthy, *Critical Theory* (Cambridge, Mass.: Blackwell, 1994); Axel Honneth, "The Social Dynamics of Disrespect: On the Location of Critical Theory Today," *Constellations* 1, no. 2 (1994): 255–69.

35. For an excellent discussion of the similarities and differences between critical theory and genealogy, see Thomas McCarthy, "The Critique of Impure Reason: Foucault and the Frankfurt School," in *Ideals and Illusions: On Reconstruction and Deconstruction in Contemporary Critical Theory* (Cambridge: MIT Press, 1994). For an excellent introduction to critical theory, see Susan Buck-Morss, *Origins of Negative Dialectics: Theodore W. Adorno, Walter Benjamin and the Frankfurt Institute* (New York: Free Press, 1977).

36. See Seyla Benhabib, *Critique, Norm, and Utopian: A Study of the Foundations of Critical Theory* (New York: Columbia University Press, 1986), 34.

37. This method reflects Walter Benjamin's statement that "historical materialism wishes to retain that image of the past which unexpectedly appears to man singled out by history at a moment of danger" ("Theses on the Philosophy of History," 255).

38. Michel Foucault, "Two Lectures," in *Power/Knowledge: Selected Interviews and Other Writings, 1972–1977*, ed. Colin Gordon (New York: Pantheon, 1980), 83.

Chapter 2. Space and Politics

1. Wendy Brown, "Feminist Hesitations, Postmodern Exposures," *Differences* 3, no. 1: 63–84.

2. Jean-Jacques Rousseau, *Politics and the Arts: Letter to M. d'Alembert on the Theater,*

trans. and ed. Allan Bloom (Ithaca: Cornell University Press, 1960), 16–17. See also Paul Thomas and David Lloyd, *Culture and the State* (New York: Routledge, 1998).

3. Michael Walzer, "The Communitarian Critique of Liberalism," *Political Theory* 18, 1: 6–23; Michael Sandel, *Liberalism and the Limits of Justice* (Cambridge: Cambridge University Press, 1982); Amitai Etzioni, *The Essential Communitarian Reader* (New York: Rowman and Littlefield, 1998), Robert Bellah, *Habits of the Heart: Individualism and Commitment in American Life* (Berkeley: University of California Press, 1985).

4. Bonnie Honig, *Political Theory and the Displacement of Politics* (Ithaca: Cornell University Press, 1993); William Connolly, *The Ethos of Pluralization* (Minneapolis: University of Minnesota Press, 1995). For example, William Connolly criticizes a nostalgic politics of place for assuming a correspondence "between the scope of common troubles and a territorial place of action to form the essence of democratic politics"; Connolly, "Democracy and Territoriality," *Millennium: Journal of International Studies* 20, no. 3 (1991): 464. See the postscript for a more detailed discussion of the relation of the local in an era of globalization.

5. Hannah Arendt, *The Human Condition* (Chicago: University of Chicago Press, 1958), 194.

6. Sheldon Wolin, *Politics and Vision: Continuity and Innovation in Western Political Thought* (Boston and Toronto: Little, Brown, 1960), 7.

7. These distinctions are a slightly adapted version of the discussion in David Harvey, *Justice, Nature, and the Geography of Difference* (Oxford: Blackwell, 1996), 208.

8. See George Mosse, *The Nationalization of the Masses: Political Symbolism and Mass Movements in Germany from the Napoleonic Wars through the Third Reich* (New York: Howard Fertig, 1975).

9. Charles Tilly, "Spaces of Contention," *Mobilization* 5 (2000): 135–60. See Aldon Morris, *The Origins of the Civil Rights Movement: Black Communities Organizing for Change* (New York: Free Press, 1984), for a discussion of movement halfway houses.

10. James C. Scott, *Domination and the Arts of Resistance: Hidden Transcripts* (New Haven: Yale University Press, 1990), 118. See also Sara Evans and Harry C. Boyte, *Free Spaces: The Sources of Democratic Change in America* (New York: Harper and Row, 1986); Robert Couto, "Narrative, Free Space, and Political Leadership in Social Movements," *Journal of Politics* 55 (1993): 57–79; Eric Hirsch, "Protest Movements and Urban Theory," *Research in Urban Sociology* 3 (1993): 159–80; William Gamson, "Safe Spaces and Social Movements," *Perspectives on Social Problems* 8 (1996): 27–38.

11. See the classic work by Jane Jacobs, *The Life and Death of American Cities* (New York: Vintage, 1961); Iris Marion Young, "The Ideal of Community and the Politics of Difference," in *Feminism/Postmodernism*, ed. Linda Nicholson (New York: Routledge, 1990).

12. Cited in Dolores Hayden, *Redesigning the American Dream: The Future of Housing, Work, and the Family* (New York and London: Norton, 1984), 101.

13. Gaston Bachelard, *The Poetics of Space* (Boston: Beacon Press, 1994).

14. For a revealing discussion of the relationship between the planning of domestic space and the modernist agenda of social transformation, see James Holston, *The Modernist City: An Anthropological Critique of Brasilia* (Chicago: University of Chicago Press, 1989).

15. Bachelard, *Poetics of Space*, 3.

16. Harvey, *Justice, Nature, and the Geography of Difference*.

17. Hayden, *Redesigning the American Dream*.

18. Robert Fishman, "Bourgeois Utopias," in *Readings in Urban Theory*, ed. Susan Fainstein and Scott Campell (New York: Blackwell, 1997), 23–60. See also Mike Davis, *City of Quartz: Excavating the Future in Los Angeles* (New York: Vintage Books, 1992).

19. See Gregory D. Squires, "Partnership and the Pursuit of the Private City," in *Readings in Urban Theory*, ed. Susan Fainstein and Scott Campell (New York: Blackwell, 1997), 266–90; Susan Bickford, "Constructing Inequality: The Purification of Social Space and the Architecture of Citizenship," *Political Theory* 28, no. 3 (2000): 355–77.

20. Michel Foucault, *Discipline and Punish: The Birth of the Prison* (New York: Vintage Books, 1979), 24.

21. See Edward Casey, *The Fate of Place: A Philosophical History* (Berkeley: University of California Press, 1997); Henri Lefebvre, *The Production of Space*, trans. Donald Nicholson-Smith (London: Basil Blackwell); Richard Sennett, *Flesh and Stone: The Body and the City in Western Civilization* (New York: Norton, 1994).

22. Foucault wrote that "a whole history remains to be written of spaces—which would at the same time be the history of powers (both these terms in the plural)—from the great strategies of geo-politics to the little tactics of the habitat . . . passing via economic and political installations"; Michel Foucault, "The Eye of Power," in *Power/Knowledge: Selected Interviews and Other Writings, 1972–1977*, ed. Colin Gordon (New York: Pantheon Books, 1980), 149.

23. Marshall Berman, *All That Is Solid Melts into Air: The Experience of Modernity* (New York: Penguin, 1988).

24. For an excellent critique of Laclau's position, see Doreen Massey, *Space, Place, and Gender* (Minneapolis: University of Minnesota Press, 1994), 249–55.

25. Ernesto Laclau, *New Reflections of the Revolution of Our Time* (London: Verso, 1990), 68.

26. Cited in Kristin Ross, *The Emergence of Social Space: Rimbaud and the Paris Commune* (Minneapolis: University of Minnesota Press, 1988), 8.

27. Jacques Derrida writes, "Levinas also intends to show that true exteriority is not spatial, for space is the Site of the Same. Which means that the Site is always a site of the Same"; Derrida, *Writing and Difference*, trans. Alan Bass (Chicago: University of Chicago Press, 1978), 112. See also Martin Jay, *Downcast Eyes: The Denigration of Vision in Twentieth-Century French Thought* (Berkeley: University of California Press, 1994). Although the focus of the book is vision, Jay notes that many theorists denigrated the fixity of the visual image that they conflated with space. For a complete analysis of the hostility to place in Enlightenment thought, see Casey, *Fate of Place*.

28. Michel de Certeau, *The Practice of Everyday Life* (Berkeley: University of California Press, 1984), 34–36.

29. Ibid., 36.

30. Ibid., 35.

31. Ibid., 93.

32. Ibid., 103.

33. Laclau, *New Reflections*, 41.

34. Massey, *Space, Place, and Gender*.

35. Laclau recognizes this possibility, stating that "the representation of time as a cyclical succession . . . is in this sense a reduction of time to space. Any teleological conception of change is therefore also essentially spatialist" (*New Reflections*, 42). I contend that this admission invalidates the distinction between space and time; both have elements of fixity and disruption.

36. See Berman, *All That Is Solid Melts into Air*, 131–72. See also Ross, *Emergence of Social Space*.

37. Guy Debord, "Theory of the Derive," in *Situationist International Anthology*, ed. and trans. Ken Knabb (Berkeley: Bureau of Public Secrets, 1981), 50.

38. This is analogous to the principle behind Michel Foucault's archeological method as outlined in Foucault, *The Archeology of Knowledge* (New York: Pantheon Books, 1972), 41.

39. Michel Foucault, "Two Lectures," in *Power/Knowledge*, 78–108.

40. For an excellent critique of the concept of the Third World, see A. Ahmed, *In Theory: Classes, Nations, Literatures* (London: Verso, 1992).

41. "Pro-Cooperazione," *Giustizia* (Reggio Emilia), Dec. 9, 1906. Unless otherwise noted, all translations from the French and Italian are my own.

42. Jacques Greux, *Peuple*, special edition, April 1899. I thank Nicole de Coteau for help translating this passage.

43. "Pro-Cooperazione," n.p.

Chapter 3. The Bourgeois Public Sphere

1. Carlo Goldoni, *The Coffee-House: A Comedy in Three Acts*, trans. Henry B. Fuller (New York: Samuel French, n.d.). Further evidence that Goldoni is parodying the cross-class contact of the café is the following statement, made by the café-proprietor's servant on the first page of the play's text: "Really, it is enough to make a man burst with laughter to see even the porters coming to drink their coffee" (7–8).
2. Ibid., 11.
3. Jürgen Habermas, *The Structural Transformation of the Public Sphere: An Inquiry into a Category of Bourgeois Society* (Cambridge: MIT Press, 1991), 32–33.
4. Jürgen Habermas, "The Public Sphere: An Encyclopedia Article (1964)," *New German Critique* 3 (1974): 49.
5. John Timbs, *Clubs and Club Life in London* (London: Chatto and Windus, 1899), 215, 299.
6. Ibid., 232.
7. Jodi Dean, "Publicity's Secret," *Political Theory* 29, no. 5 (2001): 624–49.
8. Habermas, *Structural Transformation*, 35.
9. J. M. Roberts, *The Mythology of the Secret Societies* (New York: Charles Scribner's Sons, 1972); Ira Wade, *The Clandestine Organization and Diffusion of Philosophic Ideas in France from 1700 to 1750* (Princeton: Princeton University Press, 1938); Margaret Jacob, *The Radical Enlightenment: Pantheists, Freemasons and Republicans* (London: George Allen and Unwin, 1981).
10. I follow the convention of using the term *speculative Masonry* to distinguish the largely bourgeois/aristocratic lodges from their precursors, "operative" Masonic lodges that were essentially guilds of practicing artisans.
11. The Latin root *corporare* means "to form into a body" and was used to describe society as an organic and unitary entity.
12. Mary Ann Clawson, *Constructing Brotherhood: Class, Gender, and Fraternalism* (Princeton: Princeton University Press, 1989), 38.
13. Roberts, *Mythology of the Secret Societies*, 99.
14. Jacob, *Radical Enlightenment*. One of the appeals of Masonry was its cosmopolitanism. Lessing, in "Die Gespräche über Freimaurerei," arges that the main purpose of Masonry is to counterbalance the divisive effects of nationalism and parochialism. This is also reflected in Masonic documents, such as the Records of the Chapter-General of the Knights of Jubiliation at Gaillardin (1710).
15. There is some doubt about what actually constituted the "higher teachings," since there is even less documentary evidence. John Rath argues that the higher levels included a vow to "cooperate in the destruction of tyrants and despots" rather than to uphold "sentiments of virtue and respect for the law," as required of the apprentices; R. John Rath, "The Carbonari: Their Origins, Initiation Rites and Aims," *American Historical Review* 69, no. 2 (1964): 362.
16. *Memoirs of the Secret Societies of the South of Italy, Particularly the Carbonari* (London: John Murray, 1821), 69.
17. Rath, "Carbonari," 353–56. See also the chapter titled "The Secret World" in Rath, *The Provisional Austrian Regime in Lombardy-Venetia, 1814–1815* (Austin: University of Texas Press, 1969), 190–242.
18. George T. Romani, *The Neapolitan Revolution of 1820–1821* (Evanston, Ill.: Northwestern University Press, 1950).
19. The first statement comes from a document found in the Venetian archives, cited in Rath, "Carbonari," 367; the second comes from a document cited in *Memoirs of the Secret Societies of the South of Italy*, 95.
20. Rath, "Carbonari," 370.
21. *Memoirs of the Secret Societies of the South of Italy*, 54.
22. There are scholars who question whether the public sphere ever existed, at least in its

idealized form. See Michael Schudson, "Was There Ever a Public Sphere? If So, When? Reflections on the American Case," in *Habermas and the Public Sphere*, ed. Craig Calhoun (Cambridge: MIT Press, 1992), 143–63; Wolfgang Jaeger, *Öffentlichkeit und Parlamentarismus. Eine Kritik an Jürgen Habermas* (Stuttgart, n.d.), 14.

23. Oskar Negt and Alexander Kluge, *The Public Sphere and Experience: Toward an Analysis of the Bourgeois and Proletarian Public Sphere* (Minneapolis: University of Minnesota Press, 1993); Pierre Bourdieu, *Language and Symbolic Power* (Cambridge: Harvard University Press, 1991).

24. Jürgen Habermas, "Some Further Reflections on the Public Sphere," in Calhoun, *Habermas and the Public Sphere*, 425.

25. See Nancy Fraser, "Rethinking the Public Sphere: A Contribution to the Critique of Actually Existing Democracy," in Calhoun, *Habermas and the Public Sphere*, 116.

26. My discussion focuses on the political inclusion of the working classes. On gender, see Mary Ryan, "Gender and Public Access: Women's Politics in Nineteenth Century America," in Calhoun, *Habermas and the Public Sphere*, 259–88; Catherine Hall, "Private Persons versus Public Someones: Class, Gender and Politics in England, 1780–1850," in *Language, Gender, and Childhood*, ed. Carolyn Steedman, Cathy Unwin, and Valerie Walkerdine (London: Routledge and Kegan Paul, 1985).

27. Habermas, *Structural Transformation*, xviii.

28. Ibid., 177.

29. Since E. P. Thompson's pathbreaking work, this literature has become extensive. Some of the most prominent examples include the following: E. P. Thompson, *The Making of the English Working Class* (New York: Penguin, 1968); William Sewell, *Work and Revolution in France: The Language of Labor from the Old Regime to 1848* (Cambridge: Cambridge University Press, 1980); Maurice Agulhon, *Marianne into Battle: Republican Imagery and Symbolism in France, 1789–1880*, trans. Janet Lloyd (Cambridge: Cambridge University Press, 1981); idem, "Working Class and Sociability in France before 1848," in *The Power of the Past: Essays for Eric Hobsbawn*, ed. Pat Thane, Geoffrey Crossick, and Roderick Floud (Cambridge: Cambridge University Press, 1984); Joan Scott, "Popular Theater and Socialism in Late-Nineteenth-Century France," in *Political Symbolism in Modern Europe*, ed. Seymour Drescher, David Sabean, and Allan Sharlin (New Brunswick, N.J.: Transaction, 1982), 197–215; Alain Cottereau, "The Distinctiveness of Working-Class Cultures in France, 1848–1900, in *Working-Class Formation: Nineteenth-Century Patterns in Western Europe and the United States*, ed. Ira Katznelson and Aristide R. Zolberg (Princeton: Princeton University Press, 1986), 111–54; John Merriman, *The Red City: Limoges and the French Nineteenth Century* (New York: Oxford University Press, 1985); John Merriman, ed., *Consciousness and Class Experience in Nineteenth-Century Europe* (New York: Holmes and Meier Publishers, 1979).

30. Maurice Agulhon, *The Republic in the Village: The People of the Var from the French Revolution to the Second Republic*, trans. Janet Lloyd (Cambridge: Cambridge University Press, 1977). See also Maurice Agulhon and Maryvonne Bodiguel, *Les associations au village* (Le Paradou: Actes Sud, 1981); and Maurice Agulhon, *Le cercle dans la France bourgeoisie, 1810–1848: Étude d'une mutation de sociabilité* (Paris: A. Colin, 1977).

31. Günther Lottes, *Politische Aufklaerung und Plebejisches Publikum: Zur Theorie und Praxis des englischen Radikalismus im späten 18. Jahrhundert* (Oldenburg, 1979), 216.

32. E. P. Thompson, "Patrician Society, Plebian Culture," *Journal of Social History* 7, no. 3 (1974): 399–401.

33. Habermas, *Structural Transformation*, 176.

34. See Guy Debord, *The Society of the Spectacle* (New York: Zone Books, 1995).

35. See Jürgen Habermas, *Theory of Communicative Action*, vol. 1, trans. Thomas McCarthy (Boston: Beacon Press, 1984); idem, "Legitimation Problems in the Modern State" and "What Is Universal Pragmatics," in *Communication and the Evolution of Society*, trans. Thomas McCarthy (Boston: Beacon Press, 1979); idem, "A Reply to My Critics," in *Habermas: Critical Debates*, ed. John B. Thompson and David Held (London: Macmil-

lan, 1982); idem, *Between Facts and Norms: Contributions to a Discourse Theory of Law and Democracy*, trans. William Rehg (Cambridge: MIT Press, 1996).

36. The literature on this topic is vast. An excellent overview can be found in the following secondary sources: Thomas McCarthy, *The Critical Theory of Jürgen Habermas* (Cambridge: MIT Press, 1978); Maeve Cooke, *Language and Reason: A Study of Habermas's Universal Pragmatics* (Cambridge: MIT Press, 1994); William Rehg, *Insight and Solidarity: The Discourse Ethics of Jürgen Habermas* (Berkeley: University of California Press, 1997); Simone Chambers, *Reasonable Democracy: Jürgen Habermas and the Politics of Discourse* (Ithaca: Cornell University Press, 1996).

37. Habermas, *Between Facts and Norms*; idem, *The Inclusion of the Other: Essays in Political Theory* (Cambridge: MIT Press, 1998).

38. Seyla Benhabib, "Toward a Deliberative Model of Democratic Legitimacy," in *Democracy and Difference*, ed. Seyla Benhabib (Princeton: Princeton University Press, 1996); Chambers, *Reasonable Democracy*; James Bohman, *Public Deliberation: Pluralism, Complexity, and Democracy* (Cambridge: MIT Press, 1996).

39. Habermas, *Structural Transformation*, 27.

40. Anthony Giddens, *The Constitution of Society: Outline of the Theory of Structuration* (Berkeley and Los Angeles: University of California Press, 1984), 122–26.

41. Habermas, *Structural Transformation*, 51.

42. Richard Sennett, *The Fall of Public Man* (New York: Knopf, 1977).

43. Habermas, *Structural Transformation*, 51.

44. Negt and Kluge, *Public Sphere and Experience*, 38–39.

45. Charles Tilly makes a similar argument in "Spaces of Contention," *Mobilization* 5 (2000): 135–60.

46. Negt and Kluge, *Public Sphere and Experience*, 39.

Chapter 4. The Disciplinary Factory

1. Adam Smith, *An Inquiry into the Nature and Causes of the Wealth of Nations* (Chicago: University of Chicago Press, 1976), esp. 302–19. Smith's nuanced reflections on the impact of the division of labor are especially prominent in book 5.

2. Marx and Gramsci are the focus of this chapter. For an interesting discussion of Lenin on the factory, see Vladimir Lenin, "Immediate Tasks of the Soviet Government," in *The Lenin Anthology*, ed. Robert Tucker (New York: Norton, 1975); James Scoville, "The Taylorization of Vladimir Ilich Lenin," *Industrial Relations* 40, no. 4 (2001): 620–26; James Scott, *Seeing Like a State: How Certain Schemes to Improve the Human Condition Have Failed* (New Haven: Yale University Press, 1998), 147–80.

3. For an excellent study of the diverse nature of work sites (as well as labor markets, production processes, and labor relations), see Chris Tilly and Charles Tilly, *Work under Capitalism* (Boulder: Westview Press, 1998).

4. Marx's criticisms of utopian socialism are found in the *1844 Manuscripts* and *The Holy Family*. In a similar vein, Marx writes in a September 1843 letter to Ruge, "Two facts cannot be denied; religion and politics. . . . No matter how these may be, we must begin with them, not oppose them with any one fixed system, as for example the *Voyage to Icaria* [by Etienne Cabet]"; Marx, *Writings of the Young Marx on Philosophy and Society*, ed. Lloyd D. Easton and Kurt H. Guddat (Garden City, N.Y.: Anchor Books, 1967), 213.

5. Karl Marx and Friedrich Engels, *The German Ideology* (New York: International Publishers, 1970), 53.

6. Friedrich Engels, *The Condition of the Working Class in England in 1844* (New York: Macmillan, 1958), 12.

7. Karl Marx and Friedrich Engels, *The Communist Manifesto*, in *The Marx-Engels Reader*, 2d ed., ed. Robert C. Tucker (New York: Norton, 1978), 479.

8. Ibid.

9. Karl Marx, *Capital*, vol. 1, in Tucker, *Marx-Engels Reader*, 409.

10. Marx and Engels, *Communist Manifesto*, 480.

11. Developments that seem to belie Marx's prediction include the rise of a professional and managerial middle class, the persistence of small farming in agriculture, and the expansion of outsourcing, subcontracting, and home production along with large-scale heavy industry. After Eduard Bernstein's pathbreaking *Evolutionary Socialism* (New York: Schocken Books, 1961), the literature on this topic was extensive.

12. Marx, *Capital*, 407.

13. Cited in C. Douglas Lummis, *Radical Democracy* (Ithaca: Cornell University Press, 1996), 82.

14. See, for example, David Montgomery, *Workers' Control in America* (Cambridge: Cambridge University Press, 1979).

15. Most of the specific details cited in the subsequent section come from socialist newspapers (especially the column "The Prison of the Factory"), studies performed by the Milan nonprofit organization Umanitaria, or government reports. Some of the most appalling details, especially regarding unsafe and unsanitary working conditions, I do not summarize here because they are only marginally related to the topic.

16. Unless otherwise specified, the following examples of discipline in the factory are drawn from Stefano Merli, *Proletariato di fabbrica e capitalismo industriale. Il caso italiano: 1880–1900* (Florence: Nuova Italia, 1972), 146–241. All translations from the Italian are my own. For example, see "Per l'onore delle nostre operaie," *Eva* (Ferrara), Oct. 6, 1901; *Unione diocesana di Bergamo, primo saggio d'inchiesta industriale* (Bergamo, 1900).

17. Giuseppe Berta documents how the introduction of the factory system in Biella served as a barrier to the formation of political and economic organizations. See "Dalla manifattura al sistéma di fabbrica: Razionalizzazione e conflitti di lavoro," in *Storia d'Italia*, vol. 1, *Dal feudalismo al capitalismo* (Turin: Einaudi, 1978).

18. Ministero di Agricolture, Industria, e Commercio, *Sul lavoro dei fanciulli e delle donne* (Rome, 1880), 402. Also, for a good overview of factory regulations in this period, see *I rapporti tra lavoranti e imprenditori nei regolamenti di discipline per gli stabilimenti sociali* (Milan, 1903), 14.

19. "Lo stato e l'industria in Italia," *Gazzetta dei Cappellai*, Sept. 1, 1897.

20. "Nei reclusori dell'industria," *Ragione* (Bari), Nov. 1 and 8, 1903.

21. Cotonificio Legler Hefti, *Regolamento generale* (Bergamo, 1893), 8.

22. *Regolamento per la classe operaia addetta alla manifatture nazionali dei tabacchi nelle province toscane* (Florence, 1861).

23. *Lotta di classe*, Oct. 9–10, 1897. *Regolamento per gli operai della Fonderia Negroni di Bologna* (Bologna, 1898), 5.

24. *Rapporti tra lavoranti e imprenditori nei regolamento*, 25.

25. *Corriere Biellese*, Oct. 30, 1901.

26. "Regolamento degli stabilimenti industriali di Rivarolo Ligure," reported in *Nei reclusori delle industrie*, cited in Merli, *Proletariato di fabbrica*, 164.

27. "Un'orgaizzaione operaia femminile in formazione," *Difesa delle Lavoratrici* (Milan), Dec. 8, 1912.

28. *Regolamento disciplinare per il personale addetto alla Officina Galileo* (Florence, 1884), pt. 3, article 51, as cited in Merli, *Proletariato di fabbrica*, 165. See also G. Procacci and G. Rindi, "Storia di una fabbrica. Le 'Officine Galileo' di Firenze," *Movimento Operaio*, January 1954.

29. Merli, *Proletariato di fabbrica*, 164.

30. Ibid., 165.

31. *Fascio Operaio* (Milan), July 2–3, 1887, as cited ibid., 156.

32. Merli, *Proletariato di fabbrica*, 166.

33. Cited ibid.

34. Speech given on Mar. 18, 1902, as cited ibid., 241.

35. Donald Howard Bell, *Sesto San Giovanni: Workers, Culture, and Politics in an Italian Town, 1880–1922* (New Brunswick, N.J.: Rutgers University Press, 1986), 24.

36. Ibid.

37. Cartiere Fasana, Gemonio, e Trevisago, *Regolamento per gli operai* (Varese, 1889), 6, specifies a fifty-cent fine for leaving one's assigned post; cited in Merli, *Proletariato di fabbrica*, 158.

38. C. Brielli, *Osservazioni spase sulla trattura* (Milan, 1886).

39. "Echi delle fabbriche," *Gazzetta dei cappellai* (Milan), Nov. 1, 1897.

40. "L'inchiesta del Sindaco di Cremona sulle filatrici della filanda Trissino ex Guerri," *L'Eco del Popolo* (Cremona), Sept. 20–21, 1896; cited in Merli, *Proletariato di fabbrica*, 172.

41. E. Gallavresi, *Sul lavoro delle donne e dei fanciulli*, 24, cited in Merli, *Proletariato di fabbrica*, 208.

42. Rinaldo Rigola, *Il movimento operaio nel Biellese: Autobiografia* (Bari: Laterza, 1930), 123–25.

43. Louise Tilly, *Politics and Class in Milan, 1881–1901* (Oxford: Oxford University Press, 1992), makes an important contribution to our understanding of the events known as the Fatti di Maggio, the demonstration in Milan that was crushed by the government and culminated in the banning of almost all socialist organizations nationwide. Tilly analyzes the class composition of the 1,700 participants arrested in connection with the demonstration and finds that the proportion in the group of unemployed and recent immigrants reflected their proportion in the general population. Although participants were almost entirely from the subaltern classes, neither industrial workers nor the *lumpenproletariat* were overrepresented. In proportionate terms, construction workers and small shopkeepers were the most important groups.

44. Richard Humphreys, *Futurism* (New York: Cambridge University Press, 1998).

45. Antonio Gramsci, "The Factory Worker," in *Pre-Prison Writings*, ed. Richard Bellamy and Virginia Cox (Cambridge: Cambridge University Press, 1994), 152.

46. Ibid.

47. This discussion refers to Gramsci's early writings. After the failure of the factory councils and the founding of the Partito Comunista Italiano (PCI), Gramsci emphasized the primary role of the political party; Antonio Gramsci, "The Factory Council," in *Pre-Prison Writings*, 163–67.

48. Martin Clark, *Antonio Gramsci and the Revolution That Failed* (New Haven: Yale University Press, 1977).

49. P. Spriano, *L'occupazione delle Fabbriche* (Turin: Einaudi, 1964).

50. See, for example, Donald H. Bell's review in *Social History* 1 (1976): 129–33.

51. Merli challenges the statistics about the composition of the working class in 1900. Although he is correct that the categories make it impossible to distinguish between artisanal and industrial production in certain sectors, this does not belie the fact that Italy was an overwhelmingly agricultural country. As late as 1936, 52 percent of the country was employed in agriculture. For a more complete discussion of class composition in Italy, see chapter 4.

52. See Tilly and Tilly, *Work under Capitalism*, for a nuanced sociological analysis of the diverse ways of organizing work in capitalist economies: volunteer, household, informal, artisanal, and labor market (31).

53. Harry Braverman, *Labor and Monopoly Capital: The Degradation of Work in the Twentieth Century* (New York and London: Monthly Review Press, 1974); Michael Piore and Charles Sabel, *The Second Industrial Divide: Possibilities for Prosperity* (New York: Basic Books, 1984); Charles Sabel, *Work and Politics: The Division of Labor in Industry* (Cambridge: Cambridge University Press, 1982).

Chapter 5. The Cooperative Movement

1. Mario Montagnana, *Ricordi di un operaio torinese* (Rome: Edizioni Rinascita, 1949), 137–38.

2. Erving Goffman, *Encounters: Two Studies in the Sociology of Interaction* (Indianapolis: Bobbs-Merrill Educational Publishing, 196), 17.

3. For a good general overview of the implications of Goffman's work on encounter for social theory, see Anthony Giddens, *The Constitution of Society: Outline of a Theory of Structuration* (Berkeley and Los Angeles: University of California Press, 1984), 60–93; and idem, *Social Theory and Modern Sociology* (Stanford: Stanford University Press, 1987), 109–40.

4. Michel Foucault, *Discipline and Punish: The Birth of the Prison* (New York: Vintage, 1979).

5. Goffman, *Encounters*, 31.

6. Antonio Gramsci, "Alcuni temi della quistione meridionale," in *Le opere*, ed. Antonio A. Santucci (Rome: Riuniti, 1997), 179–204.

7. John Timbs, *Clubs and Club Life in London* (London: Chatto and Windus, 1899).

8. Maurice Agulhon, *The Republic in the Village: The People of the Var from the French Revolution to the Second Republic*, trans. Janet Lloyd (Cambridge: Cambridge University Press, 1982), 150.

9. Lega Nazionale delle Cooperative Italiane, *Statistica delle società cooperative: Annuario statistico* (1903); G. D. H. Cole, *A Century of Cooperation* (London: Allen and Unwin, 1944). On cooperatives in France, see also Henri Desroche, *Histoires d'economies sociales: D'un tiers etat aux tiers secteurs, 1791–1991* (Paris: Syrols Alternatives, 1991); Ellen Furlough, *Consumer Cooperation in France: The Politics of Consumption, 1834–1930* (Ithaca: Cornell University Press, 1991). In 1917 there were 11 million cooperative members in Russia; by 1919 their membership had expanded to 18 million. See Daniel Orlovsky, "State Building in the Civil War Era: The Role of the Lower-Middle Strata," in *Party, State, and Society in the Russian Civil War*, ed. Diane Koenker et al. (Bloomington and Indianapolis: Indiana University Press, 1989). In Belgium there were 831 cooperatives in 1908 with a total membership of 324,700.

10. Antonio Vergnanini was born in Reggio Emilia in 1861. While a student at the University of Bologna, he became a socialist. In 1901 he became secretary of the newly created chamber of labor in Reggio Emilia. In 1912 he was elected head of the national cooperative organization, a position he retained until the organization was disbanded by fascists in 1926.

11. Antonio Verganini, "Riordinamento del campo della cooperazione e della previdenza," *Giustizia*, Feb. 22, 1903.

12. Carol Pateman, *Participation and Democratic Theory* (Cambridge: Cambridge University Press, 1970); Robert Dahl, *A Preface to Economic Democracy* (Berkeley: University of California Press, 1985).

13. Mabel Berezin, *Making the Fascist Self: The Political Culture of Interwar Italy* (Ithaca and London: Cornell University Press, 1997).

14. For an excellent overview of social movement theory, including the political process model, see Sidney Tarrow, *Power in Movement* (Cambridge: Cambridge University Press, 1994).

15. See Guiliano Procacci, *La lotta de classe in Italia agli inizi del secolo XX* (Rome: Riuniti, 1992).

16. Sergio Zaninelli, ed., *L'ottocento economico italiano* (Rome: Manduzzi Editore, 1993).

17. Maurice Neufeld, *Italy: School for Awakening Countries* (Ithaca: ILR Press, 1961), 298.

18. Martin Clark, *Modern Italy, 1871–1995* (London and New York: Longman, 1996), 30.

19. Vera Zamagni, *The Economic History of Italy, 1860–1990* (Oxford: Clarendon Press, 1993), 117.

20. The relationship between productivity, growth, inflation, and real increase in workers' wages is also an area of continued scholarly debate. According to the annual statistical report of 1886, at the advent of Italian unity workers experienced an absolute decline in standard of living. Whereas in 1862 the average worker required 90 days of work to make enough money to acquire enough wheat for the subsistence needs of a family of five for a year, by 1873 that figure had increased to 94 days. Subsequently, living standards rose for a few years, before undergoing a second setback during the worldwide recession

and agricultural crisis of the late 1880s. Although the estimates of real per capita national income from 1891 to 1925 suggest a steady but very modest advance, this does not mean that workers' actual purchasing power increased during this period. Neufeld concludes that "the price of foodstuffs basic to the workers' diet increased so frequently that the cost of living outran nominal wages constantly from 1899 to 1920, except for one year, 1909" (*Italy*, 161, 312).

21. Friedrich Engels, "Socialism: Utopian and Scientific," in *The Marx-Engels Reader*, 2d ed., ed. Robert C. Tucker (New York: Norton, 1978), 687.

22. April 15, 1898, Pontremol. This and all subsequent primary documents are from the archive on working-class associationalism at the Biblioteca Nazionale Centrale di Firenze.

23. Even in England, artisans played an important role in class struggle. See Craig Calhoun, *The Question of Class Struggle: Social Foundations of Popular Radicalism during the Industrial Revolution* (Chicago: University of Chicago Press, 1982).

24. For the classic statement of this argument, see Michael Piore and Charles Sabel, *The Second Industrial Divide* (New York: Basic Books, 1984).

25. There were 80,550 members of Catholic cooperatives in 1910. In contrast, in 1914 there were an estimated 956,085 members in the socialist-oriented Lega Nazionale delle Cooperative Italiane. Ministero dell'Agricoltura, Industria, e Commercio, *Le organizzazioni operaie cattoliche in Italia* (Rome, 1911).

26. R. Zangheri, G. Galasso, and V. Castronovo, *Storia del movimento coopertivo in Italia. La Lega Nazionale delle Cooperative e Mutue (1886–1986)* (Turin: Einaudi, 1987).

27. Carlo Trigilia, "Small-Firm Development and Political Subcultures in Italy," in *Small Firms and Industrial Districts in Italy*, ed. Edward Goodman, Julia Bamford, and Peter Saynor (New York: Routledge, 1989), 174–97.

28. Data are from the 1914 elections, the first elections based on near universal suffrage. A correlation of $r = .5$, which indicates that the independent variable (industrialization) explains 25 percent of the variation in electoral support for the PSI, is considered reasonably strong by social science standards. However, the correlation is not as strong as it first appears because it reflects the strength of the difference between the north and the south rather than variation within the regions.

29. Occupational data come from *Censimento della populazione Italiana;* voting results are from A. Schiavi, *Come hanno votato gli elettori Italiani* (Turin, 1914).

30. Karl Marx, "The Eighteenth Brumaire of Louis Bonaparte," in Tucker, *Marx-Engels Reader*, 608. Although Marx refers to France's peasant proprietors, the spatial dispersion is also true of sharecroppers.

31. For a picture of the truly desperate living conditions of the Italian peasantry in the late 1800s, see S. Jacini, *Relazione finale sui risultati dell'inchiesta agraria*, vol. 15 of *Atti della giunta per la inchiesta agraria e sulle condizioni della classe agraria* (Rome, 1884).

32. Marx, "Eighteenth Brumaire of Louis Bonaparte," 608.

33. Agulhon, *Republic in the Village*.

34. Freedom of association was pioneered in Piedmont, where it was protected by article 32 of the Albertine Law, unlike in France, where mutual aid societies did not emerge out of co-fraternities and guilds. Out of 443 mutual aid societies that existed in 1862, only 66 were founded before 1848. See Arnaldo Cherubini, *Beneficenza e solidarietà: Assistenza pubblica e mutualismo operaio, 1860–1900* (Milan: F. Angeli, 1991). On France, see William Sewell, *Work and Revolution in France: The Language of Labor from the Old Regime to 1848* (Cambridge: Cambridge University Press, 1980).

35. Unless otherwise specified, all statutes cited are found in the Fonti Minori collection of the Biblioteca Nazionale di Firenze. For a helpful introduction to this archive, see Fabio Dolci, *L'associazionismo operaio in Italia (1870–1900) nelle raccolte della Biblioteca Nazionale di Firenze* (Florence: Nuova Italia, 1980).

36. This phrasing is from the statute of the Fratellanza Artigiana Giuseppe Garibaldi of Livorno, founded in 1891.

37. Carlo Trigilia, *Grandi partiti e piccole imprese* (Bologna: Mulino, 1986), 77.

38. Ministero di Agricoltura, Industria, e Commercio, *Statistica delle società di mutuo soccorso e delle istitutioni cooperative annesse all medesime* (Rome, 1878).

39. Anna Pelligrino, ed., "L'associazionismo in Toscana negli opuscoli della Bibliteca Nazionale Centrale di Firenze," Florence, 1998. Note that the real number engaged in political work was much higher, but this was not made explicit in the statutes due to continued fear of repression and dissolution by the government.

40. Luigi Trezzi, *Sindicalismo e cooperazione dalle fine dell'ottocento all'avvento del fascismo* (Milan: Franco Angeli, 1982).

41. Lega Nazionale delle Cooperative Italiane, *Statistica delle società cooperative esistenti in Italia* (Milan: Tip Coop, 1903); *Annuario statistico delle società cooperative esistenti in Italia* (Como, 1917). The figure of 956,085 members in 1914 is based on a survey done by the Lega Nazionale. Given that there were a large number of unaffiliated cooperatives, the actual number of members could be as high as 1.5 million.

42. *Almanacco socialista italiano* (Milan, 1921), cited in Trigilia, *Grandi partiti e piccole imprese*, 90.

43. Statute of the Associazione Generale fra i Coloni del Pistoiese (1919), located in the Fonti Minori collection.

44. For example, the Unione Operaia Cooperativa di Consumo di Firenze, founded in 1892, returned 80 percent of profits to members in proportion to their purchases; it retained 10 percent for reserves and 10 percent for a social fund. Similarly, the Società Cooperative Santa Croce al Pino returned 88 percent of profits to members, 10 percent to reserves, and only 2 percent for propaganda and mutualism. This individualist-oriented distribution is typical of consumer cooperatives founded in Tuscany at the end of the nineteenth century. With the growth of socialist ideas, however, some cooperatives shifted the balance in favor of solidaristic initiatives. The Cooperative Sociale, founded in San Niccolò in 1910, distributed 60 percent to members, 15 percent to mutualism, 15 percent to reserves, and 10 percent to a special fund for the benefit of the cooperative's employees.

45. Umberto Sereni, "La cooperazione sindicalista nel Parmenese, 1907–1922," in *Il movimento cooperativo nella storia d'Italia*, ed. F. Fabbri (Milan: Feltrinelli, 1979).

46. Luigi Tomassini, *Associazionismo operaio à Firenze fra '800 e '900: La Società di Mutuo Soccorso di Rifredi (1883–1922)* (Florence: Leo S. Olschiki, 1984), 121.

47. Ibid., 240.

48. Giuliano Procacci, "Italian Working Class from the Risorgimento to Fascism," working paper, Harvard Manuscripts on Europe, 1981.

49. Charles Tilly, "Spaces of Contention," *Mobilization* 5 (2000): 135–60.

50. For a good introduction to this extensive literature, see the collection of essays edited by Ira Katznelson and Aristide Zolberg, *Working-Class Formation: Nineteenth-Century Patterns in Western Europe and the United States* (Princeton: Princeton University Press, 1986).

51. Tilly, "Spaces of Contention."

52. Ibid.

53. Comune di Milano, *Sei anni di amministrazione socialista luglio, 1914–luglio 1920* (Milan: Relazione al Consiglio Comunale, 1920), 198.

54. Jacques Rancière provides an excellent analysis of the contradictory impulses within the nineteenth-century French workers' movement and criticizes the tendency in social history to romanticize workers as mythic figures of resistance. See Jacques Rancière, *The Nights of Labor: The Workers' Dream in Nineteenth-Century France*, trans. John Drury (Philadelphia: Temple University Press, 1989).

55. David Harvey, *Spaces of Hope* (Berkeley: University of California Press, 2000).

Chapter 6. The House of the People

1. Henri Lefebvre, *The Production of Space*, trans. Donald Nicholson-Smith (London: Basil Blackwell, 1991), 73.
2. Most work on space has focused on urbanism or other macrolevel analyses of social aggregation. Some of the most important reference points in this literature include David Harvey, *The Urban Experience* (Oxford: Oxford University Press, 1989); Manuel Castells, *The Informational City: Information Technology, Economic Restructuring, and the Urban-Regional Process* (Oxford: Oxford University Press, 1989); Manuel Castells, *The Urban Question* (London: Edward Arnold, 1977); and Edward Soja, *Postmodern Geographies* (London: Verso, 1989).
3. Franco Andreucci and Alessandra Pegcarolo, eds., *Gli spazi del potere: Aree, regioni, stati: Le coordinate territoriali della storia contemporanea* (Florence: Usher, 1989). Kristin Ross makes a similar argument in *The Emergence of Social Space: Rimbaud and the Paris Commune* (Minneapolis: University of Minnesota Press, 1988).
4. David Harvey, *Justice, Nature and the Geography of Difference* (Cambridge, Mass.: Blackwell, 1996), 221ff.
5. Michel Foucault, *Discipline and Punish: The Birth of the Prison* (London: Allen Lane, 1977).
6. Karl Polyani, *The Great Transformation* (Boston: Beacon Hill, 1957); Ferdinand Braudel, *La dynamique du capitalisme* (Paris: Arthaud, 1985).
7. Marshall Berman, *All That Is Solid Melts into Air* (New York: Penguin, 1982).
8. Lefebvre, *Production of Space*, 164, 165.
9. James C. Scott, *Seeing Like a State: How Certain Schemes to Improve the Human Condition Have Failed* (New Haven: Yale University Press, 1998).
10. Ibid., 346.
11. William Connolly, *Ethos of Pluralization* (Minneapolis: University of Minnesota Press, 1995), 93.
12. Michel Foucault, "Of Other Spaces," in *Rethinking Architecture: A Reader in Cultural Theory*, ed. Neil Leach (London and New York: Routledge, 1997), 352. See also Thomas Dumm, *Michel Foucault and the Politics of Freedom* (Thousand Oaks, Calif.: Sage Publications, 1996).
13. Foucault, "Of Other Spaces," 352.
14. Ibid., 356.
15. For a discussion of recent articles that treat heterotopia as a locus of emancipation, see David Harvey, *Spaces of Hope* (Berkeley: University of California Press, 2000), 182–89.
16. Sara Evans and Harry Boyte, *Free Spaces: Sources of Democratic Change in America* (New York: Harper and Row, 1986). For an extensive bibliography of the literature on free spaces (and an interesting critique), see Francesca Polletta, " 'Free Spaces' in Collective Action," *Theory and Society* 28 (1999): 1–38. On the role of squatters in Amsterdam's center, see Edward Soja, *Third Space: Journey to Los Angeles and Other Real-and-Imagined Places* (Cambridge, Mass.: Blackwell, 1996).
17. For a critique of this position, see Polletta, " 'Free Spaces' in Collective Action."
18. Maurice Agulhon, *Le cerle dans la France bourgeoise, 1810–1848* (Paris: Colin, 1977).
19. Foucault, "Of Other Spaces," 354.
20. Ibid., 355.
21. Jürgen Habermas, *The Structural Transformation of the Public Sphere: An Inquiry into a Category of Bourgeois Society* (Cambridge: MIT Press, 1991), 18.
22. See, for example, Luigi Tomassini, *Associazionismo operaio à Firenze fra '800 e '900: La Società di Mutuo Soccorso di Rifredi (1883–1922)* (Florence: Leo S. Olschki Editore, 1984), 118.
23. See, for example, A. Varni, *Associazionismo, mazzinianismo e questione operaia. Il caso della Società Democratic Operaia di Chiavenna* (Pisa: Nistrinel, 1978); L. Minuti, *Il Comune*

Artigiano di Firenze della Fratellanza Artigiana d'Italia (Florence: Tipografica Cooperativa, 1911). See also the collection of statutes preserved in the minor documents cata-
logued in F. Dolci, *L'associazionismo operaio in Italia (1870–1900) nelle raccolte della Biblioteca Nazionale Centrale di Firenze* (Florence: Nuova Italia, 1980).

24. The classic statement of the argument that private property provides an area of sub-
jective control crucial for developing subjectivity is found in G. W. F. Hegel, *Philosophy of
Right* (London: Oxford University Press, 1975).

25. Habermas, *Structural Transformation*, 46.

26. Giuseppe Mazzini, the prominent advocate of Risorgimento nationalism, was also
the founder of a radical-republican political movement in postunification Italy. For the
best discussion of the relationship between Mazzini and the workers' movement, see
Nello Rosselli, *Mazzini e Bakunin: Dodici anni di movimento operaio in Italia (1860–1872)*
(Turin: Einaudi, 1967). Giovanni Bacci, *Provincia di Mantova*, Jan. 5, 1901.

27. Luigi Arbizzani, ed., *Storie di case del popolo: Saggi, documente, immagini d'Emilia-Romagna* (Bologna: Grafis, 1982), 48.

28. Ibid.

29. G. Viciani, "Come sorgono le nostre case," in *L'almanacco socialista italiano* (1918).

30. Ibid., 247.

31. The suffrage reform of 1912 granted veterans as well as all men over the age of thirty
the right to vote, whether they were literate or not. This reform expanded the electoral
rolls from 3 million to nearly 8.5 million. Thus 1912 would probably be the date for the
transition from a liberal system based on elite competition into a minimally democratic
state based on the inclusion of the masses. See Martin Clark, *Modern Italy, 1871–1995*
(London: Longman, 1996).

32. Maurizio Degl'Innocenti, "Per una storia delle case del popolo in Italia, dalle origini
alla prima guerra mondiale," in *Le case del popolo in Europa: Dalle origini alla seconda guerra
mondiale*, ed. Maurizio Degl'Innocenti (Florence: Sansoni, 1984).

33. Arbizzani, *Storie di case del popolo*, 106 (my translation).

34. Ettore Zanardi, "La casa del popolo," *Squilla*, Oct. 10, 1908, excerpted ibid., 105.

35. Guy Vanschoenbeek, "Il significato del Centro '*Vooruit*,'" in Degl'Innocenti, *Case del
popolo in Europa*.

36. See V. Serwy, "Les maisons du peuple" and "La cooperation en Belgique," in *Album
du 1er mai* (Brussels, 1929), 24–25.

37. Robert Flagothier, "Contributo allo studio delle case del popolo in Vallonia e a Brux-
elles (1872–1982)," in Degl'Innocenti, *Case del popolo in Europa*.

38. Clark, *Modern Italy*, 156.

39. These figures refer to 1919. Luigi Arbizzani, "Case del popolo in Italia dopo la prima
guerra mondiale," in Degl'Innocenti, *Case del popolo in Europa*, 113.

40. *Inchiesta sul movimento associativo ferrarese*, Biblioteca Scienze Sociali, ARCI-Ferrara,
21–25, cited ibid.

41. Palmiro Togliatti, *Quaderno dell'Attivista* (Rome), Jan. 21, 1956.

42. Victor Horta, *Memorie*, 48–49, cited in Franco Borsi, *La maison du peuple: Sindicalismo come arte* (Bari: Debalo Libri, 1978), 20–21 (my translation from the Italian).

43. See Flagothier, "Contributo allo studio delle case del popolo in Vallonia e a Brux-
elles," 307–10.

44. Borsi reports that Horta traveled to Bayreuth, where he learned a new technique of
employing fabric as an absorbent material for improving acoustics (Borsi, *Maison du peuple*, 29).

45. Under fascism in Italy, the houses of the people that were not destroyed by fascist
squads were often requisitioned by the government. Although some continued to serve
as recreational centers, participation was low, and many were eventually turned into office space for government organizations. See Arbizzani, *Storie di case del popolo*.

46. Polletta, "'Free Spaces' in Collective Action," 19.

47. For a brilliant discussion of the fascists' use of public space, see Mabel Berezin, *Mak-*

ing of the Fascist Self (Ithaca: Cornell University Press, 1997). Berezin traces how the fascist regime became adept at using public space and political ritual such as commemoration, celebration, demonstration, and symposia to forge a link between the individual and the state.

48. See Richard Etlin, *Modernism in Italian Architecture, 1890–1940* (Cambridge: MIT Press 1991), 377–479; Thomas Schumacher, *Surface and Symbol: Giuseppe Terragni and the Architecture of Italian Rationalism* (New York: Princeton Architectural Press, 1991).

49. See Jeremy Howard, *Art Nouveau: International and National Styles in Europe* (Manchester, U.K.: Manchester University Press, 1996).

50. Jean Delhaye, *La maison du people de Victor Horta* (Brussels: Atelier Vokaer, 1987).

51. Etlin, *Modernism in Italian Architecture*, 439.

52. One example of this result is in The Netherlands, where the houses of the people were born out of charity effects and were generally unsuccessful. In 1928 there were only fifty such institutions; they were used primarily as recreational centers for children and youth, and had little relationship with the workers' movement and no political influence. See Arie de Groot, "La casa del popolo come tempio della Fede Sociale," in *Case del Popolo: Un'architettura monumentale del moderno*, ed. Marco De Michelis (Venice: Marsilio, 1986), 69.

53. De Michelis, *Case del popolo*, 90.

54. Homi Bhabha, *The Location of Culture* (London and New York: Routledge, 1994).

55. Bonnie Honig, "Difference, Dilemmas, and the Politics of Home," in *Democracy and Difference: Contesting the Boundaries of the Political*, ed. Seyla Benhabib (Princeton: Princeton University Press, 1996), 269.

Chapter 7. The Chamber of Labor

1. Vasco Pratolini, *Metello* (Boston and Toronto: Little, Brown, 1968), 27.

2. Ibid., 57.

3. "'Now we'll see whether or not we are a people,' they said. 'Getting Del Buono [the head of the chamber of labor] released [from jail] has become a question of principle, and even more, getting them to re-open the Labour Centre'" (ibid., 214).

4. Ibid., 112.

5. Pierre Bourdieu, *Language and Symbolic Power*, ed. John B. Thompson (Cambridge: Harvard University Press, 1991).

6. Osvaldo Gnocchi-Viani, "L'organizzazione dei lavoratori improduttivi," in *Dieci anni di camere del lavoro e altri scritti sul sindacato italiano (1889–1899)*, ed. Pino Ferraris (Rome: Ediesse, 1995), 126.

7. The quotation is from the inaugural speech at the founding of the chamber of labor. Cited in Gnocchi-Viani, "Dieci anni di camere del lavoro," in Ferraris, *Dieci anni di camere del lavoro*, 148 (my translation).

8. Ibid., 132.

9. Rinaldo Rigola, *Rinaldo Rigola e il movimento operaio nel Biellese* (Bari: Laterza, 1930), 132.

10. J. K. Hyde, *Society and Politics in Medieval Italy: The Evolution of Civil Life (1000–1350)* (London: Macmillan, 1973); David Waley, *The Italian City-Republics*, 2d ed. (New York: Longman, 1978).

11. See Richard Sennett, *Flesh and Stone: The Body and the City in Western Civilization* (New York and London: Norton, 1994), 231.

12. For a literary account of this shift from the perspective of the bourgeoisie, see Edmondo De Amicis, *Primo maggio* (Milan: Casa Editrice Garzanti, 1980), written in the early 1890s. The opening scene depicts a bourgeois family's fear as the workers march through the center of town on the first of May.

13. The term "right to the city" comes from Henri Lefevbre, *Writings on Cities*, trans. and ed. Eleonore Kofman and Elizabeth Lebas (Oxford and Cambridge: Blackwell Pub-

lishers, 1996). Lefebvre uses this term to suggest nonconsumerist needs for information, symbolism, the imaginary, and play.

14. See G. Angelini, *Il socialismo del lavoro, Osvaldo Gnocchi-Viani tra mazzinianesismo e instanze libertarie* (Milan: Franco Angeli, 1987).

15. This quote and the account of these events come from Louise Tilly, *Politics and Class in Milan, 1881–1901* (New York and Oxford: Oxford University Press, 1992), 112.

16. Ferraris, "Osvaldo Gnocchi-Viani: Un protagonista dimenticato," in Ferraris, *Dieci anni di camere del lavoro*, 43.

17. Tilly, *Politics and Class in Milan*, 111–12.

18. Rigola, *Rigola e il movimento operaio nel Biellese*, 140–46.

19. Ferraris, "Osvaldo Gnocchi-Viani," 28 (my translation).

20. Nicla Capitini Maccabruni, *La camera del lavoro nella vita politica e amministrativa fiorentina (dalle origini al 1900)* (Florence: Leo S. Olschki, 1965).

21. Diego Robotti and Bianca Gera, *Il tempo della solidarietà: Le 69 società operaie che fondarono la camera del lavoro di Torino* (Milan: Feltrinelli, 1991), 76.

22. For example, in Sesto Fiorentino the chamber of labor was the product of an initiative of the socialist municipality. Ernesto Ragionieri concludes that this top-down formation was responsible for its relative weakness. According to Ragionieri, it had a bureaucratic rather than a participatory character. See Ragionieri, *Un comune socialista: Sesto Fiorentino* (Rome: Edizioni Rinascita, 1953), 146–60.

23. Robotti and Gera, *Tempo della solidarietà*.

24. Nora Carignani, Rosella Luchetti, and Graziella Poli, *La camera del lavoro di Piombino: Dalle origini agli anni sessanta* (Florence: All'Insega del Giglio, 1985).

25. In 1902, at the prewar highpoint, the membership in Milan was 44,440 or 16 percent of the labor force.

26. Renzo Casero, "La camera del lavoro di Milano dalle origini alla repressione del maggio 1898," in *La camera del lavoro di Milano dalle origini al 1904* (Milan: Sugarco, 1975), 181 (my translation)

27. Ibid.

28. This is the assessment of Martin Clark in his very centrist history *Modern Italy: 1871–1995*, 2d ed. (London and New York: Longman, 1996).

29. Minimalists supported the PSI's minimal, consensus program, which emphasized such provisions as tax reform, elementary education, and social insurance. Abstentionists made up the most extreme wing of the PSI and argued against electoral participation. They claimed that Parliament was exclusively a tool of the bourgeoisie and that no transformation was possible under capitalism.

30. Adriano Ballone, Claudio Dellavalle, and Mario Grandinetti, *Il tempo della lotta e dell'organizzazione: Linee di storia della camera del lavoro di Torino* (Milan: Feltrivelli, 1992), 61.

31. Clark, *Modern Italy*, 141.

32. Ibid., 142.

33. Statute of the Fratellanza di Greve in Chianti (1890) and of the *camera del lavoro* in Scandicci (1896), in the Fonti Minori collection of the Biblioteca Nazionale Centrale di Firenze. The Scandicci statute also specified that members "conduct themselves with dignity in order to bring prestige to the section."

34. Claudio Treves, "Debbono le camere del lavoro diventare socialiste?" in *La Critica Sociale*, vol. 2, ed. Mario Spinella, Alberto Caracciolo, Ruggero Amaduzzi, and Giuseppe Pertonio (Milan: Feltrinelli, 1959), 186.

35. Ibid., 186 (my translation).

36. These figures refer to 1901, the year the article was published.

37. Osvaldo Gnocchi-Viani, "Il socialismo e le sue scuole," in Spinella et al., *La Critica Sociale*, 1:25–28.

38. Ferraris, "Osvaldo Gnocchi-Viani," 16.

39. Gnocchi-Viani, "Organizzazione dei lavoratori improduttivi," 121–23.

40. It is interesting that Ragionieri's study of Sesto Fiorentino confirms Marx's contention that the *lumpenproletariat* was essentially a conservative force. He looks at the membership of the liberal-conservative electoral organization, which had 450–500 members. Although the leaders were local notables—landowners, industrialists, and professionals—the membership allegedly consisted of members of the working class. He concludes that the members were, in fact, "aspiring workers," members of the *lumpenproletariat* who joined the organization in hopes of getting a letter of recommendation that would open the doors to a job at Richard-Ginori, the main employer in town, who refused to hire socialists (Ragionieri, *Comune socialista*, 173).

41. Mario Montagnana, *Ricordi di un operaio torinese* (Rome: Edizioni Rinascita, 1949), 22 (all quotations from this text are my own translation).

42. Ibid., 26. Terpsichore is the Greek muse of dance.

43. Ibid., 108.

44. Ibid., 233–34.

45. Donald Howard Bell, *Sesto San Giovanni: Workers, Culture, and Politics in an Italian Town, 1880–1922* (New Brunswick and London: Rutgers University Press, 1986), 162.

46. Victoria de Grazia, *The Culture of Consent: Mass Organization of Leisure in Fascist Italy* (Cambridge: Cambridge University Press, 1981).

47. Francesca Polletta, " 'Free Spaces' in Collective Action," *Theory and Society* 28 (1999): 19.

Chapter 8. Municipalism

1. Agricultural employment in Sesto declined from 85 percent at unification to 2.7 percent in 1921. See Luigi Trezzi, ed., *Sesto San Giovanni, 1880–1921* (Milan: Skira, 1997).

2. The story of the political, social, and cultural developments of Sesto San Giovanni provides a useful illustration of the type of transformations in power that have been discussed thus far. It is a history recovered in rich detail by the careful archival work of social historian Donald Howard Bell. Unless otherwise cited, all information in this section is from the fascinating study of Donald Howard Bell, *Sesto San Giovanni: Workers, Culture, and Politics in an Italian Town, 1880–1922* (New Brunswick and London: Rutgers University Press, 1986).

3. Ibid., 3

4. This is similar to Raymond Williams's distinction between alternative and oppositional culture. See Williams, "Base and Superstructure in Marxist Cultural Theory," *New Left Review* 82 (November/December 1973).

5. It is interesting that Bell does not note whether it was located in Old or New Sesto. Although a complete list of the members' occupations is lacking, there were members from the trades of printer, mason, bookbinder, and housepainter, as well as multiple metal workers.

6. Based on the occupational lists provided in Bell, *Sesto San Giovanni*.

7. Instead of using the actual party designations, I am loosely translating them in order to communicate more clearly to non-Italianists their respective positions on the political spectrum.

8. Bell, *Sesto San Giovanni*, 100.

9. Ibid., 98.

10. Joan W. Scott, "Mayors versus Police Chiefs: Socialist Municipalities Confront the French State", in *French Cities in the Nineteenth Century*, ed. John M. Merriman (New York: Holmes and Meier Publishers, 1981), 245.

11. There were several major policy victories at the national level during the Giolittian era. These included a 1902 law limiting working hours for women and children; a 1910 statute setting up a maternity fund financed by state, employer, and employee contributions; and a series of laws regarding health and safety. Still, enforcement of these statutes was inconsistent, so municipalities still played an important role in implementation.

12. Out of a total of 8,268 communes in Italy (see appendix 4). See also Direzione del Partito Socialista Italiano, *Il congresso nazionale delle amministrazioni comunali e provinciali socialiste. Bologna 16–17 gennaio 1916* (Milan: Libreria dell'Avanti, 1916), 75.

13. Maurizio Ridolfi, *Il PSI e la nascita di una partita di massa, 1892–1922* (Rome and Bari: Laterza, 1992), 64.

14. Bolton King and Thomas Okey, *Italy To-day* (London: James Nisbet and Co., 1909), 263.

15. Scott, "Mayors versus Police Chiefs," 230–45.

16. King and Okey write, "Among the many communal councils that are dissolved every year, the offence is sometimes that they have a Socialist majority or have made themselves unpleasant to the local Deputy" (*Italy To-day*, 269).

17. These examples all come from ibid., 269.

18. The law places restrictions on both the *dazio* and the property tax, which theoretically could not be more than one-half of the duties collected by the central government. King and Okey report that these restrictions, however, were routinely violated (ibid.).

19. Because the distinction between democrats and republicans is not important for our purposes, I use the generic term *moderates*, which will help clarify for non-Italianists the groups' position on a left-to-right ideological spectrum.

20. Atti del Comune Sesto Fiorentino, *Azienda elettrica municiaplizzata*, cited in Ragionieri, *Un comune socialista: Sesto Fiorentino* (Rome: Riuniti, 1953).

21. Before 1913 the suffrage restrictions were lower for communal elections than for parliamentary elections, which explains why the more "popular" communal councils could advocate positions different from those held by the prefect or Parliament.

22. Ragionieri, *Comune socialista*, 120.

23. Alessandro Schiavi, "Quattro anni di amministrazione socialista in Milano" (1918), in *La Critica Sociale*, vol. 2, ed. Mario Spinella, Alberto Caracciolo, Ruggero Amaduzzi, and Giuseppe Pertonio (Milan: Feltrinelli, 1959), 522–36.

24. Margaret Cole, *The Story of Fabian Socialism* (Stanford: Stanford University Press, 1961); G. D. H. Cole, *History of Socialist Thought* (London: Macmillan, 1953–60).

25. Giuseppe Zibordi, "Primavera di vita municipale," *Avanti*, Sept. 8, 1910.

26. Filippo Turati, "Comune moderato e Comune popolare," *Critica Sociale* 20 (1910): 135 (my translation).

27. Peter Gay, *The Dilemma of Democratic Socialism* (New York: Collier Books, 1972); Manfred Steger, *The Quest for Evolutionary Socialism: Eduard Bernstein and Social Democracy* (Cambridge: Cambridge University Press, 1987).

28. Spencer DiScala, *Dilemmas of Italian Socialism: The Politics of Filippo Turati* (Amherst: University of Massachusetts Press, 1980).

29. Ibid., 20. The articles in *Lotta di Classe* were not signed but are credited to Turati, one of the editors, on the basis of their style and substance.

30. This schema is indebted to and adapted from the typology in Fred Dallmayr, *Twilight of Subjectivity: Contributions to a Post-Individualist Theory of Politics* (Amherst: University of Massachusetts Press, 1981), 137–43.

31. Jean-Jacques Rousseau, *The Government of Poland*, trans. Willmore Kendall (Indianapolis: Hackett Publishing, 1985).

32. Mancur Olson, *The Logic of Collective Action* (Cambridge: Harvard University Press, 1965).

33. Michael Sandel, *Liberalism and the Limits of Justice* (Cambridge: Cambridge University Press, 1982).

34. Ibid., 150. See also the discussion of this topic in William Cortlett, *Community without Unity: A Politics of Derridian Extravagance* (Durham, N.C., and London: Duke University Press, 1989).

35. Sheldon Wolin, "What Revolutionary Action Means Today," in *Dimensions of Radical Democracy: Pluralism, Citizenship, Community*, ed. Chantal Mouffe (London: Verso, 1992).

36. Carlo Trigilia, *Grandi partiti e piccole imprese: Comunisti e democristiani nelle regioni a economia diffusa* (Bologna: Il Mulino, 1986), 47.

37. In Europe, economic relations of dependence were a crucial barrier to equal citizenship. In other contexts, such as that in the United States, the struggle against racial prejudice and subordination was the vehicle of mobilization.

38. Victoria de Grazia, *The Culture of Consent: Mass Organization of Leisure in Fascist Italy* (Cambridge: Cambridge University Press, 1981), 115.

39. See Margaret Kohn, "Civic Republicanism versus Social Struggle: A Gramscian Approach to Associationalism in Italy," *Political Power and Social Theory* 13 (1999): 201–35.

40. For a study updating and confirming Putnam's results, see Tamara Simoni, "Il rendimento istituzionale delle regioni: 1990–1994," *Polis* 11, no. 3 (1997): 417–36.

41. Although provisions for regional government were already included in the 1948 Italian constitution, they were not inaugurated until 1970. For a fuller account of the implementation of regional governments, see Peter Gourevitch, "Reforming the Napoleonic State: The Creation of Regional Governments in France and Italy," and Sidney Tarrow, "Local Constraints on Regional Reform," in *Territorial Politics in Industrial Nations*, ed. Sidney Tarrow, Peter J. Katzenstein, and Luigi Graziano (New York: Praeger, 1978), 28–63 and 1–27, respectively.

42. Robert Putnam, *Making Democracy Work: Civic Traditions in Modern Italy* (Princeton: Princeton University Press, 1993). There are many persuasive criticisms of Putnam's work. See, for example, Sidney Tarrow, "Making Social Science Work across Space and Time," *American Political Science Review* 90, no. 2 (1996): 389–97; E. Goldberg, "Thinking about How Democracy Works," *Politics and Society* 24, no. 1 (1996): 7–18; Carlo Trigilia, "Dai communi medievali alle nostre regioni, *L'Indice* (1994): 36; A. Bagnasco, "Regioni, tradizione civica, modernizzazione italiana: Un commento alla recerca di Putnam," *Stato e Mercato* (1994): 93–104.

43. There is extensive literature on political subcultures, most notably Trigilia, *Grandi partiti e piccole imprese*. Two of the early works were Giorgio Galli, *Il bipartitismo imperfetto* (Bologna: Il Mulino, 1966); and F. Alberoni, *Il PCI e la DC nel sistema politico italiano* (Bologna: Il Mulino, 1967).

44. Kohn, "Civic Republicanism versus Social Struggle."

45. The reason for doing this is that correlation does not necessarily establish causality. If two variables are correlated with each other, the causal arrows can go in either direction. By looking at the density of association before the regions existed, we can safely exclude the possibility that good regional government caused the political associations to flourish.

46. Kohn, "Civic Republicanism versus Social Struggle," looks at both the interwar period and the contemporary period. The data include Catholic associationalism (1910), red associationalism (1902–10), PSI strength (1914 and 1920), index of red subculture (1982–92), and index of white subculture (1982–92).

47. Putnam uses four indicators of civic community: preference voting and referendum turnout (as indicators of clientelistic politics), newspaper readership, and presence of sports and cultural associations. Only the last factor, however, plays a role in the causal story he tells to explain institutional performance. In "Civic Republicanism versus Social Struggle," I used a more recent and thorough survey of civic participation (attendance at meetings, membership in voluntary organizations) done by ISTAT, the Italian statistical institute, in 1994.

48. Ragioneri, *Un comune socialista*, 177.

49. Ibid., 178–79.

Conclusion

1. Maurice Halbwachs, *The Collective Memory* (New York: Harper and Row, 1980).

2. Jacques Greux, *Le Peuple*, Apr. 1, 1899, special edition commemorating the inauguration of the Maison du Peuple.

3. Rinaldo Rigola, *Il movimento operaio nel Bielese: Autobiografia* (Bari: Gius, Laterza and Figli, 1930): "La politica si fa li signori."

4. Henri Lefebvre, *The Production of Space* (Oxford: Blackwell, 1991), 419.

5. Robert Putnam, *Making Democracy Work: Civic Traditions in Modern Italy* (Princeton: Princeton University Press, 1993); see also chap. 8.

6. Following William Connolly, I call this the visceral register; Connolly, *Why I Am Not a Secularist* (Minneapolis: University of Minnesota Press, 1999), 175–77.

7. Erving Goffman, *Encounters: Two Studies in the Sociology of Interaction* (Indianapolis: Bobbs-Merrill Educational Publishing, 1961), 31.

8. Charles Tilly, "Spaces of Contention," *Mobilization* 5 (2000): 135–60.

9. To my knowledge, the term *lifeworld* comes from Edmund Husserl's phenomenology. Husserl, in *The Crisis of the European Sciences and Transcendental Phenomenology* (Evanston: Northwestern University Press, 1970), 22, defines the lifeworld as the "manifold pre-logical validities" that lay the groundwork for objective knowledge.

10. Hannah Arendt, *The Human Condition* (Chicago: University of Chicago Press, 1958). For a nuanced discussion of this distinction in Arendt, see Hanna Fenichel Pitkin, "Justice: On Relating the Public and Private," *Political Theory* 9 (1981); and the chapter on Arendt in Bonnie Honig, *Political Theory and the Displacement of Politics* (Ithaca: Cornell University Press, 1993), 76–125.

11. C. Douglas Lummis, *Radical Democracy* (Ithaca: Cornell University Press, 1996).

12. This point is made by Roberto Unger, *False Necessity: Anti-Necessitarian Social Theory in the Service of Radical Democracy* (Cambridge: Cambridge University Press, 1987).

13. This phrase comes from a description of Walter Benjamin's dialectical image. Ester Leslie, "Space and Westend Girls: Walter Benjamin and Cultural Studies," *New Formations* 38 (summer 1999): 117.

14. Walter Benjamin, *Gesammelte Schriften*, ed. Rolf Tiedemann and Hermann Schweppenhäuser (Frankfurt: Suhrkamp Verlag, 1972), 1233, cited in Leslie, "Space and Westend Girls," 118.

Postscript

1. See, for example, the essays in Frederic Jameson and Masao Miyoshi, eds., *The Cultures of Globalization* (Durham, N.C.: Duke University Press, 1998); Neil Smith, "The Satanic Geographies of Globalization: Uneven Development in the 1990's," *Public Culture* 10, no. 1 (fall 1997).

2. Mike Featherstone, Scott Lash, and Roland Robertson, eds., *Global Modernities* (London: Sage, 1995).

3. Fredric Jameson, "Globalization as a Philosophical Issue," in Jameson and Miyoshi, *Cultures of Globalization*.

4. William Connolly, "Democracy and Territoriality," *Millennium: Journal of International Studies* 20, no. 3 (1991): 464.

5. Gilles Deleuze and Felix Guattari, *A Thousand Plateaus: Capitalism and Schizophrenia* (Minneapolis: University of Minnesota Press, 1987), 9.

6. Ibid., 326. Connolly reaches a similar conclusion in "Democracy and Territoriality," 481, suggesting that "[these growing interdependencies] provide the need and the condition of possibility, not for the globalisation of democratic elections or the liquidation of territorial democracy, but for the pluralisation of democratic energies, alliances and spaces of action that exceed the closures of territorial democracy."

7. See Saskia Sassen, *The Global City: New York, London, Tokyo* (Princeton: Princeton University Press, 1991); Manuel Castells, *The Informational City: Information Technology, Economic Restructuring, and the Urban-Regional Process* (Oxford: Oxford University Press, 1989).

8. Leslie Sklair, "Social Movements and Capitalism," in Jameson and Miyoshi, *Cultures of Globalization*, 305.

9. Jameson, "Globalization as a Philosophical Issue," 76.

10. G.W.F. Hegel, *The Encyclopaedia Logic* (Indianapolis: Hackett Publishing, 1991), 181–92.

11. Darin Barney, *Prometheus Wired: The Hope for Democracy in the Age of Network Technology* (Chicago: University of Chicago Press, 2000).

12. Cass Sunstein, *Republic.com* (Princeton: Princeton University Press, 2001).

INDEX

war of position, 63, 139, 157
Web. *See* Internet
Wolin, Sheldon, 15
workers, industrial, 50–58, 60, 62, 65, 124, 132

workers' movement, 70, 82, 110, 126
working class, 36–37, 46–49, 60, 63, 79, 83, 94, 100, 117–18, 130
World War I, 5, 72, 126, 133
World War II, 9, 144